SHOOTER DOWN

MY STORY: THE MASS SHOOTER WHO NEVER WAS

RALPH TARSO

SILVERSMITH
PRESS

Published by Silversmith Press—Houston, Texas
www.silversmithpress.com

ISBN 978-1-961093-78-2 (Softcover Book)
ISBN 978-1-961093-79-9 (eBook)

This book is dedicated to my mother and father, to Bic,
and to those in this story who are no longer alive.

CONTENTS

INTRODUCTION

And when He got into the boat, he who had been demon-possessed begged
Him that he might be with Him. However, Jesus did not permit him, but
said to him, "Go home to your friends, and tell them what great things the
Lord has done for you, and how He has had compassion on you."

Mark 5:18-19[1]

More than a decade before Columbine, around the beginning of
1986, I was a depraved young man actively planning a mass mur-
dering rampage. It never took place due to an extraordinary intervention. In the years since, every time some new horror takes
place, I have always had one question: How is it that I was stopped
and they were not? What saved my potential victims without their
knowledge? And what am I doing here, still walking above the
ground almost forty years later, when I should have been burning
in Hell for decades?

   In an effort to answer these questions, I here attempt to tell

---

1   All scriptures quoted are New King James Version (NKJV) unless otherwise
noted.

my story as accurately as I can. I am now an ordained minister with the Assemblies of God, and so I can frame my story with the theological understanding that I now have. I have also been a professional physicist for many years, a job which requires concentrated thought and attention to detail. In sharp contrast, there were times as a young man that I was so demonized that I was unable to hold more than four or five thoughts in succession.

In my account I merge these two worlds. I endeavor to tell this tale from my own point of view at the time, rather than the way I view the world now—yet with the current understanding that a lifetime of reflection has given me. I understand the danger Warfield noted, commenting on Charles Finney's memoirs:

> The account of [his conversion experiences], written in his old age, is more or less adjusted to his subsequent modes of thought, and closes with a couple of odd paragraphs in which he "improves" his conversion by representing it as impressing then and there indelibly on his mind his later doctrines...[1]

I have taken every precaution to avoid this. I include the voices of others to indicate what this all looked like from the outside. Two whole chapters primarily consist of the personal recollections of others, and I likewise quote official reports from psychologists who were examining me at the time. The discerning reader will also detect the perspective of those who did not commit their memories to writing as I attempt to recount what I learned from them. These perspectives from without combined with mine from within do not reveal my own condition so much

---

[1]   Warfield, Benjamin B., The Works of Benjamin B. Warfield, Volume VIII, Oxford University Press, 1932, Reprint Baker Books, 2003, pp. 15-16.

as the human condition: that we are not the masters of our own destiny, and our stories are not merely our own. Our lives are, in fact, thoroughly enmeshed in the experiences and decisions of others, both the living and the dead, for good or for ill.

I also do my best to clearly distinguish my current reflections from what I know I was thinking at the time. This was not easy, because I can no longer relate to the person I once was. But I couldn't tell the story without dredging these things up. And I think it *is* important to tell the story for the following reasons.

First of all, an inside look at what would have been the weeks running up to a mass shooting is useful in its own regard. Had things continued as they were, my inner convictions would have entered the outer world and impacted many people. I have to explain why I turned against God, then how I became a Satanist, and then again why this shifted to planning a mass shooting[1].

I take this account beyond the final few months to go through my entire life up to that point, from earliest childhood. I want to show the experiences, decisions, and turning points that were involved all the way through to almost the end. I would summarize these processes into two phenomena: anti-socialization and demonization. Here I must be absolutely clear that I am not speaking of figurative demonization, but literal.

Many simply will not accept the involvement of literal demons. Not just unbelievers but even some Christians will attempt to reduce my account to merely mental or metaphorical phenomena. Therefore, I must have extended discourses to argue for what actually happened—a combination of my own bad

---

1   Not something a serious Satanist would normally do—to throw one's life away openly rather than seeking power. I accurately understood this development at the time as a demotion.

ideas and decisions, and the advantage taken of them by actual satanic forces.

Once this is understood, a second reason to tell this tale appears. Fellow Christians will begin to notice a continual one-upmanship, a constant back and forth between God and Satan's kingdom over my life. I did not craft the narrative to reflect this, but it emerged and I noticed it as I wrote. And I think this aspect of the story reveals a great deal to us about both our God and His enemy.

Thirdly, I hope that the account will illustrate what the church must do to reach the current generation. In an age in which Satan is operating so much more openly, many of the newly redeemed will have sustained significant damage to body and soul. Consequently, I also hope that this tale demonstrates the extensive pastoral work that will be required to deal with this aftermath. I comment on such things in full knowledge that I haven't done such a great job myself. But I trust that the picture I paint of the extensive ministry infrastructure which helped me through will serve as a guide to others more capable than myself.

Finally, there is something else to consider. Almost all of what we see and read is, by definition, written by the 'winners' in life. This is because they are the ones who have the wherewithal to get their story out there, and so their narrative becomes the narrative of us all. But this is not how we all experience life. To anyone who has eyes to see, people are despairing, and dying of that despair, all around us. It would seem to be worthwhile, in the light of what is happening, to present the world from the loser's point of view, as this apparently defines the experience of so many of us.

The first priority, when faced with an active shooter, is to take the shooter down. But what if the entire process can be stopped before it even gets to that point? My goal is to describe what such an intervention looked like from the inside out. In contrast, I say very little about the planning of the actual shooting. It is difficult to face the picture of myself, as I once was, that I am forced to paint here—the narcissism, disregard for human suffering, and inability to distinguish between the guilty and the innocent. Nevertheless, it is necessary to tell the truth in order to arrive at the solution—a moral renovation that penetrates so deeply to the root of the problem that you could be described as an entirely different person on the day that it takes place, yet so comprehensive that it takes a lifetime to complete.

CHAPTER 1

DOWNWARD MOBILITY

The sound of the Gion Shoja [temple] bells echoes the impermanence of
all things; the color of the sala flowers reveals the truth that the pros-
perous must decline. The proud do not endure, they are like a dream on
a spring night; the mighty fall at last, they are as dust before the wind.

The Tale of the Heike[1]

1969 – 1974

My father's parents had a house with a swimming pool in a nice
part of New Orleans, for those were still the days of their prosper-
ity. I knew Dad's father as Grandpa. At fifteen years old Grandpa
became a scullion[2] on the United Fruit Company ships going back
and forth to Central America. He began studying to become a doctor, but his father, a fire captain, died around 1930, so he had to
leave Louisiana State University to support the family. He eventually got a job as a construction worker making around $10 a week.

---

1   Excerpt as translated from Japanese by Helen Craig McCullough
2   An unskilled cook's assistant

After rising in the ranks, he managed to buy out that construction company and become one of the owing partners in the 1940s.

I knew Dad's mother as Grandma. Grandma's mother died when she was around four years old. Her father remarried, and without the protection of her mother, Grandma was passed from house to house and felt like no one really wanted her around. The events in Grandma's life after the death of her mother produced in her an iron determination to completely control her environment and fix everything around her. This had long term consequences for my father, but in the medium term my paternal grandparents lived a great life.

I always knew my mother's father as Gramps and her mother as Granny. Gramps grew up in poverty, so he took up boxing and other hustles to get his mother and siblings through. They mainly just ate crackers dipped in coffee. But when Gramps broke all kinds of bones while boxing, they told him he had to find a way to get milk. So Gramps settled into a routine where he set up a stand in a department store and sold Cokes in the morning, boxed in the afternoon, and went to night school at Delgado in the evenings to study engineering. This greatly helped his family get through hard times—especially the Coke stand, until the department store shut it down and took over the business themselves.

Pearl Harbor happened shortly after Gramps' eighteenth birthday, just in time for him to be enlisted. He spent some time in the Pacific as a chief engineer on a troop transport, and married Granny during the last year of the war.

My mother was born several months after the war was over. Mom was convinced that her parents did not want her. This perception of being unloved by everyone entered deeply into her personality. Yet I always remembered how she seemed to be doing her best to help me. I perhaps didn't see my father much, but what I remember is how much I loved doing things with him.

BEFORE THE DAWN OF WORDS

I was born in 1969 in Metairie, immediately across the Parish line from New Orleans. But my earliest memories begin in Baton Rouge, where my parents moved not long before my second birthday. I have surprisingly vivid memories of those very earliest years. In fact, I have at least one memory of what it was like to think before I could talk, even in my own head, and of the phantasmagoric[1] world of a very young child before the focusing of the eyes and the rules of perspective are set.

That would be the last time I ate a cricket. My mother could not understand why I wasn't starving even though I was refusing all her food—until one day I looked up at her, with two legs wiggling out of my mouth. Then she saw that I was crawling all over the house and grabbing crickets as fast as I could and stuffing them in my mouth.

But I can only remember that final day when such feasting had to come to an end. I saw something like a worm coming out of the cricket I was eating. Whatever I was eating tasted rotten, and my nose was burning. I still remember the difficult to conceive process of thinking—really feeling and sensing without the power of speech—but just knowing that something had gone terribly awry and that this cricket was probably already dead when I ate it. There was also a wordless determination never to do this again.

I say this was all phantasmagoric because I lacked perspective. One second the worm-like object looked giant, the next second there was a small cricket in my hand. Then it seemed all mixed

---

1   Means a dreamlike scene in which objects rapidly change size, blend into each other, etc, as in optical illusions. A Phantasmagoria was a 'magic lantern-box' used to create such scenes in prior centuries.

up with me so that I could not tell the difference between myself, the cricket, or the worm. Then the floor looked gigantic because my eyes were near it. In contrast, when I rolled over on my back, looking at the ceiling, the whole world seemed to flee away.

Some of these very early memories are happier. I remember my mother taking me with her into the voting booth during the 1972 Nixon/McGovern election, not long after I became three. And, before this, I remember my second birthday very clearly. I remember what I got—a Nerf-mobile and a Nerf football—and I remember my parents looking at me, saying "Look how cute he is!" as I hugged my Nerf-mobile and pretended to be asleep. And as I grew older there were many similarly happy times.

However, things were not normal for me. I suspect that part of the reason for the vividness of those extremely early memories was the skewed nature of the brain I was born with. It was strong on internal calculations and memory, but extremely weak on input/output and understanding what was going on in the world outside—most especially the world of social interactions. This caused problems. My parents tell me that I barely talked or responded to them—that there was no saying "Momma" or "Daddy" or any kind of baby talk, but that I just looked at them. This went on until I suddenly started talking in complete sentences when I was around two or so. When I did laugh or cry, it didn't seem to have any relation with what was going on around me. My own memories bear this out—that I lived in a very vivid inner world but that my dealings with people in the outside world left me into a constant and deeply frustrating fog of confusion. This state didn't really lift until around the 4th grade.

This absorption in an inner world and constant confusion toward the outside social world made me a prey. In those days we wandered around a lot our neighborhoods, even as very young children. I was regularly being harassed and beaten by the local kids. At one point I took a real blow to the head when several of us were playing and fighting with baseball bats. Another time I had two boys about my age repeatedly kicking me in the face until the blood ran down, while their older brother held me down. My personality did not help. My parents reported that they often saw me playing in the sandbox or something similar when other children were harassing me. I would neither fight nor flee, but simply continue what I was doing as if they were not there.

My father was very concerned and agitated that I was not defending myself properly. He made it clear to me that I was not allowed to "run home crying," and I would get spankings at home if I did not fight back. This made every incident not only bad in itself, but a problem to face at home as well. It was the spanking at home part that I was really worried about. I did not think it was fair that Dad was accusing me of "running home crying," because I thought I was just running home without the crying part. But, on the positive side, my father was doing his best to teach me how to fight. This was based on his own experience, for as he himself wrote in his own words many years later,

> While I was still six years old a new kid joined our group and started pushing everyone around. I'm not sure why, maybe it was his cocky attitude, but we were all scared to death of him. Everyone started running away and he chased me, punching me in the back of the head all the way home. I was frightened and crying as I slammed the door behind me and ran to my mom. She held me and assured me that I was in no danger, then, surprisingly, told me I should go back outside and face him. She told me that she understood my fright at first, but said that the boy appeared to be about the same age as me and smaller. She led me

outside and the only instructions she gave me were, "Don't run because he's faster than you." My mom closed the door behind me and I felt that I had to give it my best. Within minutes this boy was after me again. This time, he and I found out for the first time in my life that, although I couldn't run well, I was very strong and could hit very hard. The fight only lasted seconds but that's all it took to make me a legend in the minds of all first and second graders in the neighborhood.

It seemed so great at the time, but, as I look back on it, this event may have started a series of events that caused a serious decline in my ability to reach my potential as a person.

MY FATHER'S WORLD

My father had three main things going against him. First of all, he was an extremely brittle diabetic from about the age of eleven or so—brittle meaning that his blood sugar level could fluctuate wildly and was difficult to keep stable via the normal means used by diabetics. Besides this brittleness, Dad had a strategy to always keep his blood sugar as low as he thought he could get away with, believing that in this way he could avoid amputation and blindness later in life. In this he was successful. But the price was fairly regular insulin reactions that were constantly getting him into trouble. This could be real trouble for both himself and others, as the episodes of low blood sugar would at times violently affect his mind.

His adrenaline induced 'berserker[1]' modes, combined with his natural strength and fighting ability, could lead him to cause

---

1   Berserkers were old Norse warriors who would go into a frenzy which gave them superhuman strength in battle.

serious damage and in turn receive severe beatings from the police and others. So, from an early age, well before my teen years, I had to be familiar with dealing with police and paramedics. I would come out to see Dad all beat up and bruised and bleeding, explain his situation to the police and medical professionals, and eventually get him home.

Dad's 'berserker' mode, the second major problem in his life, was related to his intense claustrophobia. My father died years ago, but I can still let him explain in his own words how everyone first came to be aware of this from a brief description of his life that he wrote:

... I was attacked by a boy I hadn't seen since I was five years old. He was two years older than me and was the bully of my old neighborhood. He backed me into a chain link fence and leaned against me. He pushed my neck against the twisted wire and put his forearm against the front of my neck, choking me. He kept pulling his arm up every few seconds so I could take a breath or two and then started leaning on and choking me again. He laughed while he was doing this and I was screaming for help.

I can remember seeing adults close by and I was looking right into their faces and pleading for help. No one seemed to notice, and I can remember seeing them looking at me and smiling and rocking in their rocking chairs. The back of my neck was bleeding, I was confined and hardly breathing, and I was terrified. I don't remember anything else until the sound of sirens. A police officer was picking me up and pulling me back and two ambulances were parked on the sidewalk.

I looked down and saw the bloody, almost lifeless body of the guy who had attacked me. My hands, elbows, and all of my clothes were bloody, and I was confused. I was later told that I picked him up over my head and threw him on the sidewalk in a fit of rage. I then proceeded to beat him until he was unconscious and continued seemingly trying to beat him to death. I was told that many people tried to pull me off but couldn't keep me away. When the police got there and I heard their sirens I stopped and seemed to be in a trance ...

And yet my father's intentions were mostly good, so unlike myself when I was a boy. He was a naturally compassionate man—as were his parents—even to those outside his immediate circle. His primary desire in life was to have a happy family. But in this fallen world, good intentions are not enough. As good as my father's parents were, that very goodness became a kind of third problem for him. For they practiced an overprotectiveness with him that in many ways left him unprepared for life. The spirit is willing, but the flesh is weak. The corrosive cultural and spiritual forces working throughout our society in those years, together with a personal lack of discipline and spiritual focus, seemingly buried Dad's family dream. But not entirely. Our family remained intact throughout all my childhood, and was still my haven in spite of the worst that was going on for me, both inside myself and in the outside world. I certainly have no grievances.

Dad eventually learned what he needed to know the hard way—at least by the end of his life. But only after most opportunities were past and all of our family's money was gone. I suppose that is the way it is for us all. The briefness of our productive life mocks the wisdom we have gained—after it is too late to put to effective use. From this we learn two things. The first is not to put our ultimate hope in this life, but in the world to come. The second is that the best gift that we can ever leave to our children is wisdom and self-control—for we will surely run out the clock if left to learn it on our own.

In fact, Dad allowed me to make a decision on my own when I was around four or five, which continues to impact me to this day. I had repeatedly asked to learn boxing. One day my mother handed me the phone telling me Dad had something to say to me. He told me he found a boxing hall and asked if I wanted him to sign me up. I asked him to describe it for me, and for some reason as he did so, I was temporarily scared and said I was not sure if I wanted to go. He just asked, "Are you sure you don't want to go?" and, after some hesitation, that was the end of it. I deeply regret that he allowed me to make that decision on my own, when I was too young to see the big picture—instead of pushing me through, willing or not.

I regret that about many things. But how could any of us have known? At this time in their life both my father and mother had their own problems.

CHAPTER 2

THE BATTLE BEGINS

"And forgive us our sins, for we also forgive everyone who is indebted to us."

Luke 11:4

FEBRUARY 1974 – FEBRUARY 1976

I knew what year it was for the first time in the Fall of 1974, when we were asked to write down the month, day and year every morning in kindergarten at St. Thomas More Catholic School. Earlier that same year, my mother resolved to do something different for Lent—that is, to perform some positive action rather than giving up something. Her choice was to read the Bible some minimal amount each day. But, once she started reading, she found that she could not put the Bible down.

That was the joyful part, but there was also a painful and difficult part. She had to forgive her own mother—Granny. Mom felt utterly rejected by her parents—that they did not want her at all, especially her mother. This belief, and my mother's perspective of how she was treated, was entrenched deeply in her soul. Decades later when recounting it, she could barely hold back the tears, saying, "If even your own parents don't love you, who in the world would ever love you?"

As she continued to read the Scriptures, unable to put them down, she knew the command to forgive was not optional. She had to do it. Through many real tears, she did forgive her mother. And, in that one act of obedience a great battle began, one that would bring us all to the knife's edge of Good and Evil, of eternal salvation or everlasting ruin.

OPENING SHOT

The opening salvo of this battle occurred one night about a year later, in the spring of 1975. Dad was in New Orleans and Mom, pregnant with my younger sister, was at home alone with my older sister and me. She had not slept for some time and was completely exhausted. Shortly after she finally put me to sleep, I got up and vomited all over the place. She got up, cleaned up the mess, and put me to bed again. Just as she was beginning to drift off to sleep I promptly got up and vomited all over the place again—projectile vomit that stuck deeply into every crack and crevice. She began the whole process of cleaning up the mess again from square one. While this was going on, my older sister came in, telling my mom that she was hearing loud, extremely angry voices from outside, speaking in a foreign language. Mom calmed her, finished cleaning my mess, and put us back to bed. She was within seconds of finally drifting off to sleep again, when I threw up everywhere a third time. This was just too much.

An overwhelming impulse to take her own life overtook my mother and, though it may seem a frivolous reason for such a drastic action, in the moment the urge had an overpowering compulsion to it that was beyond the reach of reason.

Or so it seemed. Within minutes, an even more powerful force swept in. My mother recognized this as the Holy Spirit, although she did not know much about the Holy Spirit at that time. She instantly saw the folly of it all. Then an equally intense but opposite rage—that she could have possibly thrown away her soul and suffered eternal loss over something so foolish—swept over her heart and mind in the other direction. And, though she knew so little about the Holy Spirit, she understood that night that It was precisely who had saved her life.

My mother wasn't the only one with suicide on her mind in those days. That same night, my father was thinking the same thing as he was driving back from New Orleans. His construction business was failing and we were going bankrupt. He was thinking to himself that it would be best for the rest of us if he could arrange his death to get the insurance money for us all, rather than continuing to spiral into financial ruin. He drank heavily so that his death, for the sake of life insurance purposes, could be disguised as a traffic accident. Yet he has often stated that the Lord somehow spoke to him that night and told him that it would be a terrible mistake, that he himself was needed by all his family more than the money. How exactly this was communicated to him, none of us know. But it was absolutely true.

What I do know is that around this time Dad had a dream in which he clearly saw that we would turn out very badly if we continued to have a lot of money. He seemed to see some sort of future where I in particular would turn out to be a very evil person indeed unless our wealth was wiped out.

Strangely enough, sometime after this, I myself, a five-year-old boy, expressed similar thoughts to my mother. The context was this. My early years were the aftermath of the 1960s, and so I was always hearing adults discussing how bad this or that kid turned out when they became teenagers or young adults—selfish or getting into drugs and the like. I also overheard some of my older relatives talking about me one day, how I didn't care about anyone but myself. What I took from all this was that there was a general trend of kids such as myself going bad as we grew older. If anyone was going to go bad, I thought to myself, it would certainly be me.

From an early age, I had a strong sense of the reality of heaven and hell. I also had a strong sense of my own sinfulness. But, being a small child, I believed that at this particular point in my life I would go to heaven upon death. It was in the future, I supposed, as I grew older, that my exposure to the risk of eternal damnation would grow ever more acute. But I really wanted to go to heaven. I reasoned that the best possible outcome was for me to die now and go to heaven, where I already wanted to be, and thus avoid the ever-increasing risk of damnation.

I expressed this conclusion to Mom as clearly as I could, basically asking her why I couldn't just kill myself now. Her answer rocked my little world. She told me that the Church had made it clear that all suicides went to hell, so I'd better not even consider this. With that answer, the Lord seemed so unfair and unreasonable to my young and self-centered mind. Why wouldn't He let us all just end things while we were ahead, and go to heaven with Him? Why did we have to risk the fires of Hell? And why did this life of mine, that I already really hated, have to drag on?

Yet it was at that very time that a serious respite from my problems, a kind of brief golden age, was about to begin.

CHAPTER 3

A BRIEF GOLDEN AGE

When I was my father's son, Tender and the only one in the sight of my mother...

Proverbs 4:3

FEBRUARY 1976 – OCTOBER 1977

Throughout all of 1975, my father's construction business was going through an agonizing bankruptcy. In a desperate attempt to save the business, my dad started holding onto the payroll taxes, which got us into trouble with the IRS. As things got worse, Dad put up our house for sale, but the IRS put an immediate lien on it to recover their money.

The result of the bankruptcy and the loss of our home is that we moved to Jackson, Mississippi, when I was six years old. My father would work at a Burger King owned, or rather jointly owned, by Gramps. While I don't know the details, this was a kind of partnership between my paternal and maternal grandparents. Grandpa put up the money and Gramps was going to run the place. In the mind of my father's parents, a big part of this deal was that Gramps would provide Dad with a job as a manager. But the whole venture was ill-fated, and in the end doomed, so that nothing worked out as planned.

I knew none of this. For me, this twenty months or so became a kind of golden age, the only genuinely joyful period of my childhood. St. Richards, the Catholic school that I went to in Jackson, had some kind of special program for learning disabled children. Unlike any other interaction I've ever had with the psychological profession, this time a significant part of what they did worked for me. But not right away. I arrived near the end of 1st grade and faced the usual total confusion I'd always faced in school thus far: I could neither understand what was being asked of me, nor focus long enough to get any of it done.

AN OBSERVATION

But the story I am telling does not rest on my personal memory alone. I left behind quite a paper trail in the school system and, to a lesser extent, the juvenile court system throughout my childhood. A small subset of this has come into my possession. According to a report from the Mississippi school system at the end of 1976:

> [Ralph] was observed by the examiner on the playground, and it was noted that he played by himself, having little contact with other children. He walked in circles on the playground, rolled on the ground, and occasionally hit himself on the head with his fists. The teacher stated that she had attempted numerous times and in numerous ways to engage other children to play with him, but that her attempts had been futile. It was noted that when the teacher called for the class to line up to go back into the classroom, that [Ralph] did not join the line, until he became visually

aware of what was happening. The teacher stated that this type of behavior was a common occurrence, such as his not being aware of verbal directions in the classroom. Also, he frequently walks in circles around the teacher or desk when conversing with her and may slide onto the floor and crawl around on his stomach. The teacher also stated that peers are beginning to tease him about his behavior.

It may seem from all this that I had difficulty communicating verbally, but that was not in fact the case—not when directly engaged in a one-on-one conversation with someone. In fact, studies like the one I quoted from consistently attributed to me a 'psycholinguistic age' a few years higher than my biological age. But once the situation moved beyond a direct, focused, one-on-one conversation with few distractions, I could not pull out of my own mind long enough or consistently enough to understand what was going on in the social world around me. For me, this was like the explosion of complexity you run into when you go from a two to a three-body problem in Physics.

This dynamic was no more apparent than in my father's failed attempt to get me involved in organized sports through T-ball. For me to comprehend what was going on in a team sport like this, to grasp all the rules and relationships, was akin to someone with a 2nd grade education opening up an advanced calculus text—written in Greek—and immediately catching on with the flow of what he was reading. I may perhaps have had a chance at T-ball if Dad had sat me down and went through each and every rule step by step, with verification at each point that I had grasped everything up until then. But that was not the way things were done. You were supposed to just pick it up naturally as you began playing—and so I didn't.

The way it actually went is that I would spend the whole time not knowing what was going on. Then a bunch of people would be yelling at me that it was time for me to try and hit the ball off the T. If I did finally hit the ball, I would just stand there with no idea that I was supposed to actually do something afterwards like run to a base, until Dad would frantically get through to me that I needed to do it now. Later I would be positioned some place out in the field and would be completely lost in my own world, until a ball rolled right up to me that I was supposed to throw to someone. But I wouldn't know this. Perhaps I would be spinning around in circles, or lying on the ground looking up at the sky, when the ball came my way. I would not be aware of anyone's frantic shouts that I needed to act.

Needless to say, this tried everyone's patience and my own, so that it did not go on for long. The issue with sports was not that I had an aversion to physical activity. I absolutely loved dodgeball, for example, and was rather good at it. It is just that the level of social-interactive complexity involved in a team sport was completely above my head. I never got to the point where I could comprehend the rules and what was going on until around 6th grade or so, but by that point I was too far behind and had forever lost all interest. This complete lack of interest in sports remains to this day.

FRIENDSHIP

And yet, by 2nd grade it seemed like some kind of light turned on. I started to be able to both communicate with people and to understand what was going on around me. At this one point in time and place, a school was able to spend considerable time and resources on a single student. This consisted of speech drills repeated as many times as it took for me to understand what was being said and repeat it back correctly—exactly what I needed to slowly emerge from my fog.

. The fact that I was in an environment where other parents were trying to figure out ways to deal with their problem children was also helpful. For the first time in my life, I had a friend, whose parents were trying to work through his extreme hyperactivity. This led to many long days where I had fun with another kid, learning how to function outside of my own mind. This soon spread to a few others, and finally showed up in the classroom. I and a boy or two in my classes started drawing pictures, and we would say things like "Look at this weird picture;" "Yeah, that's a really weird picture!" And with that I had made my first entrance into society.

A far less helpful intervention during this period was various experiments with psychiatric drugs, especially Tofranil and Ritalin, to see if they could help. I have a daily journal scratched out on a torn-out piece of notebook paper that my mother was using to try and track their effectiveness in the week or so before Christmas of 1976:

- Sun—Nervous
- Mon—Doctor
- Tues—Big Day (out with friend, played all day, skated all night, stayed up late, got up early
- Wed—Cross—Pale
- Thurs—extremely nervous, hands shaking, heart pounding, pulse 122, pale, mad, depressed
- Fri—much worse, pale, frustrated, knee pains, blow up over everything, skating—stopped to lay down because heart was pounding out of his chest, didn't sleep well

· Sat—morning—fine, happy, could take things, lunch time bad, couldn't go out to eat, no pills, grew worse while day wore on, extremely nervous + frustrated Sat nite

But at this time in my life, such problems were no more than distant thunder far off on the horizon. I had so many things to do that I loved. Both in the apartment complex where we lived initially, and later in the house we moved into, there were woods we could wander off into and discover all kinds of stuff. There were creeks, frogs, a lake full of fish, and all the things a boy could want.

Even outside of formal sports, there were so many physical activities I could enjoy. I (finally) had learned to ride a bike and rode it all over the neighborhood and through the woods continually. At school there was dodge ball. Outside there was roller skating, which I learned to do after much difficulty, and then learned to love. I would go the rounds in the skating rink for hours, dimly illuminated by disco balls, listening to literal disco music which I couldn't get enough of.

It felt like I was living in paradise. There was some trouble in paradise—too much television, for cable had just come out, and with it, HBO. But as much time as these things wasted, they were still only a portion of a life that continued to be in some sense normal, healthy and fun. Video games were barely beginning to encroach; computers were off on the horizon. The internet was far out of sight, and social media and smart phones out of all imagination. In spite of all modern encroachments, we still mostly lived in the physical world. Even movies were usually in fun, outdoor drive-in theatres.

Great things were happening in Mom's life also. She had left Baton Rouge after her near-death experience wanting to find out more about the Holy Spirit. She only knew that it was the Holy Spirit who had saved her from suicide. Sometime in the second half of 1977, my mother saw an announcement for a "Life in the Spirit" class. This was a class that in the 1970s and early 1980s served as the entrance into the Catholic Charismatic movement. From the name of the course, Mom immediately knew that it was just what she was looking for. At long last, she would finally find out more about the Holy Spirit. She told herself that, if she had really forgiven Granny, she needed to invite her to this class also. This was not difficult since we were all living in Jackson.

The course went on for six weeks, and sometime during it both Mom and Granny began speaking in tongues. Their relationship with each other also radically changed. Regardless of what her rather sinful life had been like previously, Granny became a standard late 20th Century charismatic church lady from then on, going to prayer meetings, watching 700 Club and the PTL network, etc.

But it was all coming to an end. My father was failing at the Burger King, and the relationship with and between the in-laws was falling apart. A never-ending road construction project made the restaurant all but inaccessible to the public, and an ensuing lawsuit broke the back of the considerable resources that my paternal grandparents had built up. Grandpa sold their home in New Orleans and moved to Metairie, very near to where I had been born. Around the same time Gramps had an adverse reaction to a flu vaccine that gave him Guillain–Barré syndrome, a rare nerve disease that effectively ended not just his business but his ability to work at all. Gramps and Granny would struggle with poverty for the rest of their lives.

I had one last skating party in Jackson about a week or so before my eighth birthday, which was the absolute peak of all

I had experienced there. It was a cold morning as I woke up on my actual birthday in our new home back in Baton Rouge, not far from where we had lived previously. I looked outside and saw the frost on my 'Stretch Arm-Strong' toy that had gotten left out there in all the rush to move in. The brief golden age in my mostly difficult childhood was over.

CHAPTER 4

A HARD FIT

David fastened his sword to his armor and tried to walk, for he had not tested them. And David said to Saul, "I cannot walk with these, for I have not tested them."

1 Samuel 17:39

NOVEMBER 1977 – AUGUST 1979

The passing of the life I had in Mississippi and at St. Richards was a serious blow to me. One part of my new life was going to public school for the first time. As much trouble as I may have had at school in the past—and I had a lot of it—Sherwood Elementary was an entirely new experience for me. My older sister and I didn't like it at all and wanted to get back to what we considered our normal life at Catholic school. The fog that had slightly lifted in 2nd grade returned full force.

I mostly did not understand what was going on all day in class, and never got my work done. I remember only a few scraps from those days. There was some kid that I was always getting in fights with. On a larger scale we would play 'Yankees and Rebels' out on the field, which were extremely fun, free-style, large formation group brawls. Because we lived in Louisiana, we had French lessons every week. A lady would just come and speak French without explaining anything, so I learned nothing.

But while I don't remember much of what was going on in class, I certainly remember what was going on out in the hall. That was where I met a friend, who would be a major part of my life until adulthood; I will call him Harry Robinson. He was in the 3rd grade classroom right next to mine. We would both regularly be 'punished' by being kicked out of class to sit in the hall for the rest of the day, so that the teacher could go on teaching her class in peace. It always seemed to be just to the two of us out there by ourselves. We talked, rolled 'hot wheels' toy cars up and down the hall, and became friends in spite of our extraordinarily different personalities.

However little I learned in class or even understood what was going on around me, I had intellectual interests of my own. 3rd grade was the period when my fascination with science began to take off. I started reading books about dinosaurs and other extinct creatures from the early world, and this funneled all my interest at this time toward paleontology and the evolution. Grandma and Grandpa had assured me that Darwin's theory of evolution was completely consistent with our Roman Catholic faith, and that we could safely leave Adam and Eve behind. Dad was quite a bit more skeptical. Nevertheless, I devoured all I could and became convinced of evolution down to my core. This would have ever more impact on my way of thinking over the next few years.

In the Fall of 1978, I returned to St Thomas More Catholic school for the 4th grade. In those days I had severe allergies which caused my nose to run continuously, soiling my clothes and everything around me with a constant stream of snot. I was quickly labeled 'the Booger Man' and became THE major form of entertainment. I was surrounded by the other kids and was pushed, hit and spit on every day, whenever there was an opening to do so. This went on without mitigation for some time. But there came a day when one kid, who I will call Ron Guidry, strangely began to stand up for me. He yelled at the other kids, told them I was clearly sick and that what was happening was not my fault, and we became friends.

Although he defended me, Ron was not entirely just. In fact, we were not above picking on other kids ourselves. Ron loved making mischief and getting in trouble and was always emphasizing the importance of trying to pick up girls. We were a bit young for this, so that all Ron's talk about having girlfriends was more of an idea that seemed cool to him than anything that had any real basis in physical desire. I, in turn, proclaimed loudly that I had no interest in girls, and, in fact, I developed an entire persona for myself around this.

Because Ron and I went to the same Catholic church and school, there were many opportunities for doing things together. I began going to his house regularly after school and all through the summer, and we would while away the hours either doing fun things outside or watching cartoons. We would wander all over our neighborhood collecting discarded bottles to make money and loved to go hang out at the local Kmart, and the Woolco on the other side of the highway. More than that, we loved to go to the local video game arcade. Arcades were at that time beginning their ascent as the central hangout for young boys, before they were wiped out by Nintendo and the like. We both joined the scouts, but for some reason ended up in different troops, and this turned out badly. While Ron eventually ended up doing all the things I wanted to learn to do, like camping, I ended up in an entirely female led troop that did nothing but arts and crafts. It wasn't long before

I gave up on this and quit. But in those days, there was still a lot more to do, as we roamed the neighborhoods freely, often coming home after dark.

UNDERGROUND

Due to the flatness and wetness of the terrain, South Louisiana is full of drainage canals in almost all neighborhoods, and no house is far away from this system. Unlike in New Orleans where these canals are flat, out in the open, and often concreted over, the ones in Baton Rouge could be like a wooded adventure-land, especially as you followed the canals further and further out. Among other activities, we started smoking out in these canals by making our own 'cigarettes' from small, hollowed bamboo stalks which we stuffed with either pine needles or some kind of white Styrofoam-like plant material, that we perhaps got from cattails. Needless to say, we thoroughly habituated ourselves to not fully inhaling long before we ever got to real cigarettes, and this may have saved me from addiction later on.

But the best adventure of all was subterranean. About halfway between my house and Ron's was a large metal drainage pipe that came out through the banks of the canal to empty into it, and at its opening we could fully stand up and walk in. We had to keep our feet up at angles to avoid the oily, rotten, worm-infested water trickling beneath us, which got deeper the further in we went. Dad originally showed me this. He also taught me to wrap plastic garbage bags all around our legs and feet and put old pants and shoes used to cut grass over them to avoid this contamination, changing our clothes when we finally exited.

With Dad I didn't go too far in. But I later brought Ron, showed him the garbage bag method, and over time we explored deeper and deeper. The tunnel became gradually smaller while the water got higher, meaning that we had to increasingly raise our feet further up the two sides of the tunnel and lower our head as we waddled through. We kept place by counting the large open chambers where light filtered in from the street gutters above our heads. There we would usually find dry ground to stand flat again, take a break, and get some semi-fresh air.

There were other open chambers without a street gutter above them that were completely dark. These could be a trap because, if we didn't see the chamber in the dark, our feet that were braced against the walls of the tunnel would suddenly hit air and we would go crashing down into the nasty water. We called the main such trap the 'Crescent Moon trap,' because, if you looked carefully, you could be forewarned via a thin, almost imperceptibly dim crescent shape where the faint light from the entrance reflected on the changing shape of the wall.

At the third gutter there was a 90° shift to the right and, by the time we made it to the turn, the light coming in from the main entrance became a small white circle. As we turned to the right and went in deeper, the tunnel became smaller. We eventually had to crawl on all fours, applying pressure to the sides with all four limbs to prop ourselves over the water, which was also becoming gradually deeper. Whenever we looked down, we saw the disgusting, oily, worm-filled water beneath us. The air also became thicker and thicker with swamp gas until constant puffs of fog were coming out of our mouths, as on a cold winter day in spite of the warm temperature—but much thicker, as if we were human diesel engines.

Needless to say, this was very tiring. On the way back out, as we turned the corner from the third gutter, a kind of joyful mania would set in when we saw the small dim light of the tunnel entrance off in the distance. Before long, we would be unconsciously impelled to start running. As the literal light at the end of the tunnel grew ever larger, we would run faster and faster, compelled by the gravitational force of impending freedom. As we got even nearer and the light of the exit loomed ever brighter, we would impulsively begin yelling and cheering, like Xenophon's ten thousand soldiers, shouting out 'Thalassa[1]!" all the way down the line as they saw the sea. In this last wild rush, we would abandon our waddle and plunge our feet directly into the filthy water in order to run at absolute full speed, putting all our trust in the garbage bags wrapped around our legs and feet. Nothing can describe what it was like to make the final entrance, leap to the ground below, stand on solid ground and, above all, breathe clean air again.

But there came a day when we did not make our entrance back out again in this manner. One day there were three of us—me, Ron and another kid. We all had flashlights and we arrived early in the morning, determined to go as far as we could. In the past it just looked too forbidding beyond the fifth gutter, but this time we removed the debris out the way and kept going.

The tunnels got smaller and the water deeper, and whenever we came to an open chamber and rested, the thought of going all the way back out the same way again was just too much. At every such juncture we would deliberate and then decide to keep going deeper, giving new meaning to the phrase "there is no way out of this but through it." After a long day of this, we finally arrived at

---

1   The 'ten thousand' in Xenophon's *Anabasis* were Greek mercenaries who went far away to fight for a Persian Emperor against his rival. They were betrayed, but survived to march 1500 miles through landlocked territory—unnerving for the sea-faring Greeks. They were over-joyed when they finally saw the sea, *Thalassa* in Greek (*Thalatta* for Attic purists).

the eleventh gutter. Though we could see the twelfth, the tunnel was so small, and contained so much debris, that we knew we were at the end of the line.

As we considered the misery of going all the way back the way we came, we decided on a new plan. We noticed that the opening slots on the street gutter above our heads were wider than usual, and that the chamber was low enough for us to push our way out through them—at least it seemed I could. Since I was a little bigger than the other two boys, I lifted them up where they could grab the middle bar, and then helped push them from behind as they pulled and squeezed their way out. Ron got out first and helped pull the other boy out. Now it was my turn. I jumped up, grabbed the middle bar and started pulling my way out, until I hit a block-ade—my rear end. The other boys pulled me as hard as they could, but I wouldn't budge. I finally slunk back down into the chamber. It was bad enough for all three of us to go all the way back out the way we came, but I couldn't imagine doing it all myself.

A horrible thought struck me—I was confined to the under-world of Baton Rouge forever for no other reason than the mere girth of my buttocks!!!

But help was on the way. The boys started knocking on doors in the neighborhood, and eventually a couple of burly men came out with a crowbar and lifted the heavy iron top off the gut-ter so that I could get out. Someone let Ron inside to use their phone and call his parents, and the residents explained to our parents where we were and how to get home. We returned home and decontaminated.

I did not know it at this time, but in just a few years I would be making a slow series of decisions that would lead me, sta-tion by station, into a kind of spiritual subterranean tunnel into the darkness.

ANOTHER KIND OF DARKNESS

One characteristic of mine that began to manifest in elementary school was the strange way in which my emotions operated when I was in danger or under attack. You could almost say that I would lose my temper in the manner of a snake rather than as a bear or lion. What would happen was that my blood would go cold, and my emotions would seem to completely leave me, almost as if the blood was sucked completely out of my body. It felt like I was turning into some kind of computer or robot, or that I was merely controlling some kind of avatar that was not really me.

There were varying results. The most common consequence was a Hamlet-like failure to act, a delay in waiting for the supposed perfect moment for retaliation that never came. This led to a failure to defend myself with the consequent relegation to the absolute bottom of the pecking order. At other times it led to me calmly and flawlessly getting out of some danger or difficult situation. And on a few occasions, it would lead to some carefully delayed retaliation of murderous intent.

For example, I would wait for some kid who had crossed me to climb to the top of a tall slide and then push him off without warning at just the right moment. Or once at a summer camp, I waited for a boy, who was hassling me, to climb up awkwardly on a chair to reach something, and then pulled away the chair with the intention of breaking his neck.

The camp counselor looked at me in shock and said, "You could have killed him!"

I simply looked back and said, "I know." In my mind I was weak, beleaguered, and well justified in seeking vengeance. But it was always out of all proportion, and almost always the wrong target.

In those days Ron, with his rough sense of justice, was trying hard to guide me into the normal social world of boys. But it just wasn't working. Like a shoe that wasn't sized correctly, there was just no way to force the fit without a lot of pain. Despite all this, the way of God still seemed clear before me, and that is the way I still expected to go.

CHAPTER 5

A FORK IN THE ROAD

I call heaven and earth as witnesses today against you, that I have set before you life and death, blessing and cursing; therefore, choose life, that both you and your descendants may live

Deuteronomy 30:19

FALL 1979 – SUMMER 1980

I say that the way of God seemed clear to me, as I entered the 5th grade in the Fall of 1979, because good things were happening in Mom and Dad's life. Through that, my parents were giving me an indication of the path forward. They were going to something in our church called 'Marriage Encounter,' and seemed to genuinely be getting closer to each other instead of fighting all the time. It is only fair to say, however, that if you asked my mother today, she would claim, looking back, that Dad was faking it all. There was also a strong Catholic Charismatic ministry there based on a Friday night prayer meeting, and my mother was getting ever more involved.

At first, I was not going to these prayer meetings. During them my younger siblings were in childcare at the church, and my older sister was one of those doing the babysitting. This left me at home alone most Friday nights. I greatly enjoyed this and each evening I knew where to find the same three shows. I believe I would watch the Incredible Hulk first. At the end of each episode, Bill Bixby would once again have to leave town due to having turned into the Hulk. And, as Bixby picked up his backpack and wandered off in the distance with the soft, mournful music playing in the background—a tune I will never entirely forget—I would carefully consider the course of my life. I loved the Dukes of Hazzard, which came next. However strongly I may have insisted to Ron that I was not interested in girls, I was regularly transfixed by the sublime, never-to-be-surpassed beauty of Daisy Duke. Dallas was next, which I would watch only rarely. My parents and the rest of my family would usually get back not long after Dallas was over. On those nights when I didn't watch Dallas, I would usually read the Bible.

THINGS OF THE SPIRIT

Mom had gotten me started on the Bible early. It began with a colorful ten volume set of Bible-based story books we had. I believe it was produced by the Seventh Day Adventists, and you would often see these volumes in the dentist's office. This series went through the Bible in chronological order and, by reading through it, I got a grasp of the overall flow of the Old Testament. Because the intertestamental volume was missing—my mother gave it away to someone—I got frustrated and so never made it to the Gospel and New Testament part. But I already had a fairly strong base of what was in the Gospels from hearing them read week after week in church because—despite much commentary to the contrary—there is in reality, if not in theory, a lot more actual reading of the Bible going on each Sunday in Catholic churches than there is in most Protestant churches.

I would mainly read a New Testament translation that was everywhere in those days called *Good News for Modern Man*. These Bibles had one quality that made them priceless—the line drawings by Annie Vallotton interspersed throughout the text. There came a night when everyone was taking an especially long time to come home, and I found and read through the entire book of Revelation, which I had never heard of before. Of course, it scared the tar out of me. The one thing that stood out in my mind more than anything else was the vision of the eagle flying in mid-heaven, which in that translation cried out, "O horror! horror! How horrible it will be for all who live on earth when the sound comes from the trumpets that the other three angels must blow!"[1] The last of these trumpets is blown, of course, the day the Dragon, Satan, is cast down out of heaven to the earth and empowers the Antichrist. And there, right above this scripture was an illustration of a terrifying eagle, which from then on became fixed in my mind as the symbol of the entire Revelation.

I heard an eagle

13"Then I looked, and I heard an eagle that was flying high in the air say in a loud voice, "O horror! horror! How horrible it will be for all who live on earth when the sound comes from the trumpets that the other three angels must blow!"

Around that Thanksgiving of 1979, my mother took me to a Catholic Charismatic conference. This conference was held that

---

1   Today's English Version (TEV)

time each year in Lake Charles at the Civic Center downtown, beautifully situated on the lake itself. It was a special time, I was deeply moved by the meetings, and Mom would talk to me at night about the gifts and fruit of the Holy Spirit. I remember Granny being at our house the night we returned from the conference, although she hadn't come with us. We were all out in the driveway of our house, and Granny and Mom were talking about the things of the Spirit, and perhaps also about the Last Days.

For after the rain there was a weird formation in the sky where the moon seemed to be surrounded by a big corona of light. But on that evening, as I witnessed Granny and Mom laughing and joyfully talking about the things of the Spirit—the daughter who had felt so rejected and even hated by her own mother now reconciled—it seemed as if the Spirit of Holy Wisdom Itself was smiling down on them with a warm, feminine glow.

Not long after I returned from Lake Charles, I began going to the Friday night prayer meetings with my mother, and went through the "Life in the Spirit" class. By the end of that class, I was speaking in tongues and going to the prayer meetings each week.

THE TAPERING

Meanwhile at school, throughout the first half of 5th grade my problems were as bad as they had ever been. The 'booger man' taunting continued, but for a few reasons it would gradually start to taper off. There was a kid there who was constantly hassling me. I finally challenged him to a formal one-on-one fight, where I expected to fare better than the constant group bullying I was receiving at school. The fight was to take place on the corner right outside my house. But I was never quite the fighter I would have liked to be, because it took too much to drive me into action. So this 'fight' went on for some time with us just glaring at each other, until finally the guy said, "Look over there!" and, as I did, he punched me as hard as he could in the face. When I turned around and looked back at him, he said he saw someone in the window of my house, that he knew I was a coward and would call in outside support, and left. When I told Dad about this, I was distraught. "He made up this totally fake story about someone coming to help me," I said, "I didn't get the decisive end to this fight that I needed, and now he is going to use it to tell everyone at school that I was a coward!"

"Nonsense," Dad said. "First of all, that kid was the one who got scared when he punched you as hard as he could, and nothing happened. That is why he made up that ridiculous story and left." "The key to spinning this whole thing," Dad continued, "is to get to school early, before everyone else, and start telling your version of the story as loudly and brazenly as you can." "I have done this many times before," he added, and then he laid out for me a whole plan of how to seize control of the narrative.

Whatever other problems I may have had, I was able to execute Dad's plan flawlessly. When I got there early before the other kid, I started telling my version of the story, about how he ran away in fear after making up some ridiculous story. Everybody laughed, and my story took on a momentum of its own—so much so that I could clearly see the other kid's face drop as he couldn't turn the story around. As much as this was mostly pure propaganda, it slowly started to turn things around for me. I didn't have any more problems with that kid and, while I still had to deal with a few obnoxious bullies, the overall group dynamic started to slowly and imperceptibly taper off. Also, Harry Robinson had followed me to St Thomas More, and we became reacquainted and began to hang out together.

Another thing going on in those days was that my love of science was escalating. I had some interest in the systems of the human body but most of all in atoms and electricity. This started with a book in the school library about electricity. This book eventually lost me when it got into the intricacies of vacuum tube diodes and triodes used in older computers. But it began with atomic structure, where it explained what electrons were and how they operated—and this is where it hooked me. Around the same time, Dad gave me an old college chemistry book of his, where I went straight to the periodic table, and didn't really pick anything else up. My love centered on the elements and their atomic structure, and on fission and fusion, and the house started filling up with little drawings of atoms and their nuclei everywhere. I didn't really understand how atomic electron shells worked with their probabilities, imagining them to be simple orbits, but at least I did my best to get their numbers right.

This interest in science helped mitigate my overall situation at the time. My 5th grade teacher, who genuinely cared about what was going on in my life, slowly convinced the other students that my knowledge of science was something we could all be proud of together. This caused a kind of appreciation to develop. So, as the decade of the 1980s began, my outcast position was slowly beginning to wane, and the bullying tapered off.

The first inkling of this came when, as part of the Kris Kringle campaign (secret Santa) before Christmas, I received a single gift. It was nothing more than a note boldly proclaiming, "You are not the Booger Man!"

THE TESTING PLOT

But by this time the Catholic school was done with me. They explained to my parents that in their view the school was simply not equipped to deal with a kid with my problems, and that I needed to go to a public school where perhaps I could get some help. More importantly, they were probably fed up with my parents' inability to keep up with the tuition bills. Faced with this ultimatum, my parents were desperate to get me into what was called the 'Gifted and Talented' program in the East Baton Rouge Parish School System. But there was a problem.

You needed an official recommendation from a school to even get tested for the program, and no such recommendation would be forthcoming from St. Thomas More. As always in my life, although my parents were in over their heads with their own personal problems, they were doing their best to try and help me. So, together with my 5th grade teacher, they came up with a scheme to get around this blockade. At that time the Cerebral Palsy Clinic was doing widespread free testing in the city, and part of their testing was an IQ test. The plan was to take me there, ostensibly to get me tested for cerebral palsy, and armed with the resulting IQ test, get a recommendation into the Gifted program.

The plan worked. In August of 1980 I got a dual designation of Gifted/Learning Disabled from the Cerebral Palsy Clinic, and I was let into the Gifted program at Istrouma[1] Middle Magnet School at the last minute, just as 6th grade was already beginning.

Thus elementary school ended for me. Shortly after the end of the 5th grade school term, I went to see *The Empire Strikes Back* with Ron as a kind of last hurrah for that period in my life. I was at a fork in the road. There was no reason at this point that I couldn't leave the past behind and start a completely new life. No reason except that I was still the same person.

---

1   The "Istrouma" was the 'Red Stick' after which Baton Rouge was named, a reddened cypress pole that marked the boundary between the hunting grounds of two Choctaw tribes, the Houmas and the Bayougoulas.

CHAPTER 6

TRANSGRESSION

Having received the piece of bread, he then went out immediately. And it was night.

John 13:30

1980

Why do we keep repeating the same behaviors over and over again, when at their best they no longer achieve their goals and at their worst are self-destructive? Could it be because early in life we find ourselves in some situation for which we develop a methodology to cope? This then becomes like our operating system on a computer or phone. Consider how hard it is to completely change the operating system on a computer that you have been using for years, with all your work and applications set. You may be utterly fed up with all the intrusive updates which reset all your carefully chosen settings, the spyware and surveillance, the needless forced obsolescence of useful and trusted applications, and the involuntary corralling into new and decidedly worse ways of doing things.

But do you really have the bandwidth to truly break free and change to some completely new operating system, like Linux? Can you put your life on hold while you spend many hours learning how a new operating system works, and then take the time to save what you can while you rebuild your computer from the ground up? Can you learn to do everything you used to do with new applications, and to replace the old ones that won't transfer to the new system? Can you be sure that you can transfer many years of work and files to the new system, without opening some transferred text file, for example, only to find that it has been transformed into hundreds of pages of circles, diamonds and squares?

We tell ourselves that someday, when a semi-infinite amount of time and breathing space is available, we will change all of this. But, since this breathing space never arrives, we put all this off to some ever-receding horizon. And so, we keep living the same way, and doing the same counter-productive things.

In fact, we do more than this—we are ever unconsciously seeking to reshape the world around us so that the conditions exist that are most appropriate for our preferred modus operandi. The hard-core entrepreneur, whose most formative experience in life was operating on the razor's edge of bankruptcy and ruin, will recreate the same conditions by going off on some new venture whenever financial stability arrives. That way, his preferred methods of coping can be applied. The loner repeatedly finds some way of ending all his relationships, perhaps with the Whitesnake anthem "Here I go again on my own" playing in his head like some kind of personal theme song, so that the MO he developed early in life can be properly executed.

DRIFTING IN THE DARK

And so, sometime in the winter of 1980, I also recreated my own mess. Some inward compulsion was driving me to alienate people, even to turn them against myself—in a word—to transgress. Transgress, not so much against God but against the social order. I acted out, acting crazy. But none of this began as soon as the school year started, so I need to describe a little of the path that brought me to such a place.

I was still going to the prayer meetings with my mother in the beginning of the 6th grade school year. But there was a problem—I felt I was being attacked by evil spirits. I can no longer remember any details, yet clearly remember that this was, in fact, what was happening. The means I was using to fend this off was a mixture, which included both the true means of prayer—resisting in the Name of Jesus and His blood—but also the ineffectual use of things like holy water, crucifixes and the like. And it was not working at the level I thought it should. Or maybe I was just giving up.

To give up so easily on spiritual warfare was a profound disappointment. My mother had often told me that she had been compelled to name me after the famous archangel, almost against her will, by the mere fact that her mind went blank, and she forgot all other names. Be that as it may, I noticed that when I didn't go to the prayer meetings, somehow these spiritual attacks would subside. In weakness I started drifting away.

As I was gradually pulling away from the prayer meetings, I was going to the mall more and more. There were many times when I had money, for example, from Grandma and Grandpa, and for a year or so my parents even tried giving me an allowance as a way to see if they could get my behavior under control. So, when I had money I would go to the mall on Friday nights, maybe see a movie (around $3 or $4 back then), and then go to the video game arcade. When I didn't have money, I would go to the arcade and watch other people play—especially the star players who would always have a group of young boys looking on to see what next level they could get to. When I finally stopped going to the prayer meetings altogether, and people asked about me, Mom just told them that I really liked going to the mall.

I was spiritually disturbed in other ways. My mother had taught me to read the Bible in a way that showed how it all connected together. She began with Exodus 12, where it was forbidden to break any of the bones of the Passover lamb, and then took me to the Gospels, where it showed that none of Jesus' bones were broken when He was taken down from the cross. But in those days, there came a time when I read something that was far more frightening to me than that eagle at the end of Revelation 8. It was Romans chapter 9.

To quote just part of this,

For He says to Moses, "I will have mercy on whomever I will have mercy, and I will have compassion on whomever I will have compassion." So then it is not of him who wills, nor of him who runs, but of God who shows mercy. For the Scripture says to the Pharaoh, "For this very purpose I have raised you up, that I may show My power in you, and that My name may be declared in all the earth." Therefore He has mercy on whom He wills, and whom He wills He hardens. You will say to me then, "Why does He still find fault? For who has resisted His will?" But indeed, O man, who are you to reply against God? Will the thing formed say to him who formed it, "Why have you made me like this?" Does not the potter have power over the clay, from the same lump to make one vessel for honor and another for dishonor? (Romans 9:15-21, NKJV)

When I spoke to Mom about this, she just said something like "What is there to worry about? That is good news. God has predestined us to make sure we get to heaven."

"Who is *us?*" I thought to myself. Surely if there was anyone that God was going to harden for the purpose of damnation, I was that guy.

We went to the Lake Charles Catholic Charismatic conference a second time when I was in 6th grade. While I enjoyed the beginning, I had a very depressing experience near the end of the conference. A student youth group had come, and they were giving their testimonies of how they were living out their Christian faith in school. The way they were expressing how they were living seemed to be too much for me—that I could never, ever so openly represent Christ. A dark sense of hopelessness set in that I could never be the kind of Christian that I had previously supposed I could be over the last year or so—and it was thick. It was so thick that I gradually felt more and more physically ill, until the nausea reached the point where I could no longer even sit up but had to lie down. I found a place behind some stacked chairs where no one could see me, and listened to the rest of the testimonies lying on my back. I left that conference in despair. As we drove away from Lake Charles, I felt like I was veering off into the outer darkness.

But, when I say I started drifting away from God, it was mainly from what I considered hard core—participating in the prayer meetings and seeking a personal relationship with God. Nevertheless, I continued and even increased more ceremonial activities such as prayers and the rosary. I was also always looking for other externals, such as a stairway they had at my grandparents' church in Metairie, where I could go up the stairs kneeling and praying at each of the stations of the cross. And I always put down money to light a candle or two every chance I got.

Kids at school were listening to heavy metal and playing Dungeons & Dragons, but I had been warned to stay clear of this. And I did steer clear for as long as I could hold out. A kind of wavering back and forth toward God would continue until an almost-decisive night in 1984. My religious activities numbed the despair I had felt, but what numbed it more than anything else was staying away from the prayer meetings. As far as attacks from unclean spirits were concerned, these also ceased from my awareness when I stopped attending the prayer meetings.

In the Fall of 1980, things seemed to be going well at first. I was still hanging out with Harry Robinson, who would be following me to Istrouma. At the end of that summer, Harry spent the night at my house, and late into the night we discussed our upcoming time at Middle School. Harry discussed with me the advice his own father had given him. Harry's father had said that when he was in school, he needed to build his muscles, be mean, and beat people up, even though he hated such things. His father did this to keep people from intimidating him and to get where he was today, Harry said, and we would probably have to do the same even if we hated it. I didn't buy into this, because at this early date I still had a somewhat Christian understanding of the world.

But I got a small glimpse of what Harry was dealing with early in the school year when we all went up to a small town where they had a large telescope facility to look at the stars. After we got home Dad told me, "I would sure hate to be Harry Robinson." He explained that, as he talked with Harry's parents on the way up, they kept saying things like "We don't know what's wrong with Harry. We got all straight As in school; we did everything right. We can't understand why he can't get it together" and so on. My own father may have been right to reject their line of reasoning, but I think something in between may have been in order. For, as much as he wanted to, my father did not seem to know how to steer me away from wasting my life.

BRINGING DOWN THE WRATH

Harry did not remain long with me in the 6th grade. His father was some kind of engineer in the petrochemical industry and the whole family got transferred to the Netherlands early in the semester. I had another friend who I was hanging out with, but shortly into the semester I completely alienated him for no reason at all.

Something was driving me to transgress the social norms around me, and eventually the dam burst. I would act crazy. I would deliberately cross the big guys who were always telling everyone what to do, to try and prove I wouldn't just give in. And in a final denouement[1], I stood up on the school bus and cried out, "I am gay, totally gay!![2]" and did my best to act the part—week after week.

At this point in the story, I must lift my eyes up to heaven above and thank the Lord on high that I was a kid back then in the 1980s, but not now! What terrible forces would have been activated around me and descended upon me if I had behaved that way now! How my family itself, the only real haven I had in spite of all their imperfections, would have been dismantled by bad Samaritans! How I would have been wrecked, ruined, desecrated and perhaps mutilated seemingly beyond all hope of repair should I have acted thus as a child in the present day!

As it was, I saw an inkling of the regime to come. It took about a year of increasing problems for them to bring in the psychologists. When they did, there was a social worker asking me "Do you think you may really be gay? It can be so hard to admit that

---

1   The part of the plot in a play where some final revelation or outcome takes place

2   The actual language has obviously been massaged for contemporary sensibilities.

because there is so much social pressure against it." That is when I saw that I was really playing with fire. I didn't care about the social pressure—that was the whole point—for some perverse reason I was trying to test my mettle against it. But to actually be gay, for the adults in the room to actually think that was real and to say it was okay—that was more than I could accept. I never trusted the psychologists again. And so, somewhat less than a year after it started, I left this bit of transgressive theatre behind. But in the process, I got a glimpse of the new perverted moral order that would soon gain the high ground in its campaign to displace the ancient Christian one.

But this took place in the early 1980s. The wrath of my peers came down in all its fullness, and I got what I was subconsciously looking for. The bullying that I had experienced in 6th grade, the constant being spit upon and taking blows, was the worst that I had experienced thus far in life, exceeding the elementary school years. But why?

I have already mentioned that I may have been executing the very human tendency to try and shape the world around me to fit my familiar modus operandi. In this case, it was recreating my position at the bottom of the bullying pecking order that characterized my elementary school years. But something else may have been going on.

Throughout Middle School I was constantly brooding over the problem of pain. I considered that I would have a bad life as far out in the future as I could see. I was also deeply concerned to know how I would stand up under Communist torture because, if there was anything I was constantly obsessing over in those years, it was the Cold War, and my anxiety that the Communists were winning. As I considered these things, I thought to myself that perhaps we could fundamentally change our psychology toward pain. What if the fact that we sought pleasure and avoided pain was arbitrary and we could somehow convince ourselves enough to reverse the polarity? Could I train my mind to seek pain and avoid pleasure? After all, I thought, pleasure and pain were nothing more than feelings.

This thesis, that masochism could be the possible solution to the problem of pain, would lead me in those years to slash myself, burn myself, not eat for days, expose myself to extreme cold, all in order to test the thesis against myself. And that may have been why I did what I did in 6th grade. But it was all complete nonsense, for prolonged pain is compelling in a way that cannot be denied. All these things I did were under my control. If I had been faced with constant back pain, bone cancer, chemotherapy, real hunger, or any of the things people put up with every day, my thesis would have melted away. And before long I would be pursuing a different solution to my dilemma.

CHAPTER 7

A CRUEL VISION

Then I returned and considered all the oppression that is done under
the sun:
And look! The tears of the oppressed,
But they have no comforter—
On the side of their oppressors there is power,
But they have no comforter.
Therefore I praised the dead who were already dead,
More than the living who are still alive.
Yet, better than both is he who has never existed,
Who has not seen the evil work that is done under the sun.

Ecclesiastes 4:1-3

1981

At the end of 1980, for New Year's Eve, my cousin invited my older
sister and me to an all-night rock concert on a Mississippi riverboat named 'The President.' This was to see a New Orleans band,
"The Cold," that she followed at the time. All night long until the
sun came up, the riverboat went up and down the river in New
Orleans as the rock concert rolled on inside.

I had a digital watch that I loved, and I especially liked to call the National Bureau of Standards'[1] phone number in Boulder, Colorado in order to set that watch to the official exact second. As midnight approached, I left the bacchanalia in the concert hall behind and stepped on deck to stare at the river and the New Orleans skyline. There I carefully focused on my watch until the exact second that the year on it changed to 1981, and I reflected upon the course of my life up until then. And so ended the year 1980 for me.

Everything mostly stayed the same until the 7th grade began, and then things changed only a little. One tendency that first clearly revealed itself in the 6th grade still bedevils me to this day—that of constantly studying and reading things without getting any actual schoolwork done. This continued to be a fight for me through High School, into college, years later in graduate school and even now, as I endeavor to finish this book. I had little interest in my World History *class*, for example, for all the reasons that History got renamed "Social Studies." And I certainly had no interest in projects, posters, dioramas and the like, which I was never going to put any real effort into—F or no F.

But I sure loved my actual History textbook, and I read the whole thing through during the first few weeks of class, when I should have been doing my homework. I just had to find out how different periods of history connected, for example, how we got from Roman emperors to Medieval kings. But my real love in those days was astronomy. The interest was always there, but it was kick-started by an actual school project—the kind of thing I normally didn't want to do. Our science teacher wanted us to each take a constellation and make a report, which she intended to put all together into a book that would be published. After Scorpio,

---

1   Now NIST

my favorite constellation was Leo and that is what I was assigned. Even though I waited until about 9:00 on the last Sunday of the Christmas holidays to start working on it, when it was due the next day, it stirred up my love of constellations and drove my attempts to navigate my way through the night sky.

Other things were happening at the same time. Voyager had reached Jupiter a couple of years earlier and produced stunning images in the National Geographic, and it wouldn't be long before it reached Saturn. We saw it in class. Grandma had also gotten me a bunch of books about the planets for Christmas. From then on, I was constantly getting up before dawn and often climbing up on our roof to see the stars, especially in winter when the skies were clear. From then on, I was also going to the library and bringing back a stack of books on the planets, stars, black holes and the like every few weeks, and was usually reading this instead of doing any of my homework.

CHANGES

Sometime around 1981 Dad finally got a regular job with the Louisiana Department of Transportation and Development. After a few transfers, he ended up at the Materials Laboratory as a lab technician where he tested samples of things like concrete and epoxy. He excelled at that job. The years of failed business ventures and unemployment were over. Mom had expected to be a stay-at-home mother. But, under overwhelming pressure from Dad and Grandma, she also got a job as a clerk at Blue Cross that year, where she was also employed for a good part of her working life. And yet, strangely, things seemed to get tighter. It may have simply been that reality was setting in and my parents needed to get on something like a real budget.

My parents were in different circumstances than they had grown up in. But they had mastered the art of living beyond their means—although my mother would say this was entirely Dad's fault, as proved by her frugal life alone later. But they couldn't always keep all the plates spinning, and so nothing seemed to make sense in those days. It was often feast or famine. It seems like sometimes we had big delicious meals that we could all enjoy together, and other times we ran out of food and nobody knew what to do. For years it seems we could all go together for a family meal at Godfather's Pizza every week. So the best I can tell was that there was no real lack going on but just a certain amount of disorganization.

The one thing I know that made a difference for me is that when 7th grade began, I was no longer eligible for free lunches. I got put on the reduced-price lunches first, but the reduction wasn't enough—Dad wasn't going to give me any lunch money unless I asked repeatedly, which I was unwilling to do. All my life I have intensely hated squeaky wheels. So I mostly stopped eating lunch during the school year, but not entirely. In the beginning I would hover by the area where students would turn in their used lunch treys to be cleared and washed, and whenever I saw something untouched, I would grab it before they could put it in. Sometimes I would get whole pieces of chicken, and I stayed well fed. But this got back to my parents, and I was accused of eating food out of the trash, which wasn't true. I believed that I was being careful to only take things that were entirely uneaten, or that no one's saliva had touched, before they got into the trash. Nevertheless, my parents warned me, there were authorities out there who had the power to snatch me away from my own family over such things, over appearances alone. On the inside I raged and seethed against the fact that such a thing was even possible, and in my bravado I promised in my heart to bring vengeance down on whoever would do such a thing, no matter the cost. But I took my parents warning and piped down on the food snatching.

A few other things happened at the beginning of 7th grade. I was assigned to the wrong bus stop and there met a guy, who I will call Dave Boone, who would remain a close friend and associate of mine until the day I got saved. He is, in fact, one of the few close friends from those days that is still alive, and I still keep in touch with him. He started out as a scrawny kid with glasses, but he was on a mission to become ever cooler. He got contacts, built his muscles, and was forever strumming on his electric guitar. But, more than all things, he seemed to have an encyclopedic knowledge of history, especially military history, and also the gift of the gab. This was evident the very first morning I met him, as he talked and talked. Just try to get a word in edgewise if you ever meet him one day.

I remember the teacher in our 7th grade English class trying to stump us all one day by asking about what she thought was an obscure Roman military formation. To her surprise, Dave instantly rose his hand and told us all about the Testudo. On the bus he would regale us all with tales such as the night Attila died, with all kinds of details about how he was partying too hard and how one of his wives found him dead in his own vomit—the same way Jimi Hendrix died, Dave reminded us all.

In a related vein, I started taking Latin and joined the Latin Club, which was one of the few arenas where I could accomplish something in spite of my overall academic sloth. The way that happened was a classic case of the Dale Carnegie adage about giving someone a fine reputation to live up to. Our Middle school Latin teacher was a wonderful woman and one day she asked a question about a relatively obscure mythological figure, a giant covered with eyes named Argus. I knew something about him only because of a New Orleans Mardi Gras parade in his name, and so I answered the question. A few days later, apparently based on my answer to this question, she told everyone in the class that I was their mythology expert. This really shook me, since I knew it wasn't true, and I was terrified of being revealed as a fraud. So, from then on, I studied Greek mythology continually and really did become a kind of expert.

Still trying to follow God intermittently, I stayed away from heavy metal and did my best to avoid Dungeons & Dragons. But I ultimately gave in for a season. The lure to join in the people playing it all around me was just too great. But as I carefully studied how 'clerics' and 'magicians' did their thing and differed from each other, and pored over their books of gods, demigods and demons, I knew I was getting near the realm of the demonic.

There came a night as I was reading through their lists of spells that I came to one called something like the 'Caco-Demon.' It literally described how to summon an actual demon via inscribing a pentagram, and so on. That was a bridge too far, and I pulled back. I would never go back to D&D again. But, as a compromise, I purchased a fantasy role-playing game called Gamma World, which was supposed to be about a futuristic post-apocalyptic world and so, theoretically, wouldn't have all the magic. And I kept praying my rosary and doing my novenas; yet I would soon be adopting a distinctly non-Christian vision of the world.

FROM THE BOTTOM

The bullying from 6th grade continued, but I can now see on reflection that it was nowhere near as bad as I imagined it to be at the time or for many years afterwards. Probably most of my mornings and afternoons on the school bus were spent peacefully off in some corner reading something like the Iliad. There were so many good things going on, so many opportunities, but the bullying was just what I chose to focus on. Perspective is the oxygen of the soul and, since I had almost none of it, my anoxic soul was beginning to wither.

And so, in the midst of my laser-like focus on bullying, there came a day when I noticed something while a whole group of kids were humiliating me. Since I was still near the bottom of the pecking order, I noticed that other kids who were often bullied themselves were getting some status and acceptance, and a kind of vicarious strength from participating in the attack on me. For me, this observation turned into a kind unified theory of all human behavior.

Imagine an African dictator, I thought to myself: Abusing all his people, stealing everything in the country and keeping it for himself and his cronies, driving all his people to starvation, and feeding anyone who opposes him to the alligators. From time to time, he has rallies opposing some phantom or long-vanquished threat, like 'Colonialism,' in which the humblest of people are allowed and are indeed expected to participate. And, as they do, raging against some bugaboo, they are vicariously joined to and get to participate in the strength and status of their tormentors. They in a sense become one with those ruling over them, and so transcend the misery of their lives. Not only this, but if they can find someone lower on the scale than they, someone officially designated as permissible to abuse, they get something more than mere vicarious strength. In that one context, they get to be part of the winning team, and enjoy all the camaraderie and backslapping that goes with it.

As I sat on the bus and considered these things, this became my vision of what the whole world was: one miserable pecking order from top to bottom, run through with abuse all the way down. I was convinced of Darwinian evolution to the core, and this vision cemented it in my mind as the theory of all life. It was a cruel vision, but I intended to act upon it. And so a plan formed in my mind. When I saw an opportunity, I could strategically join in the hassling of some kid, but do it better, perhaps more cruelly, perhaps in a more funny or ironic way, and so gain credibility with those doing the hassling. From there, I could seek to gain my strength, do more outrageous things, and begin a slow ascent up the ladder.

Why was that my plan?!? If I was going to try and build my strength, why bother with victims at all? Why not just build my strength, beat a few bullies who really deserved it instead of the wrong target, and get enough such victories to go on with my life undisturbed? Then I could focus on the things that really interested me—which were a lot. All I can say is that I had a complete lack of imagination, beyond myopia into a kind of tunnel vision because, being so young, I suppose, I lacked perspective. I simply could not imagine any other way. But my cruel vision was all a theory until an event took place which pushed me decisively in that direction.

THE TURNING POINT

Sometime in 7th grade, near the end of 1981, another rock concert came to New Orleans, the "Psychedelic Furs." It was around Thanksgiving, and we were all at Grandpa and Grandma's (Dad's parents) house. Mom didn't want any of us to go to the concert, as she accurately saw the world as the place full of danger—especially spiritual danger—that it was. But Grandma was more of a 'just let the kids be kids and have fun' kind of woman and, of course, relentlessly insisted on her own way as she had done all her life. Finally, she prevailed upon Dad to let my sister go. Now Mom and Dad were in a real stink with each other and were arguing on into the night. Meanwhile Dad's blood sugar was dropping. For some long-forgotten reason, I entered their room to talk about something, and as they continued to argue, Dad was becoming ever more incoherent.

By the time I was there, Dad had become almost unintelligible and was getting more and more agitated, until he cried to Mom at the top of his voice "You're the Devil!" He threw a coke can with deadly force, but Mom ducked, and it burst against the wall. He leaped toward her and started pounding at her but, fortunately for the moment, mostly missing. Then he turned around and faced me and shouted, "You're the Devil too!!" and continued to scream out in horror. We were cornered, because he was between the door and us, and we knew there was a strong possibility that he could beat us to death.

At just that moment Grandpa and Grandma returned home and could be heard coming down the hall. Mom believed they would be able to handle the situation, and in the distraction, considering herself to be the primary target, she bolted out of the room, locked and barricaded herself in the bathroom, and started praying in tongues.

But I was way on the other side of the bed and could not get out of that room without walking right up to Dad. For a few seconds that seemed like an eternity, I wasn't sure what to do, and neither did Dad. Then, for another moment, the terror of us 'being the Devil' was so much for him that he threw a sheet over his head to hide. That's when I made a dash out of the room. He soon ran after me, but at that point Grandpa came out to try and stop it all and reason with Dad. This slowed things down, but Dad struck Grandpa with a blow of such force that Grandpa hit the ground hard and bounced back up about two feet. Grandma came out, braced her legs behind her, and held up a large crucifix way in front of herself to try to stop Dad, Dracula movie style. But Dad hit that crucifix, which had an iron Jesus right down the middle of it, so hard that it broke in half, with the two pieces flying off in opposite directions like throwing stars into my grandparents' room. And the thing about this event that was the most preternatural[1] of all was finding the two halves of that crucifix deeply imbedded in the opposite walls of that room after it was all over, and we were cleaning up.

But getting back to the moment, at that point Dad had followed his parents into their room while I was still in the hall. I heard yelling and saw blood splatting on the opposite wall of the hall, and this caused me to hesitate. Mom was yelling to me out of the bathroom to get my younger siblings out of the house and, under pressure, I made an immediate decision. My grandparents were not going to survive, they were as good as dead already, I decided.

It turned out I was completely wrong—my grandparents were far more resilient than I had imagined. But, in the moment, I decided that the only useful and necessary thing I must do was to get my younger sister and brother out of the house. They were sound asleep, so when I woke them up, they were in a complete stupor. But I had to get them out as quickly as I could. This was very slow, and meanwhile Dad started lumbering toward us. He reached us in the garage. I had already gotten my younger brother outside, but my sister was still there with me and I was trying to keep her moving in her confusion. Dad was just about to strike my sister with a huge blow, when he suddenly and inexplicably

---

1   Very weird and out of the ordinary but not quite supernatural, or violating laws of physics.

56

snapped out of it all and came to. My mother's praying must have finally worked.

I brought my younger siblings to the neighbors, who we woke up while Mom and my grandparents dealt with the aftermath inside. And, as I was rousing the neighbors and trying to explain what was going on, I started crying and weeping uncontrollably. And I became deeply ashamed. I would never cry and be weak like this again, I told myself. I would harden myself and, in fact, systematically remove every part of my conscience, so that I would no longer have pity for anyone or any regard for my own pain either. I promised myself I would kill someone, somewhere, by the time I was fifteen.

When I returned to the house, I started washing the dishes, as I have always done under stress—for my main jobs as a child in our home were washing dishes and cleaning the bathrooms. I understood my father's situation and did not blame him and, despite all my plans for hardness of heart, I was concerned how he would make it through. Dad and his parents were sitting at the kitchen table. Grandpa kept saying something like "I can't believe it, that is all just like what happened with so and so." Both paternal grandparents were recovering from their injuries and trying to make jokes of them the best they could.

As for Dad, he couldn't believe what he had done and was collapsed over the table with his head in his arms in horror. But I couldn't help but notice that, even in his hour of desolation, Dad had a kind of quiet dignity about him as he sat with his head hunched over—so unlike myself crying hysterically like a baby. Grandma and Grandpa were comforting him, and Dad would make it through, for they had a love for him that would never die. The arc of my own life, however, was about to take a decidedly villainous turn.

CHAPTER 8

SO UNNECESSARY

"The lamp of the body is the eye. If therefore your eye is good, your whole body will be full of light. But if your eye is bad, your whole body will be full of darkness. If therefore the light that is in you is darkness, how great is that darkness!"

Matthew 6:22-23

JANUARY – AUGUST 1982

Early in 1982 I took my first baby steps towards the moral abyss. When the second semester of 7th grade began, I got switched to a different History class. There was a relatively weak kid that was picking on another even weaker kid in that class, and I had a chance to put my theory into practice. I joined in, did what I thought was a better job, and had instant camaraderie. This was a marked difference from the bullying that I was still experiencing. But I was already being bullied less, and it probably would have remained minor without me needing to participate myself.

Everything that was to follow over the next few years was so completely unnecessary.

Indeed, something much more prosaic and yet positive was also going on. To try and keep up with the fake reputation my Latin teacher had given me, I was studying Greek mythology day and night, leaving big charts of genealogies and the like all over the place—all the while not keeping up with my regular school-work. This was perfect for me because all I had to do was continually read and absorb without having to produce anything of assignment grade quality.

And that year was, I believe, the first time that a middle school participated as a school in the state Latin convention run by the Junior Classical League (JCL). It had previously been the province of high schools. The state JCL convention was held at Louisiana State University (LSU) in Baton Rouge, as it would be for the next several years in a row, so that most of the students were staying in dorms while we just showed up every morning. We were roundly mocked by the high school kids when they saw how little we were, and so we all doubled down and determined to win with the little time we had left.

I had slashed my arms not long ago in a fit of mental agony, and they still hurt a little, but here I was in a whole different world. We hung out all day and long into the night at the LSU student union and surrounding areas, and even I was having fun, being among friends. It was expected that I would be able to bring us a victory, and I did, getting first place in Mythology. And enough of us did so that Istrouma surprised everyone by winning first place that year. This, in the face of all the mockery we had received, was an exceedingly sweet victory.

The fact that I had new friends makes what was about to follow in my life all the more inexplicable and inexcusable. But, once certain things are set in motion, they are hard to turn around. And as we all, readers and writer, will continue to be reminded in this tale, I was still myself—and as long as that was true, regardless of external circumstances, my problems would remain.

Around that time, I started hanging out with a kid, who I will call Han Fei. I really don't understand why he was willing to hang out with me, because our personalities were so radically different. Han Fei was very high on the agreeableness scale, and one day he just started talking to me. I told him something about my life, and he said, "I did notice that you aren't very well liked." Han's mother was Thai and, although I don't know much about his father, I believe Han's father was a Wai-Shen-Ren[1] from Taiwan. With Han I started going to a Tai Kwon Do school at night taught by an incredible man who I will call Chul Yun.

Besides the Tae Kwon Do, though, I gave in to a lot of things that I was still trying to avoid before Han and I started hanging out. One of these was fantasy role-playing games. I never went back to Dungeons & Dragons, but Han and some other guys got me into a similar one called TFT[2], which, since I was still slightly trying to hold back, I justified to myself as not having as much emphasis on magic. And then there was Traveler, a Sci-Fi based fantasy role-playing game that attempted to incorporate all the favorite space narratives, such as Star Wars and Star Trek, into one big gaming universe.

All that summer, Traveler in particular consumed and wasted huge portions of my time. The National JCL (Latin) convention was looming, and my Latin teacher and new friends were counting on me as the one person who could pull in a first place for our state. But I just kept wasting time all summer, and, in fact,

---

1   Those and their descendants who fled to the island from Mainland China in the aftermath of the Communist takeover in 1949

2   The Fantasy Trip

nothing stands out more to me when looking back on my childhood than all the enormous waste.

That summer the National Latin convention was in Oklahoma.
Taking a long trip on a bus and being away from home for a week,
we had an absolute blast. Unfortunately, this gave me a greater
taste for troublemaking, hell-raising, and partying, although the
partying part would never be a big part of my life. I got third place
in Mythology, which, in light of what I should have done, was the
due reward of my sloth.

PERVERSION

There were other bad things that I gave into at this time. One
of these was pornography. Cable TV was just getting started at
this time, and the Playboy channel was supposed to be blocked
from children via a code parents had to put on the remote. But at
my house it had been left on the default code, which was widely
known by almost everyone, so I started watching. Beyond this,
Han had some uncles who were always telling tales of Thai gang-
ster life, and they had a lot of porn magazines, books and VHS
movies, which we eventually got immersed in for a season.

As I write this, I have been 100% pornography free for more
than thirty-eight years. And yet until recently I have had to spiritually fight on a regular basis against the scenarios and ideas that
were implanted in my mind all those many years ago. I say ideas
because it is the books—books with almost no pictures—that have
had the longest staying power. This would seem strange since
men are supposed to be visually triggered.

But the reality of pornography and almost all sexual lust is
that it is the case of either Satan, or our own perverted self, using
the sex drive to strengthen and energize some other, foreign

purpose or idea, just like an outboard motor. For the sex drive is a natural force with its own internal logic based on love and procreation. Satan is many things, but one thing that cannot be said about him is that he is asleep at the wheel. And he would be a poor strategist indeed if he didn't take the opportunity to commandeer this motor for all kinds of evil purposes; hence we have pornography.

The books that lured me were full of ideas—ideas which would not have such strength on their own. Seen this way, I can remember three of the main themes that the pornography of that day seemed to be trying to implant. The first was to sexualize all kinds of everyday situations and activities. Everyone laughed at this. But the true meaning of this was to bind us and take away our freedom and sovereignty to live a normal life with normal interactions. From then on, we were no longer free to engage in the normal business of life without constant sexual urges and desires. The second that I remember was a constant but cleverly gradual push to normalize all kinds of perversions. And from this, we can see the true, underground reason why attitudes about things like homosexuality changed so radically within such a short period of time.

But the most prominent of all, I think, was the theme of degrading people through sexuality. As the motor of Eros, the natural sex drive, if separated from its purpose and designed relational context, is eventually burned out and run into the ground. So, there is the need to get a little more kick to charge the ever diminishing returns. In this degradation, we can also see a logic very similar to what would occur when we broke into some car or building and there was nothing to steal there—it would almost always lead to vandalism. For at the bottom of all grasping for what is not yours is an eventual complete lack of satisfaction, which causes you to lash out. This is what I was being exposed to forty years ago, before the internet. I shudder to think how completely people's hearts and souls are rotting out today.

I also went totally into the Heavy Metal music of that time, which was to have very bad effects on me. It could not have been otherwise. First of all, you take the musical faculty, which was designed for healthy socializing, the worship of God, and the celebration of His blessings, and tie it into a continual celebration of sin. Then you play it over and over in your mind with music so compelling that it is akin to intravenously injecting the message behind the music into the inner heart of your emotional life. How could this not transform the inner desires of your heart and shape your motivations? However, the constant rebuff in those days, on the rare occasions when some religious person criticized the music, was "It doesn't affect me." But it did, in fact, 'affect' everyone, as evidenced by the radical difference between the America of the 1980s and the America of today. So many of my generation ended up believing and not believing things in recent years that would have seemed absurd to them in their youth.

And so, in 1982 I began my long slide into sin. But none of this seemed to be a very big deal to Han Fei, or outwardly affected his idea of being a good member of society or a basically good person. He saw no contradiction between pornography, or heavy metal, or low-level crime, and being a good kid at his local Baptist church. I think large numbers of people are like this. We participate in sins that are, in their underlying principle, serious and contrary to all that God wants for us; yet in the grand scheme of things, they seem to have no real impact, and so seem no big deal to us. And yet, as their effects gradually accumulate throughout society, they pile up like sand in an engine and eventually lead to widespread corruption, poverty, and heartache.

Han Fei and I represented opposite poles of the unjust judge "who did not fear God nor regard man" (Luke 18:2). I was virtually impervious to social controls but still had a residual fear of God. Han Fei did not appear to fear God—as far as I could tell. He had no problem getting in trouble, torturing animals with me, and picking on other kids from time to time. But he also was very open to the social controls which I was impervious to, so he would get upset when he thought things were going too far, saying something like "What in the world are you doing?"

DISCIPLINE

My parents could see what was happening with me and the direction I was going in. But they were unable to reach me. This fact became particularly disturbing to me after I became a parent myself, so that I have often turned over in my mind what it was that kept my parents from reaching me. There is always, of course, free will, which I suppose was the predominant factor here. But there were other factors as well. As far as I could tell, my parents had no unified system of discipline. They seemed to be pulling things from all over the place, beginning with that infamous book by Dr. Spock. Beyond this, they usually didn't agree with each other and were always arguing, making it difficult to present a unified front. Dad always had a naturally rebellious bent himself, and if he had taken my mother's ideas about our upbringing more seriously, things may have turned out differently. My father also seemed to be uncomfortable with corporal punishment. Not opposed, but unfamiliar, because I don't think Grandpa or Grandma ever spanked him.

What ended up actually happening was something that made me long for the simple arse-whippings of old. Whenever I got in real trouble, their response did inadvertently end up taking a kind of standard form. In fact, confronting my messes seemed to be one of the few unifying elements in their lives. The best way I could describe a typical response to my behavior was a combination of an interrogation and a struggle session, where they both relentlessly tried to get the truth out of me and also to get me to see the error of my ways. It could go on for hours, reminding me of Gletkin explaining to Ivanov how he had discovered his method of interrogating the peasants in Darkness at Noon[1].

In many ways, my parents were on the right course—moral suasion combined with properly carried out physical discipline. But there were some core issues that made it ineffective in the end. First, such sessions were unfocused, and could involve a certain amount of ranting and raving that seemed to go on for hours. There was no formal, disciplined corporal punishment, in which the infraction would be explained, and the punishment impartially meted out. Rather, as the session went on, my parents would get more and more worked up about whatever I had done, until Dad or perhaps Mom couldn't contain themselves anymore and would give me something like a smack across the face or the like. On it would go, waxing and waning, sometimes conversational and sometimes reaching a fever pitch, with smacks and spankings interspersed randomly and unpredictably. And I can now see clearly that so much of Dad's frustration was that he saw me throwing away all my potential by making the same bad choices that he had made—and he felt powerless to do anything about it.

Michael and Debi Pearl in their books, most famously *To Train Up a Child*, have a lot to say about the best way to handle all this. They are especially compelling when they describe how corporal punishment, properly done, relates to the penal

---

1   *Darkness at Noon*, Arthur Koestler, "The Second Interrogation," 92–94

substitutionary atonement, and frees the spirit of the child when he knows the problem issue is now officially over and the relationship is restored. But I know that I could never describe this as well as they do and am probably botching even the little that I am saying. So, I implore you! Read the book yourself!

What I can say is this. On most occasions the discipline that I received did not in any way free me as described by the Pearls. There were a few occasions when things did work out, when I ended the session with my parents feeling reconciled with them and in some sense cleansed from my sins, like I was completely starting over. For whatever their methods may have lacked, my parents' intentions toward me were good, and God could make up the difference. But the majority of the time, it did not work out this way. On the contrary, I simply became ever more convinced of my own incorrigibility, ever more dug in, and ever more determined to bury myself from sight under a mountain of lies.

But even then, I don't think the proper form of discipline was at the heart of the problem. More importantly, my parents' efforts at moral suasion weren't really directed at our duties toward God or the final judgment, but rather on the ultimate social consequences of what I was doing. This had zero impact on me because I had already entirely given up on the possibility of any good social consequences very early in life. I absolutely did not regard man, and yet I never ceased to fear God, even in the days when I hated Him. The church I was in also seemed to be becoming ever more humanistic in the long aftermath of Vatican II, with the exception of the prayer meetings, and this blunted a great deal of the moral impact I could have received.

But I think that, as a young boy, there was one issue above all that put me out of reach. For all of my mother's good influence, I needed my father to be the spiritual leader in our home. I certainly could not outtalk or outsmart my dad. At my young age his knowledge and experience were so much more than mine. Combined with his gift of the gab, I almost felt as Job said of the Almighty "If one wished to contend with Him, He could not answer Him one time out of a thousand" (Job 9:3).

Had my father been the spiritual leader, I think that I would have been reached and all that depravity and all that waste of my life through sloth could have been avoided. But as it was, I was determined to go my own way.

CHAPTER 9

THE TORMENTOR

A righteous man regards the life of his animal, But the tender mercies of the wicked are cruel.

Proverbs 12:10

AUGUST 1982 – MAY 1983

Istrouma Middle Magnet went from 6th grade to 8th. In our 8th grade year, with the older kids gone, my friends and I became a sort of invasive species cut loose from its original environment of controlling predators. Right at the beginning of the school year, my parents went on a trip with my older sister. My younger siblings stayed with my grandparents, and I stayed at Han Fei's house for the first week of the 8th grade. We egged each other on as to how we would start the school year.

In the beginning, the biggest element of this was groping and grabbing the privates of various girls that were around us. This was a complete violation, but we didn't care. We were also soon getting into all kinds of trouble, not Han Fei so much as me, but he did participate some. We just couldn't believe our good fortune, now that we were the oldest kids, and we were determined to milk it for all it was worth.

From this, we can see what an awful effect even the blessings of God can have on those whose hearts are given to sin. What God fully intends to do is "show the exceeding riches of His grace in His kindness toward us" (Ephesians 2:7). But there is a dilemma in this which was clearly illustrated to me in an event which took place in our back yard.

SPREADING THE TARES

My father wanted to grow a garden of some kind, so he dug out a patch of ground, replaced all the dirt he dug out with the richest, most fertile soil he could buy, and then added to that all kinds of fertilizers and root stimulators. But, for some reason, before he could plant anything in this perfectly prepared patch, I got it in my head to spread bird seed all over it. After some time, when no one knew what happened, we went out there to find a crop of the most horrifyingly ugly weeds imaginable, grown to an unnatural height with abnormally large thorns that none of us had ever seen before. And so it would be if God did all the good that He fully intends for us all at once and indiscriminately.

So as a twelve-year-old in 1982, as the bird seed in that heavily fertilized ground turned to weeds, so the wicked seeds that had been planted in my heart began to grow. More than anything, my goal was to move from being the tormented to the tormentor. And my bullying of other kids, whenever I had the chance, was merciless. All the spitting on and abuse by other children that I had endured as I child, I now meted out on the mostly innocent. The lockers at Istrouma were tall but skinny, and one of my friends found a way to push one kid in there and lock him in, where he yelled and banged on the door until the janitor cut him out. I felt pressure to outdo this. So the very same kid who had been put in the locker, I kicked mercilessly in the face, taking a cowardly cheap shot on a stairwell that gave him a concussion, and his cries that day still haunt me as I write this.

But my tormenting of other kids in those days was, in fact, all political, and I explicitly understood it to be so. It was all based on that cruel vision I had conceived that day on the bus, when I could see the kids who were picked on themselves getting relief as they joined in the bullying of me. One day I walked in the bathroom and there was no one there except me and one of the kids I was harassing. By his look, I could clearly see that he expected me to do something harmful. But I told him, "Don't worry, there's no one to see me harassing you here, and so it is of no advantage to me at all."

A SURREAL DREAM

In the case of one kid, however, there was a strange intervention that took place which led to an entirely different outcome. I will call him Nathan Maddox. He ended up becoming the very closest of my friends for the next several years until I became a believer, and even afterwards we were very close for several years. Nathan was an Appalachian kid whose biological father had been a nuclear physicist, perhaps at Oak Ridge. But the marriage had failed early in Nathan's life. His mother had remarried, or perhaps simply cohabitated, and moved down to Baton Rouge, where they lived in an apartment complex not far from my home.

He cut a pathetic figure in those early days, and several kids were abusing him mercilessly on the bus. At first, I joined in, but one night I had a dream. In that dream various things were happening with Nathan that I cannot recall, except for one thing. At the end of the dream, an utterly surreal event took place. Nathan

70

looked at me and his face transformed so that I was looking at myself, so that I came to the conclusion that Nathan was me. Not only this, but throughout the dream, the Lord or an angel was speaking to me and telling me that I needed to befriend Nathan or help him. All I know is that, as far as I may have run from the Lord at that time, I took this dream as a direct message from God that I should obey. Not under compulsion, as something I would want to rebel against. But rather as a deep conviction that it was something I should want to do and do willingly based on my own principles, and that it would be best for everyone in the end. I acted on that dream almost at once, if not on anything else that God wanted for me. I befriended Nathan and did my best to defend him.

Meanwhile, the rest of my life of sin rolled on, and I became worse and worse. I started sneaking out at night to engage in vandalism because hassling kids only at school was not enough. I got into more trouble and, when caught, I took refuge in ever deeper lies. Because of my parents' lengthy interrogations, I constantly practiced lying more effectively. I rehearsed whole series of answers in advance so that my change of expressions wouldn't give me away if I was caught unprepared. Then I did mental exercises to try and convince myself of my own lies to further avoid gaffes or facial expressions giving me away. If anyone got closer to the truth, I had counter stories that looked like I was finally giving up and admitting to doing something bad, but not the thing that I had actually done.

For example, when my parents caught me sneaking out after midnight, I would say we were going out to smoke pot—which was a complete lie, because I actually had only a very minor interest in drugs. I lacked interest because I really didn't like the idea of losing control. Also, getting drunk was an alternative to drugs that I could do *with* my family, which my parents had no problem with at all. At most, I smoked pot a combined total of five times in my lifetime, all in high school.

LIVING THE LIE

So, I lived a continual lie with my parents, who I nevertheless actually cared about. My life was all the more like a hall of mirrors to the outside world. I developed my own disinformation techniques whenever I caused a problem through some prank or vandalism and everyone, the school authorities and perhaps the police, was trying to circle in on who had done it. I of course wanted to boast to get the credit, but that would lead to certain detection. Their way of trying to identify the culprit was to systematically question all kinds of students until a picture developed that revealed to them who had done the deed. So I carefully considered each student, especially how naturally fearful or resistant they were, and how soon and under what circumstances they could be expected to volunteer the information they had.

For example, some may not want to give any information, unless they themselves were suspected, and then they would give up whatever they had heard. Others would volunteer immediately. So, I would find a natural occasion to 'give up' to various kids one by one 'insider' information on who had done the deed. To one group of kids I would say, "I know who did it; it was Joe," and come up with some elaborate story about how I had found out. To another, I would say, "It was Jack." I would try to arrange this in such a way that the rumor itself would pass from one person to another without pointing directly to me so that, when the authorities started systematically working the grapevine, they would find what I wanted them to find—a hall of mirrors. And this would create enough fog for me to really enjoy boasting to the few people I could relax with.

In 8th grade I was probably only successfully able to pull off this kind of disinformation campaign about two or three times. When I did not succeed, but rather got caught, I got in a lot of trouble. I was kicked off the bus for a period of time, and would have to wait long hours after school until Dad finally arrived to pick me up. I even ran away for several days, living in an abandoned building or in the woods. Because I was not yet a habitual thief, when the money ran out the hunger eventually drove me back home.

But for the most part, we were not getting caught. There was a day near the end of the school year when we had found a way to barricade some kid in a bathroom stall, until he finally came bursting out the bathroom. The assistant principal knew it was us and said she would eventually catch us for everything. But middle school would soon be over for us and she was running out of time. All of this was so exhilarating for me that I was able to put out of my mind that ever-looming Day of Final Judgment when the whole refuge of lies would be melted away like a blow torch on a wax candle.

For in those days the deep depression that had characterized most of my childhood was mostly absent, as I was thoroughly enjoying all this. I wandered around the mall and elsewhere with all kinds of punk-rock attire, spiked bracelets, chains and handcuffs for a belt, and the like.

But it was all so impractical. The chains were pulling down heavily on my blue jeans, so that, when I finally got them unlocked, there were times when my pants would drop straight down, leaving me completely exposed at the urinal. That was when I successfully got the gear off in time to urinate. But there came a day when I really had to go, and I had to spend so much time fiddling with the handcuffs that I barely made it. And with that, I made a decision to put the punk rock attire away for good. Simple ratty jeans, a T-shirt, and perhaps a leather jacket would be my standard outfit from then on.

Because I was having so much fun, the self-harm of the past was tending to fade away. It remained in vestigial form as a bunch of contests. For example, we would play chicken, which meant we would join our arms together and put a lit cigarette in between them, seeing who could go the longest without flinching. Or we had a contest in the stairway where we would go back and forth seeing who could kick the other guy in the balls the hardest. Even though one guy was especially proud of his big boots, I had a hidden technique where I could slightly shift my angle before an incoming blow arrived, so that I never, ever took a direct hit.

BROKEN ADDICTION

But as much as I thought I was enjoying myself, it was all based on sin and cruelty and a deeply disordered soul, which had to come out in other ways also. One of these ways was the torturing of animals, which I soon became addicted to. But even today, with my newly acquired conscience after salvation, it drives me to distraction and keeps me up at night sometimes to think of the terrible things I did. But, as in the case of Nathan, there was another very strange intervention that put an end to this particular perversion. There was a day when I was torturing a string of small animals and finally a lizard, whose bones I had mostly broken using a fertilizer spreader as if it was the rack. It was turning black, as they would do when they were beginning to die, but was still very much alive, and I had left it behind for something else.

But then a voice came into my head as clearly as anything outside me, "As bad as this all has been, I am giving you a chance to leave it behind forever. That lizard is still alive, and when you find it, it will turn around and look you right in the eye—and when it does, you must put it out of its misery and leave this behavior behind forever."

I grabbed a hatchet and went about some other business, until I met the lizard where I least expected to see it, at the back of the house. He came out from behind the air-conditioning condenser alive and seemingly in his full strength, turned around, looked me right in the eye, and hissed at me. And I, in pity for the lizard, in hope of freedom, and in obedience to the voice that echoed in my mind, immediately took the hatchet and cut off its head. I carefully put the body in a jar of saltpeter and buried it in the back yard, while I kept the head in a hidden place in my room, both to remember the lizard and as a reminder to never do such things again. And my addiction was broken and I never did.

But there was another addiction I couldn't break, or rather, I suppose I saw no need to do. That was my love of fire. I was constantly playing and experimenting with fire in all of its forms, from pine needles to gasoline to whatever I could find. I would fill balloons and other objects with propane to make fireballs, which would blacken all the hair on my arms to a crisp without really burning my arms.

I would burn and mix all kinds of plastics and chemicals and gasoline and, worst of all, nylon rope. When it drips, the burning drops would combine with your flesh and be absorbed into your skin while it burned with great pain, and the only way to stop it was to put it out, cool it, and then rip it out with a small piece of flesh that was meshed in with it. Not only was I getting painful outward burns, but I was often burning Sulphur. Whenever I accidentally breathed it in, it would almost knock me out, and the pain would remain in my throat, nose and lungs for longer than a month or so.

Sulphur was the type of thing I could usually get from the drug store to supplement the chemistry set I had gotten from my grandparents. My father had shown me how to make my own pyrotechnics using a mixture he had learned through experimentation when he was younger using some easily available items, including table sugar. He recalled with pride how he had made something he called a 'daylight bomb' when he was a child. Not that it was explosive, but there was enough of it to light up the whole nighttime for a brief period as if it were daylight.

But, unlike Dad, I was hooked. I worked with this more and more, doing all kinds of experiments. In the beginning my mixtures were ignited on aluminum foil which it would melt through, leaving little molten balls of aluminum that would roll like mercury before they solidified. So from then on, I used a very old iron soap dish. I tried different proportions and different ingredients added in, and as the days went by, I slowly learned some things. With a certain ingredient you got a double flame, and the two tongues blasted strongly like jets, pushing against each other so you got something like a V shape coming out. And then one day, I found out that with the right proportion of another ingredient, you could get it so hot that it would burn right through iron— because to my amazement it melted right through my iron soap dish, leaving molten balls before they cooled.

But the problem was, despite all my desperate attempts to keep everything under control, I had a really hard time stopping. One day I decided to play my hand at unrestricted warfare on a few fire ant nests in our yard, complete with fireworks, a can of gasoline, some Styrofoam cups, and a tank of propane hooked to a Bunsen burner.

Our neighbor was furious and wanted to call the police, but it seems my father calmed him down, promising to make me stop. But I was so hooked on this that I was constantly lighting small fires in my room and frantically putting them out, whenever I was bored with my homework. It seems I couldn't even wait to walk outside and do this in a more secluded place, as I apparently needed instant gratification. So, in an attempt to cover the smell in my room, I would spray large amounts of roach spray and tell my parents I was having problems with too many roaches in my room.

On one extremely cold day, my love of fire finally went too far. It was the very last day before the Christmas holidays, and a friend and I went into a very large drainage canal near our bus stop. We set a fire there which quickly blazed up, because everything was very dry and also dead from the winter cold fronts. We ran from there as fast as we could, keeping well out of sight, and laid low in our homes while the sirens blazed from all sides.

A GATHERING CREW

We returned to school after the holiday and the rest of the semester continued. I was doing better in school than I had probably ever done previously. While I had struggled quite a bit through Algebra the previous year, I was in Geometry now and I absolutely loved it. The idea of proving things from the most basic principles deeply appealed to me, and I felt like it was helping me think more clearly than I had ever been able to do before. I was able to easily get As in that class. However, I was causing all kinds of trouble in my Louisiana history class, although I enjoyed it when studying on my own. I think the way we treated that teacher was deeply sinful, considering her level of dedication. And yet for me, it was again all political as it was giving me credibility with other boys as a bad kid that needed to be taken seriously, who could also pull some hilarious pranks.

Later that year I went to the State Latin convention again, as I would every year. That year I lifted my eyes to heaven and prayed to God, requesting that, although I didn't deserve it because I didn't study enough, I would win another first place in Mythology. And I did. And this sequence where I would pray and get first place would likewise repeat itself for the three years following. I was also beginning to do some math competitions, but unfortunately, unlike the Latin, I was supplementing those victories with a lot of cheating.

At the beginning of 1983 things were slowly changing. Harry Robinson, who I had known since third grade when we were rolling Hot Wheels down the hall, was back. He was hanging out a great deal with Dave Boone and they were becoming the best of friends. A lot of that had to do with them frequenting a local place called Rusty's Arcade. Dave's parents were going to the prayer meetings together, like mine had in earlier years, and so he was free to leave the house and hang out there.

I couldn't be with them at Rusty's or anywhere else because Dad had stopped going to the prayer meetings many years ago. Mom was going less, and I could not simply ask for permission because I had already settled into a permanent state of being punished. I don't think it was my parent's intention for me to be permanently grounded, but, in reality, there would always be some new thing to punish me for, so they felt they had to raise the ante. And, as it stretched into weeks, I just stopped counting and settled into permanent punishment. From then on, I normally only did things with my friends clandestinely.

We all seemed to be undergoing a bit of a transformation around the same time. It seemed the most subtle—maybe no more than a regular linear trend—in the case of Harry. I think he did come back from Europe a bit worse, having fallen under some bad influence at the American School he attended there, and also with the heavy metal. He had always liked the image of the bad kid, who broke rules and roughed up other people and wasn't to be trifled with. But he didn't normally seem to be actively engaging in that sort of thing himself a whole lot. He rather seemed to enjoy it vicariously through others, including those that were far weaker than he was.

Harry himself was fairly strong, for he began working out early in life and, as he got older, couldn't stand being around people with bigger muscles than himself. Harry also worked hard. He got various odd jobs and made money as a pre-teen, and at twelve started working regularly at a local car remodeling shop. He ended up with his own car, which he had worked on and put together himself. This was a gold Trans-Am that you could always recognize by the "No Fat Chicks" bumper sticker on the back.

Dave seemed to be transforming from a seemingly fairly good kid into something darker. He was just starting to bully a lot of other kids, which he justified by saying he was toughening them up, which would help them in the end. He talked about how he used to cry himself to sleep every night until one day he ran out of tears and decided he was going to do something about it. He did seem to be relentlessly seeking to transform himself. But I thought what he was saying was a bunch of BS. I didn't think being bullied would ever be good for anyone, and that this was clearly just an excuse. I had my own excuse—that this was all just part of the process of evolution. My excuse was somewhat similar to his, for we were all a rather Social-Darwinian bunch. But for me this justification was very conscious and explicit, and to my young mind scientific; it also lacked the pretense that anyone that didn't end up on top would be okay.

For me this foursome—Harry, Dave, Nathan and I—would make up most of my world until the day I became a believer. I had other friends, of a more intellectual and less criminal nature, including one guy who eventually became a Catholic priest. But my interactions with them mostly stayed at school.

Yet there is one more person who I need to introduce for the purposes of telling this tale. I will call him Chuck Forten. Chuck was an extraordinarily rugged young man who had a deep fascination with military history, the Vietnam war in particular, and manliness in general. He alternated between wearing clean press jeans, a 'preppie' polo shirt, and loafers, versus wandering around with an old green military jacket and a grim scowl on his face. He always had a copy of *Soldier of Fortune* or something similar, and tales of blood and glory. Chuck's father was indeed a Vietnam War veteran, and it seems that his father was impacted by that war in ways that caused Chuck's whole family to suffer. And so, for reasons I never really understood, Chuck was deeply estranged from both his parents, but especially his father.

Chuck was a real problem for me at first, because he despised me and was quite a bit stronger than I. He would hold me down and let other kids punch me. But, for reasons I don't entirely remember, we were friends by the end of 8th grade. I think Dave had a lot to do with this, for they seem to have known each other for some time before all this. On a deeper level, I think Chuck really wanted to transgress social norms as deeply as I would, but he himself was not willing to do so. So I suspect he really enjoyed my antics.

Without some intervention, none of this was going to end well for any of us. But, if anyone would like to complain that Dave's parents should have never left him to his own devices at Rusty's Arcade while they went to prayer meetings, they should consider that out of the five of us, only Dave and I are still alive.

CHAPTER 10

THE DESIRE OF WOMEN

He shall regard neither the God of his fathers nor the desire of women,
nor regard any god; for he shall exalt himself above them all.

Daniel 11:37

SUMMER – CHRISTMAS 1983

That summer I went to the National Latin convention again, this time in Rochester, New York. Han Fei got to go with me, even though he wasn't taking any Latin, because one of his uncles wanted to be a chaperone. Apparently, they were running short. We put posters of scantily clad women up all over our dorm, played loud heavy metal, and generally sat around trying to look cool. I failed to study and got third place again.

But that previous summer I burned my time with something at least more useful than fantasy roll-playing games. I had recently learned to program in a teaching language of that time called BASIC. Inspired by my geometry class, I wrote hundreds of lines of code trying to get the simple 'high-resolution' graphics of that era to draw different polygons, make them 3D, and then calculate areas, volumes and the like. I don't know if I ever got it to work, but it looked great on paper to me. I did a lot more with Han Fei that summer and was still going to Tae Kwon Do under Chul Yun. But both would come to an end soon.

My high school years began with an orientation at McKinley High School. To understand the overall environment, it should be understood that, not just in Baton Rouge, but for much of Louisiana outside New Orleans, McKinley was THE historically Black high school. It was the kind of place that figures like Jesse Jackson or later Obama would come to speak at if they were ever in town. This is because, at the beginning of the 20th century, McKinley High was the only place a Black person could get a high school diploma throughout much of the state. Yet this storied history was not enough to save a school like McKinley from being shut down in the early 1980s era of desegregation—only the numbers mattered. But, as various schools were being mixed and matched and shut down all over the city, some kind of deal was struck to keep McKinley open, which involved the gifted program. And that's how I ended up there.

While Istrouma had been about 60% White and 40% Black, McKinley was now 60/40, the other way. This was still a very rough balance, and Whites were better able to defend ourselves in those days. There wasn't a whole system of presumption against us, and there was still some fighting spirit which our people seem to have lost presently. During all my teenage years, White and Black mainly lived in our own worlds with little interaction for either good or bad. The small amount of interracial bullying my first year was a result of me trying to enter a criminal underworld while being exceedingly naïve and stupid.

I soon wisely pulled back into my own world, which was changing fast. I still experienced a small amount of bullying, but this was mostly a thing of the past. At the very beginning of the school year my friendship with Han Fei ended. I blabbed about something that set him off, which was entirely my fault. I am sure it was best for him at that time of our lives, for I was a bad influence.

The result was that I was now moving much closer to Harry and Dave. I was spending a lot of time with Nathan too—although outside of school—because he was a grade behind us. This was going to set the course of my life until the day I became a believer. We wanted to be actual criminals and not just vandals, so we made our start with shoplifting. Besides this, we all really wanted to get into the 1980s partying lifestyle, where the sex, drugs and rock and roll would presumably flow. But this is where a clear demarcation had to take place—for, although Harry had me dreaming of parties, there was an impenetrable barrier. I could neither reconcile myself to normal social life nor to the opposite sex.

AN INEXPLICABLE RAGE

My desires for women were boiling, but I 'knew,' in an utterly fatalistic kind of way, that not one of them would ever accept me. Beyond this, I had convinced myself in all those earlier years of bullying that the girls were driving it all and the boys were doing it to impress them. During the worst of those days, the burning anger would keep me up all night as I lay in my bed. And so I hated, and I hated, and I hated, and I hated, through long dark watches of the night, year after year, until it seemed that the force and heat of it was melting my mind into something that was becoming less than human.

But what was the source of something so completely insane and out of all proportion to individual differences? For, although something akin to what I was perceiving was going on, it could hardly be applied to an entire gender. I myself did not apply it to my own family. But I was clearly already falling under the influence of dark spiritual forces.

Something more prosaic was also going on too. I understood myself to be outside of normal society, to which the door would remain shut. I understood women to be the custodians of that social life, and hence my natural enemies. I myself wanted nothing to do with the compromises that acceptance into that world would entail—being civilized, self-controlled, polite, productive. And I certainly didn't want to lose my friends and the camaraderie of our lifestyle to this.

I have heard that in these days many young men are dealing with similar issues and attitudes that seemed entirely unique to me at the time. In light of this, I feel compelled to speak a few words. Due to my extremely limited perspective at the time, my ideas about women were mistaken. Since then, I have seen the true loyalty of many women; this amazing and genuinely tenacious thing was often directed at those who did not deserve it at all. It goes without saying that I did not believe them capable of such things when I was young, but it is real and it cannot be denied. They are, in fact, capable of being entirely on your side through all the wars and struggles of life.

And this is the life we should want to live: a life in which the true adventure is to produce the next generation, without them being brainwashed, so that both genes and memes are intact. For our life is not a video game that can be started over. It is rather a relay race in which we make irreversible mistakes, learn some things, and pass the baton on to the next generation. And we cannot have a portion in that next generation without a woman, or perhaps a single life dedicated to God so that He can make an impact through us on those future generations. But in those days

I could see none of these things because I had no concept of God, nor of His creativity, nor the Life He offers, nor that anything good could happen to me at all.

Back in 1983, all this rage against the feminine was on the inside, never making its way into the open until the conversations with Harry forced it out. In these conversations Harry was trying to reconcile me to women. Harry had, in fact, been trying to lead me this way, if not since the third grade, at least since I knew him at St. Thomas More. But I raged against them all. This made absolutely no sense to Harry, and he looked on with baffled amazement. But he accepted where I stood and we moved on. Dave just let me know that he thought I was full of crap and also moved on. He didn't waste time trying to understand my attitude. He just didn't want anything to do with it—unless, perhaps, he really needed to channel my rage to get revenge on someone. For Dave was radically and seemingly successfully transforming himself in the social realm.

A SETTLEMENT

But, though my friends believed I was being foolish, they didn't let it stand in the way of our friendship. And so, the bifurcated nature of our relationship was set. As far as crime went, we were all in it together. But, as far as partying and socializing went, that was a world for Harry and Dave but not me—except we all got to talk and laugh about it together. And, of course, any of their talk of sexual escapades was almost all bluff and bluster anyway. In the meantime, ever since that dream in 8th grade, I was getting even closer to Nathan. For, even if he didn't quite have my attitude, Nathan's problems were similar to my own.

And so, we all attempted to begin our life of crime with mostly shoplifting. While this was something I could just barely pull off, Dave was turning out to be extraordinarily good at it. So much so that we were soon having open bazaars on the school bus in the morning asking people their shirt sizes and the like. Nathan wasn't at high school with us but this all became so well known that he would often bitterly complain that he was tired of Dave acting like he was the world's greatest shoplifter. But when word got to the principal of what we were doing on the bus, we had to tone it down.

As for me, I was doing little more than stupid teenage things, like vandalism, public drunkenness and disorder, and continuing to pull all kinds of pranks. I was stealing little more than condoms, which I was only using to put all over the place such as the door knob to the principal's office to freak people out. Besides this, I was mostly just stealing music. For Heavy Metal music was becoming an ever more important part of my life, especially Black Sabbath, Judas Priest and Iron Maiden.

It was stealing such music that led to my first arrest. In those days, music was mostly on cassettes or larger plate size record albums called LPs[1]. We still had record players and would often get the LPs of the albums we liked so that we could record them on blank cassettes for listening later. We used razor blades and other tools to remove tracking devices and other barriers. Dave and I were in a music store in the mall. I slipped an Iron Maiden album into one of his bags of things he had already purchased or pretended to purchase. After a short interval of shopping around, he was soon at the checkout counter with me a close distance away. This is because we almost always actually bought something as a token when shoplifting so that we didn't just look like we were

---

1   Stands for "Long Play", an album with maybe 10–12 songs.

there for no other reason than to steal. However, there must have been a tracking device I didn't see on the album, or the clerk must have just seen it and realized it was from the store, because he soon had security there to arrest Dave.

Although we were used to cooperating this way, in this particular instance, I hadn't really let Dave know what I was doing when I slipped the album in his bag. That is why it probably remained so poorly concealed. And now I had a problem. For, though I was very immoral, I had a code that would not let me leave a friend in the lurch like this due to my own actions. For I had very few friends, and believed that I needed to be fanatically loyal to those I did have. So I walked up to the officer and told him I was the one who stole the album and not Dave. This didn't make any sense to the officer since Dave was the one who had gotten caught, so he marched us both all the way through the mall and out to the squad car.

Dave and I had very different reactions to all this. Dave was very upset and visually emotional about finally getting arrested because, despite all his bluster, he really wasn't ready for this kind of life yet. In contrast, I went into a state I often went into in these kinds of situations, where it seemed like all the blood drained out of me, all my emotions left, and I became something like a machine. This detached state went on all the way to the station downtown, and all through the interrogations and discussions that went on at the station. I eventually convinced the police to let Dave go and keep me. So I was there much longer than him, until after midnight. Finally, when Dad showed up in a very visibly angry state, all my detachment left and a deep fear set in that went all the way down to my bones.

FEAR

As I struggle to understand such fear, the best I can explain it is this. Somehow in my mental architecture, all the risks I might face, from bullies, to the police, to the very severe dangers I would be facing if I went to jail, were all just external challenges that only seemed to exist to test my mettle. I didn't want to face them, but I figured I would steel myself for them anyway, and so any fear was only skin deep. Even the catastrophe beyond which no greater earthly catastrophe could be imagined—the final victory of international communism—still seemed like some external event for which I would likewise steel myself. (Even if, in this case, I wasn't quite convinced that I could hold up through all their tortures until the end.) It somewhat bothers me that now, after so many good things have happened and I feel like I have so much to lose, I no longer have that steely feeling. But such was I at the time. Yet when Dad showed up, his intense displeasure seemed to produce a kind of existential dread that went deep down beyond the surface.

From this, we can get a glimpse of how Freud came up with his delusions. It would seem that our fathers really do represent to us the delegated authority and power of God before we are grown, and can symbolically bring the fear of Him with them. Freud just reversed the polarity by making up stories about how the real fear was of our parents and we invented God to be its symbol, rather than the reality—that the fear of God was the original and our fathers just symbolized it. This would explain why the Fifth Commandment[1], to honor our father and our mother, seems to

---

1   According to the Evangelical reckoning, but Fourth for Roman Catholics (and Lutherans)

88

occupy a place between the two tables of the law, our duties toward God and our duties toward man.

The reality that my fear of my father issued from this symbolic connection with the divine, and not from my father and what he could do himself, was made clear to me on another occasion. Here it seemed to me that Dad was obviously in the wrong. He accused me of something that I simply could not agree I was guilty of, and demanded that I admit it. When I looked into his eyes and calmly told him the exact opposite of what he wanted to hear, he flew into a rage and came back with a belt to mete out the traditional punishment that he had mostly been averse to during my growing years.

I was sitting at my desk without a shirt, and was determined not to move or flinch. So, when he hit me on the back, the tip of the belt curve would come over my shoulder and snap, in the process taking a bit of flesh off my chest here and there. When I noted Dad's reaction upon seeing my torn chest, I sensed fear, that perhaps I would report this as some sort of abuse. But there was no one on earth that was less likely to do so than myself, as I internally raged against the idea that there were state actors who could break up families.

But the main point was this: that deep existential dread I had previously felt when he came to pick me up at the police station was entirely absent. It was replaced by a serene sense of composure, which came from knowing I was the one who was in the right. This proves that the true fear of my father that I felt throughout my young life came not from what he himself could do but from what he represented, which I believe has been built into the architecture of our minds by the creator Himself. And, only when we come to understand this, will we fully comprehend what an utter catastrophe the present-day epidemic of fatherlessness has become.

LEAVING THINGS BEHIND

But, at the time, I was, in fact, rather proud of the trajectory I had taken. It seemed at the time that all that weak and shameful past was finally beginning to fade off into the horizon. I had always been smoking whenever I was with my friends in those days, because it seemed like a necessarily tough and cool thing that needed to be done. But I was by no means committed enough to smoke when I was by myself or spend a bunch of money on it on my own. There came a day when we were walking together as a bunch of guys, and Harry asked "Do y'all want some smokes?" We all asked for a cigarette and started smoking except for one guy, who explained that he didn't smoke because he was on the foot-ball team—and nobody cared. I myself was trying to get stronger. I had started lifting weights with Dad at the YMCA, and was still doing the Tae Kwon Do. I asked myself, 'why do I have to smoke to look tough and bad when I have done enough bad things and crimes to gain those credentials without it, and this guy is per-fectly free to say he doesn't smoke just because he is on the football team?' So right there I finished my last cigarette and immediately quit for good shortly after my fourteenth birthday.

However, my time of doing Tae Kwon Do with Chul Yun was about to come to an end for a season. This was due to the sec-ond of three episodes of sickness I will describe shortly. For the first sickness I need to explain that the psychologists, or rather the psychiatrists, were once again called in due to my escalating behavior. They were trying different types of drugs but mainly Tofranil and, because I couldn't remember to take it regularly enough, it was throwing off their calculations when I had blood tests. So they kept upping the dose. I was also taking antihista-mines due to my extreme allergies, and I eventually found myself in a bit of a mental haze much of the time. One day at lunch break, I was in a real stupor, trying to slowly follow something Dave was talking about. He finally said "You know, Tarso, I think it's terrible what they are doing to you, experimenting on you like a &#@$ animal." With that, I decided I'd had enough and quit everything cold turkey.

I paid a price. I got very sick, so that I was retching so hard that I was holding onto the toilet seat with both arms for dear life, while my two feet shot out like a donkey behind me and hit the wall above. It was one of those sicknesses where you get so dehydrated that every sip of water makes you dry-vomit, so that without Gatorade you are not coming back. But, after a few days I got through, and I gained something for the price I paid. I got all of their garbage out of my body, and all these years I have never put any back in.

The second illness was prolonged, and was entirely my fault. 1983 was a year of extreme weather in Baton Rouge. That winter of 1983, right before Christmas, was the coldest anyone could remember. I was at the same bus stop with Harry at the time. That morning Harry had brought about two six-packs of beer, and we were all amazed when the spilled beer actually froze on the ground. With this phenomenon I saw an opportunity to show off. I announced to everyone the importance of mind over matter, and said that we could resist the cold if we convinced ourselves that we liked it. To demonstrate, I took off all my layers right there, including my t-shirt, and stood there motionless and shirtless with my arms folded in the bitter cold, trying to look smug. It was especially important for me not to shiver, and I used up a great deal of my strength simply for that.

This was exceedingly foolish because I could directly feel my body's resistance cracking on the inside as I refused to shiver.

Yet I persisted and my whole torso clearly turned a light shade of blue. When I felt I had made a sufficient demonstration, I put my clothes back on as nonchalantly as I could and got on the bus.

By that evening, I was horribly sick. This persisted through the whole holiday and beyond. I tried to go back to Tae Kwon Do but I had a cough that wouldn't stop whenever I exerted myself; it was similar to the 'Katrina[1] cough' so many of us got decades later. So the Tae Kwon Do had to end, and I couldn't get back into it. For, despite all my talk of the power of the will, I am a very inertial person with a relatively weak will. Once I get going on something, I can keep charging through but, when forced to stop, it is extremely hard for me to get started again.

These setbacks shook but did not end my sense that I was on the trajectory I had put myself on. For, even though I knew myself to be a rather sad sack at the time, I believed that with persistence and steady progress I would eventually become the hardened criminal I wanted to be. But, in spite of all this, I still had to contend with the Lord and His final judgment, and I hadn't entirely given up on the possibility of repentance. I just hoped to be able to kick the can down the road for a very long time. The third episode of illness directly challenged this concept of deliberately putting off repentance. But that came later, so I will discuss it in chapter 12, about that wild year of sin.

---

1   The famous 2005 hurricane that submerged New Orleans

CHAPTER 11

A NIGHT OF APOSTASY

He who does not love does not know God, for God is love.

1 John 4:8

JANUARY – MAY 1984

My story has now reached the point where a truly decisive event was about to take place. The opposing forces that had been gathering strength throughout my childhood would finally come to a head on a single late night. The decision I made not long after midnight would determine the course of my life for the next two years. Had an extraordinary intervention not taken place, the result would have been terrible. Yet this decisive moment all happened within the hidden counsels of my own mind. So, I will need to describe at length my thought processes and conclusions which led to this moment.

EVOLUTION

By 1984 it was beginning to dawn on me that I was on the road to hell. For this reason, I was really beginning to hope that the

Bible was not true. I dreamed of a world without God. The primary Western alternative for anyone who didn't want Christianity to be true was still a mechanistic and atheistic view of the world—at least it was for me. Not only was I constantly reading science books from famous atheists like Isaac Asimov and the like, but Grandma had gotten me a subscription to a magazine called *Discover* around 1980 that aimed to popularize science. Due to a bunch of controversies in the early 1980s, *Discover* was constantly attacking Creationism, led by Stephen Jay Gould. No such article in those days would be complete without some liberal preacher weighing in about how shocked he was that anyone thought there was some conflict between evolution and religion. Of course, there are religions that are entirely compatible with evolution, but whether the core message of the Bible could be counted among them was another matter entirely.

I was no Creationist back then. I was all in with evolution, but I really wanted to know how this could have all worked. Years earlier, maybe around 3rd or 4th grade, I was showing Dad some pictures of dinosaurs and told him that they had ultimately evolved all the way from bacteria. Dad told me that was too much for him to believe and he didn't buy it. I thought he didn't know what he was talking about, but it still bothered me.

By 9th grade I felt I had to follow the whole thing through to satisfy myself. The occasion was a science paper for my Biology class—just the kind of thing that I would so often fail to complete. But this time curiosity impelled me and I really plowed into it. I spent almost all my time on it. In fact, as I try to recall how it was that I was getting anything else done, I suspect I must have started the summer before and just took the opportunity to use it for an assignment during the school year.

This was before computers, word processors and the like

were widely available. So what actually moved this project beyond good intentions was that Grandma was willing to help me by typing it all out. Writing legibly was very slow and painful for me. I had learned typing in 7th grade, on non-electric typewriters that made for more muscle memory. But I was error prone, and on typewriters the logistics of constantly revising with liquid paper, sliding back to the exact right spot, and the like, could also be very daunting. But Grandma knew how to do it right. With the help of a little questioning, she could produce passable results, no matter how chaotic and illegible the content I passed to her. So I pushed on, trying to briefly explain in this paper each stage in the evolution of life, from the origin of life from nonliving matter (abiogenesis) to the descent of man, until I reached somewhere between fifty to a hundred pages.

At the end of this paper, there were four things I couldn't believe had evolved without divine intervention. They were: abiogenesis itself, the move from prokaryotes to eukaryotes, the move from mitosis to meiosis (asexual to sexual reproduction), and the move from one-celled to multicellular organisms. I was also tied up by other standard issues—eyesight forming independently at least three times with mollusks, insects, and fish; and flight independently four times with insects, flying reptiles, birds, and bats.

Now in one sense, I was still a true believer. For I was convinced that it was undeniable that evolution had actually happened in the sequence described, because I thought this history was clearly shown in the fossil record. I just didn't think it could happen on its own, but that there had to be some guiding hand behind it. Therefore, what I actually became convinced of was not pure evolutionism but a mostly metaphorical understanding of Christianity. This was also encouraged by my church and religion classes at the time.

CONSCIOUSNESS

Convinced evolutionists will see my difficulties as a simple case of personal incredulity, issues that will eventually be fully explained if we maintain a commitment to the scientific process. But the great fact that struck me the most in those days is one that none of us can deny, for it is something we are almost always immediately aware of. That fact is the reality of our own consciousness: that "I" was and still am here, observing the world, experiencing it and thinking about it to myself. I am in that sense aware of myself even when I am not being introspective but paying attention to something else. I only know about the outside world because it is piercing through into my consciousness—the self-consciousness that was the one thing I knew prior to all others.

This I knew even before I had words or the power of speech, as my earliest memory with the cricket shows. Our awareness that we ourselves exist is the one immediate apprehension on which all our other simple apprehensions[1] are based on and pierce into.

I had been taught that science itself is based on empiricism[2] and observation. Therefore, it seemed obvious to me that science could only begin with *something* for the sense impressions to pierce into, and *someone* to do the observing. And if that *something* is a *someone*, then the only way to describe it is to say that it is a soul—eternal or not. However, science can never explain what that soul is. Why? Because the whole process of science by

---

1   Simple apprehension is the very first step in logic, where you perceive something and form a concept of it without judgment. Only from there can you make judgments about the things you perceive, and from those judgments, inferences, that is, reason.

2   Empiricism is the theory that sensory experience is the only source of knowledge.

its nature strictly confines itself to observing and systematizing and predicting what things are observed to *do*—not some deeper meaning of what things are or what sentient[1] things *experience.*

Rather, science itself is entirely dependent on that consciousness or soul that it cannot account for or describe. For it is the soul that does the observing and induction and sensing and systematizing upon which science is built. I could see that the soul is the source of science, so that we could no more explain our sentient souls through the scientific method than we could grasp the bottom of our feet and pull ourselves up into the air.

It turned out that in 1984 this issue of Consciousness was THE core issue for me. For, if the most fundamental thing—my self-awareness and experience of life—could not be explained within the scientific method, then a mechanistic and atheistic view of the world simply could not explain reality as it is. It was already beginning to dawn on me that the core choice in life is not some antithesis between 'Atheism' and 'Religion.' Rather, atheism is just part of the spectrum of religious conceptions, going from the most 'personal' god to the least.

Using atheism as our example, imagine that I said that god existed, but he only ever 'did' certain things—such as make Maxwell's laws happen, cause the law of Gravity to take place, and other such natural laws—and never anything else. No atheist could really say that such a 'god' did not exist, for such a god would only be doing the things we universally agree we are observing. Since they are empiricists whose conclusions are based on observation, there would be nothing else to say. The one and only element that would be missing in this 'god' would be Will and Consciousness, because his actions would be so unvarying as

---

1   A sentient being is conscious, capable of feeling or perception.

to leave no place for a 'Will.' This means the ONLY thing atheism is saying is that consciousness, and hence will, emerges from physical things, whose behavior is mostly deterministic.

So now I understood my choices in terms of a spectrum of belief, which would include Christianity, Atheism, and everything in between. In such a spectrum, the Christian faith would have the most personal God who loved His people, became a man, and died on behalf of their sins. Judaism would be second, because it is presenting the same God—at least in the Hebrew Old Testament. In Isaiah, for example, we read about such a personal God:

> For He said, "Surely they *are* My people,
> Children *who* will not lie."
> So He became their Savior.
> In all their affliction He was afflicted,
> And the Angel of His Presence saved them;
> In His love and in His pity He redeemed them;
> And He bore them and carried them
> All the days of old.
> But they rebelled and grieved His Holy Spirit;
> So He turned Himself against them as an enemy,
> *And* He fought against them. (Isaiah 63:8-10, NKJV).

Next on the spectrum would be Islam, where, even though you still have a monotheistic god, he is becoming less personal and more distant. Then on to the Eastern religions where the ultimate is becoming more like a universal principle than a singular intelligence or person as we understand it. Then you get to Atheism where god is simply natural law itself, although even natural law has been becoming increasingly mysterious since the advent of modern physics. I may even put Buddhism further past Atheism on the spectrum, due to their sense of transitory unreality that applies even to the self.

By this point, I felt that I could not deny that God existed. But so much of this was against my will, against the way I really wanted things to be. Soon I would be looking up and down that spectrum, seeing if there was any way of escape. But, in a partial way, it would soon become clear that there was a good reason for me to really want God to be there, and that I, in fact, could not bear it if He was not.

THE BLUFF

I have been talking about the way I was thinking in the year 1984, but I was also reading the book *1984*. In those days, the terrible fear of Communism, and what looked to so many of us as their likely victory, loomed over everything. In this context, I had probably read Orwell's *Animal Farm* about five or six times, and his *1984* maybe two or three. There was a scene in *1984*, which I partially quote. This was a conversation between the totalitarian official O'Brien and his prisoner Winston that made the consequences of God's existence frightfully clear to me:

> Feebly, without arguments, with nothing to support him except his inarticulate horror of what O'Brien had said, he returned to the attack.
>
> "I don't know—I don't care. Somehow you will fail. Something will defeat you. Life will defeat you."
>
> "We control life, Winston, at all its levels. You are imagining that there is something called human nature which will be outraged by what we do and will turn against us. But we create human nature. Men are infinitely malleable. Or perhaps

you have returned to your old idea that the proletarians or the slaves will arise and overthrow us. Put it out of your mind. They are helpless, like the animals. Humanity is the Party. The others are outside—irrelevant."

"I don't care. In the end they will beat you. Sooner or later they will see you for what you are, and then they will tear you to pieces."

"Do you see any evidence that this is happening? Or any reason why it should?"

"No. I believe it. I know that you will fail. There is something in the universe—I don't know, some spirit, some principle—that you will never overcome."

"Do you believe in God, Winston?"

"No."

"Then what is it, this principle that will defeat us?"

"I don't know. The spirit of Man." ...

...

"You are the last man," said O'Brien. "You are the guardian of the human spirit. You shall see yourself as you are. Take off your clothes." ... As he slid them to the ground he saw that there was a three-sided mirror at the far end of the room. He approached it, then stopped short. An involuntary cry had broken out of him.[1]

As the full impact of this hit me, I told myself that I would never deny God's existence. Not only could I not deny that He was there, but I wanted Him to be there! There would be no 'spirit of Man' for me. It may be that I myself was too selfish, too weak, too

---

1   (1984, George Orwell (Eric Blair), Three, III, pp. 221—223)—Please read the whole thing!

vengeful, and that I could never be reconciled to God in the end. Let it be. I would die and go down to my damnation like a man, and not like the atheist Winston.

In light of this terrifying vision of where we would be if secularism was real, I had to grapple with the fact that this very unreal concept ruled all our institutions. In those days I had an experience, with a game I was playing on our Commodore 64, that clearly illustrated to me how it was that secularism was able to conquer the West without actually explaining reality.

This computer game was called 'The Temple of Apshai.' It was like a simple combination of a graphical video game and a text-based role-playing game like Zork. You would move through its geography and dungeons, have conversations, fight monsters, find treasure, and the like. One day I decided to take a look at the executable code behind the game. Though I expected to find an incomprehensible machine code that had been cranked out by some compiler, I discovered to my delight that the entire game was written and run in a computer language I knew well: BASIC. This programming language was easy to understand, which meant that I could easily go into that code and manipulate the game.

Manipulate, but NOT genuinely understand. For I did not take the time to figure out the algorithms that really made the game work. I could see the upper and lower limits where attributes like 'strength' and 'dexterity' were set. Being lazy, I simply upped those limits. I thereby made my characters become super powerful and quickly overtook every monster in the game—without understanding the procedures and subroutines that actually ran the combat. Likewise, I could manipulate the numerical limits on the 'haggling' and make everything I wanted to buy super cheap so that I no longer had to make hard choices, without understanding those algorithms either. I could also find stretches of text without understanding what really drove the dialogue and, being a teenage boy, turn it into something obscene for us to laugh at. In short, I had basically become like a god in the Temple of Apshai, without truly understanding that world or the principles under which it operated.

Similarly, I could see that the actual ideas behind secularism and atheism would not have been taken seriously by very many people if they did not have the power and prestige of technology behind them. By focusing on a few key attributes of nature, scientists had released titanic forces that have genuinely brought previously inconceivable solutions and real power into the world. Advocates of secularism had seized on this power to give their ideas a prestige they would not have otherwise had, and also to create the impression that 'science' had explained things that it really had not. Just like I was able to achieve godlike powers inside the Temple of Apshai without really knowing what was going on in that world, so had they used the power and prestige of technology to seize the Western mind.

But I asked myself, what necessary connection was there between the ability to develop science and technology, and a worldview which claims that the scientific method can explain everything? The widespread Christian beliefs of so many great scientists before the late 19th century seemed to belie this. Weighing it all, I came to a conclusion. Both the claim that science has fully explained reality, and the claim that we need secularism to develop and live in a technologically advanced world, was all one big bluff.

NO EXIT

I was disillusioned. The thinkers of the West who had secularized our society had failed us in a deep way—a way that involved very willful blindness. Due to their control of certain core institutions, we were now like passengers on an airplane in which the pilots, in the fog, had become convinced that the airplane was going up when we were really going down. We wouldn't die instantly, but there would ultimately be a collision after some lapse of time. In the meantime, we were living our lives as normal, oblivious to the pending crash. I did not want to live in the world that I could see they were creating, and I would soon be looking for ways to live outside it as an outlaw.

Furthermore, their failure was entirely emotional—for I have never met a single one of them whose real reasons didn't come down to the "Problem of Evil" in the end, whatever other more technical sounding arguments they may have started out with.

But, while the 'Problem of Evil' was apparently compelling to them, it never made even the slightest sense to me in those days, when I was young, sinful, and rebellious. It struck me back then as one of the dumbest things I'd ever heard. If God exists, I thought, then, by definition, He can do whatever He wants and no one can call Him to account. Why, under these circumstances, would He be under some kind of pressure to prevent evil from existing in the world, as if the presence of any evil would thereby negate His existence?

Now I must admit that, after having been a Christian for many years and having my conscience developed, I sometimes feel disturbed by this problem and feel its weight. But the fact that this 'Problem of Evil' had no weight with me when I was a sinner, and only does now when I have been a Christian for many years, clearly tells us something. Secularism has only ever existed as a parasite atop a Christian civilization. So, if and when it finally kills its host, whither will it go, and how will it survive?

Moreover, even though as a Christian I can now feel the

103

weight of this 'Problem of Evil,' I can nevertheless see all the more clearly that it is a phantom. It ultimately indicates nothing whatsoever other than that God is running things differently from our own preferences. Now in those days the reality that God was running and allowing things different than what I wanted was indeed the core problem of my personal life. However, beyond me it had no significance. Who cares what any of us think? But our secular overlords were disturbed by the problem of evil, and every other argument, no matter how unrelated it seemed, was merely a rationalization to get rid of God based on this one concern.

Or perhaps another concern—to avoid accountability on the Day of Judgment. Most secular people, including some of the thinkers who led us down this path, were relatively moral by conventional human standards—indeed virtual saints compared to me in those days. This isn't entirely surprising, because it takes a certain level of moral earnestness to be bothered by the problem of evil. It seemed to me, therefore, that they would have no need to escape from accountability to God. Yet so many were and are clearly motivated to avoid such accountability. This I think is clear evidence of just how deep and searching and thorough the Law of God is, and how little chance any of us has of passing it on our own. Which is why, when I have read anything they had to say on the subject, it all has the feeling of an attempt at wish fulfillment.

I had the same wish, for I knew that I was already in serious trouble with God. Despite this, I was absolutely unwilling to fool myself and not face reality as it was, however difficult it may have been to accept. To turn from reality would have been what a line in a popular Heavy Metal song of the time referred to as "eating sugar with my brain." There was absolutely nothing to be gained by such dreaming. The Lord cannot be dreamed away.

And yet, if the biblical God did exist, I could see real value in steeling myself to this fact no matter how unlikely it may have seemed at the time that I could ever be reconciled to Him. As long as I accepted reality and never tried to completely put it out of my mind, there would remain some small hope that I could be reconciled to God in the end. There was nothing to lose and everything to possibly gain, however slight that possibility may have seemed.

Now, from what I have said, it may seem that I was a convinced Christian at this point. So why would I consider the possibility of being reconciled with God only slight? I was indeed convinced that the God of the Bible was real. But I was not convinced that I could live by His laws, or that He was not, in fact, dead set against me. There was my history of anti-socialization, convincing me that I could not live in normal society but only on its fringes as some kind of outlaw. There was my overwhelming desire for revenge. And there was my conviction that I had to live by 'the Cruel Vision' if I was ever to exist in a tolerable situation.

DILUTION

The irony of all this was that I was in the middle of my Confirmation[1] at this time. Yet I had a very hard time accepting what I was hearing in church, which exacerbated my dilemma. I did not get the impression that my church was trying to fight the secular system, or even create a parallel society in a kind of counter-culture. Rather, the goal seemed to be to exist within the secular system as a particularly nice set of people. I think a great deal of this came out of a desire to modernize in the wake

---

1   Confirmation is a sacrament in the Catholic church that signifies a person has reached maturity and is now able to take responsibility for their own faith.

of Vatican II, as well as a Christianized humanism that has been a part of the Roman Catholic Church throughout all its history.

A perfect example of this is an interpretation we were given of Jesus' feeding of the five thousand. What really happened, they said, was that the crowd was so inspired by Jesus sharing the five loaves and two fishes that those who had food with them shared with those who didn't, and thus all five thousand were fed. Under such an interpretation, the miraculous power of God, in which Jesus expressed His divinity, was reduced to a lesson about human morality and sharing.

While this kind of reduction was by no means universal in my church, I got a whole lot of it in the actual religion classes. Knowing what kind of persons I and the people around me were, this brought me to despair. In the end, much of the Bible was reduced to inspiring myth pointing to a kernel of humanistic morality. That kernel would be the Sermon on the Mount, but only a small part of it. The Sermon on the Mount is certainly the core expression of all that Jesus wants His people to be in the world. But this sermon loses its meaning when it is explained through a humanistic lens, when the focus is taken off the Second Coming of Christ and the world to come, and in particular when it is contrasted with the Old Testament rather than being explained in continuity with it. Nothing that slices and divides the Bible, rather than bringing it all together, can produce a workable path to living a genuinely godly life.

Jesus Himself was and will be the fulfillment of the messianic promise made to King David, who was a both a man after God's own heart and a hard-core warrior. In fact, the 'Commander of the army of the Lord' that appeared to Joshua in chapter 5, right on the eve of Joshua carrying out God's death sentence on every man, woman and child in Jericho, was the Angel of the Lord, literally

Jesus Himself, as we know from the command, "Take your sandal off your foot, for the place where you stand is holy" (Joshua 5:15). Yet, even this command was not without mercy, even for enemies, for Rahab the harlot and all her family were saved.

This same Angel of the Lord appeared to the generation after Joshua with an equally uncompromising message:

> Then the Angel of the Lord came up from Gilgal to Bochim, and said: "I led you up from Egypt and brought you to the land of which I swore to your fathers; and I said, 'I will never break My covenant with you. And you shall make no covenant with the inhabitants of this land; you shall tear down their altars.' But you have not obeyed My voice. Why have you done this?" (Judges 2:1-2, NKJV)

And yet we see that this very same uncompromising Angel of the Lord was overflowing with love for His people, as when we previously described Him using Isaiah 65 when discussing the 'spectrum of religions.'

And so we see the unfolding of our deeply passionate God, showing a depth within Himself beyond all the deepest emotions of any being who has ever existed. He can say that "... a fire is kindled in My anger, And shall burn to the lowest hell" (Deuteronomy 32:22) and yet have such incredible love for His people "...that neither death nor life, nor angels nor principalities nor powers, nor things present nor things to come, nor height nor depth, nor any other created thing, shall be able to separate us from the love of God which is in Christ Jesus our Lord" (Romans 8:38-39).

When the Bible is taken as a complete unit, with its entire worldview, like gold it becomes indigestible to the surrounding philosophies of this world. And hence we can avoid twisting and contorting its message into whatever the worldview of the day is—in our case, an absurd secular progressive value system. This cutting of the New Testament from the Old Testament, and the "demythologizing" of the Bible's record in attempt to boil it down into a message of humanistic moralism, led me to not believe, in spite of my Confirmation.

I couldn't accept it because it wasn't a real picture of who God is. This false perception has, in fact, led to the self-doubt and cultural suicide of the West and its peoples that we see all around us today. I sensed this even then. It would seem impossible, but much of what I was hearing in my church had managed to turn the Lord of creation, existence Itself, the dread Lord of all the earth, into some kind of girlie-man in my eyes.

And yet I knew enough of the truth. I remembered what I had learned in the prayer meetings and other Catholic Charismatic gatherings and teachings. I had the Bible and all that my parents, in particular my mother had taught me, and I heard the truth in Bible readings and much of the liturgy read week after week. So many people have never had such chances as I had.

But I truly grasped none of these things—least of all, the love of God for all mankind, in spite of the hard stands He and His people have had to take. Furthermore, I was still my sinful self. This led to a split. At times I would be indulging in all kinds of sinful behavior, and at other times I was still trying to seek God and make amends. In such seasons I would be praying my rosary, lighting my candles and even reading my Bible, doing whatever I could to try to get back. With all these unresolved issues, I still went on to my Confirmation.

Going through with Confirmation at that time, I believe, was a mistake. I wasn't really ready to cut loose from the old me and follow Christ. Dave refused to get confirmed, saying it was all hypocritical, and I couldn't believe he did this. To me, this seemed a profound disloyalty to my family and my religion, and I was unwilling to add this to all the things I was already doing to make them ashamed. Yet my loyalties were misplaced. We must set our relationship with God aright first, for that relationship is the true foundation upon which everything else must be built. From there, we can then be true to our families, our church and then the outside world. Nothing works when we fail to build everything on a proper foundation, but rather try and build backwards.

In this way, I went back and forth, and for a short period of time I was away from my friends and really seeking God. Then one day Dave and Harry saw me in church after service doing something like praying. Dave said, "What are you doing up there, you holy-moly boy! Come back here and talk to us; we've got some plans." So we sat in the back of the church and discussed plans to graduate from mere shoplifting and start doing some break-ins. For Dave, the irony was too much. He started laughing and saying, "Here we are, sitting in the back of a Catholic church and planning all of our crimes, just like in a Godfather movie!"

At this point we weren't very successful, pulling off only a few botched break-ins and theft out of cars at night. But one day we came up with a bigger plan. The church had an annual fundraising fair called Mission Day, and we planned to break in and steal that money right out of the rectory. I knew that this was one of the most sinful things I could imaginably do, and of course I wavered to and fro.

As stereotypical as this must sound, when the appointed night came, it really was dark and stormy and lightening and thundering. I couldn't believe what I was about to do. On the other hand, I was determined to harden myself, not be a victim and embark upon this course of life, as I had promised myself a few years before. So, I began to try and bargain with God and look for a way to pay for my sins in advance.

In the end, due to the ferocity of the storm, we never actually went out and did the deed that night. Yet something worse took place within me. As I continually tried to pray the rosary to pay for my sins in advance[1], I realized the utter futility of it all. I called out to heaven, "I know this is fake. What is the one thing I must do to be clear with You?" As soon as I prayed this, an answer dropped in my spirit: "What you must understand is love."

I couldn't accept that answer and raged against it. The lightening flashed, the thunder clapped and, with my eyes wide open, I threw my rosary down, stormed out of the laundry room, and made what I believed was a permanent decision to never attempt to follow God again.

---

1   Some will protest that Rome explicitly teaches no such thing. Fair enough, but to my young mind the possibility of gaining indulgences through a treasury of virtue built up by the saints suggested such a possibility.

CHAPTER 12
A WILD YEAR OF SIN

"For My people have committed two evils:
They have forsaken Me, the fountain of living waters,
And hewn themselves cisterns—broken cisterns that can hold no water."

Jeremiah 2:13

SUMMER 1984 – SPRING 1985

The next summer and school year in many ways started out similar to the year before. I had gone to the State Latin convention in the Spring of 1984, prayed at the last minute because I wasn't fully prepared like every other year, and got another first place in mythology. This was a peak year because I also got third in Roman History and was a member of the first place 'Certamen' team, a kind of quiz bowl, because of certain answers I could provide with great speed. We were very pleased when McKinley got first place, especially against the rather snooty Baton Rouge High. Even though the old team from Istrouma was scattered, there was still enough of us who had moved to McKinley to pull off a victory, even against former teammates.

I also went to the National Latin Convention for the last time that summer of 1984. Fewer of us went because of a new policy of only letting people who were likely to win an award go. Those of us who actually did win some things were thereby demoralized, because our motivation to win lay in our desire to be there with our friends. I, for example, got tenth place that year, which was a significant drop even from where I'd been.

We went completely out of control at that convention. There were watermelons smashed against walls, lamps and pieces of furniture thrown out of third story windows, and the like. In the process of all this dissipation I flushed some guy's toothpaste and underwear down the toilet. A day or so later the toilet started overflowing into a few of our rooms and, in desperation, we tried to soak it up with all our sheets. We temporarily stored them in the trash cans in our rooms, and our plan was to try and go to a laundromat and wash everything and get everything back to normal like nothing ever happened. But we didn't know there were facility people who had keys and were coming into our rooms, and so they came while we were gone and threw all the sheets away. Now we were really in trouble, and were about to be sent home at our families' expense. They relented at the last minute, but we had to come up with the money for the sheets and plumbing.

This was typical of the deep ingratitude I expressed all my growing years. Since my parents could not have afforded to send me to these conventions, my attendance was made possible by Grandpa and Grandma, who were always watching from afar and wanted things to go well for us, no matter how much we messed up. All such dissipation is a betrayal of our ancestors, who did what they did in order to build a future for their posterity.

I was rightfully not allowed to go back to the National Convention again. But that was a minimal issue at this point, because by that summer the four of us were in full crime mode.

All that year we were sneaking out shortly before midnight and breaking into cars, businesses, houses and, because I was there, setting fires all over the place.

We did our deeds in different combinations, for it was rare for all four of us to be together in one night. The main combinations were Harry and Dave on one side and Nathan and I on the other. I was spending most of my time with Nathan at his apartment, but eventually his parents realized I was a bad influence and wouldn't allow me there. So, I had to sneak out the window whenever they were seen coming home, as Nathan's step-dad was an exceedingly dangerous man.

During those days I did discover that I had a few skills. I was very good at hopping fences, even when they were taller than me, and I was better than the rest of us in getting through barbed wire and razor wire. I think this was both because I was very slow and methodical and because I didn't mind as much when I got cut. I also developed a skill which I still have to some degree today, which is an ability to halfway memorize a room or area when the lights were on so that I could operate in it with some ability in pitch darkness.

While all of this was exhilarating, it was also extremely nerve-wracking business, because we didn't want to get caught, and we certainly didn't want to get shot. This made breaking into houses the most nerve wracking of all. We went to great lengths to try and determine if the homes were occupied or not, and often commiserated with each other that, if only we had those 'life form detectors' we saw in Star Trek, everything would be so much easier. We commiserated even more about what we called the 'Roverlert,' where one dog barking would set off a cacophony of responses throughout the entire neighborhood.

A BAG OF HOLES

And yet for all this, we had very little to show for any of it. Many of our attempted break-ins were unsuccessful, although perhaps we should have gotten an 'A for effort.' For businesses, we were trying to break in through convoluted ways that would presumably bypass the alarm systems. At one music store, we spent almost the whole night trying to get through some hatch on the roof, dangerously going through razor wire and leaping over gaps in roofs to get there. We tried all night, decided we didn't have the right tools, came back another night, and still failed.

More than half of what we did was just breaking into parked cars. From these, we mostly got more music to fuel more crime, spare change, and maybe some knives—although Dave did get a pistol out of jeep he and I were breaking into, which greatly emboldened us for future break-ins. From restaurants or clubs, we got mostly liquor to fuel more crime. From schools and similar places, maybe audio-visual equipment which we sold for pennies on the dollar. One home break-in was very 'successful,' where I got a leather jacket and a pillowcase full of jewelry. But when I stored this loot at a friend's apartment, who I will call Johnny Slade, the cat got into its hiding place, strewed it all over the place, and Johnny's mother in fear disposed of it all. In other words, pretty much everything that was happening was pure dissipation—it was like putting all our loot into a bag full of holes. Yet in our blindness we were somehow convincing ourselves that we could go on leading a 'life of crime.'

Like gamblers winning a rare jackpot while we mostly lost all our money, the few times when we got something we considered really cool were enough to convince us that it was all worthwhile. For example, one time we found a stash of cane-swords, that is,

114

walking canes where you could twist the head to pull out a small, rapier-like sword. We danced and pranced with those canes under a midnight moon, making up words about what we would do with them in various situations to the tune of a popular song at the time called "Putting on the Ritz."

But one thing I was never into in any major way was drugs. I quit smoking when I was fourteen. I kept count back then and so know that I smoked pot a combined total of five times. But near the end, even though I wasn't interested in the drugs themselves, it started to dawn on most of us that we couldn't make any real money without selling drugs—if the opportunity presented itself. Or perhaps selling guns or car parts, if we ever got better at what we were doing.

We loved fire extinguishers and were stealing and constantly using them in ridiculous ways. There was a popular video game in all the arcades at the time called 'Spy Hunter,' which featured a James Bond style spy car being chased by all kinds of enemies, equipped with such features as machines guns, oil slick, and smoke screen. This game had an unforgettable theme song always playing in the background. So we would all start humming the theme song to each other, riding around perhaps in Harry's 'No Fat Chicks' Trans-Am, and let out a smokescreen of our own in the road behind us with the fire extinguishers.

This gave us the idea to carry at least one fire extinguisher around on our break-ins, just in case we got in some situation and needed a 'smoke screen' to get out. But Nathan just couldn't control himself when it was in his hands, and had to give it quick little squeezes every few minutes. So all night long we kept hearing '*psst, psst*' as he released small amounts of charge, and all night long we kept retorting back in loud whispers: "Will you stop that!!," '*psst, psst*', "Will you knock that off!!!" Nathan also drove us crazy because, while we were all sneaking around and keeping low and out of the light, trying not to be seen and trying not to get shot, he would just walk up to everything nonchalantly and stand up straight like he was Mr. MaGoo. Yet for all this, Nathan had an uncanny ability of knowing just how to break into things and just how to get things to open.

Darker things were going on with Nathan, for he often seemed almost like he was trying to get caught. People in Nathan's situation often do not have the full mental capacity to understand everything that is happening to them, but Nathan was both mentally disturbed and extremely intelligent. He therefore considered and framed his whole life in a context that seemed to be crushing his soul, for Nathan could not stand how bad he felt things were for him. This would cause him to engage in behaviors that drove us to distraction. One night, for example, when Dave and Johnny Slade had just successfully used suction and glass cutters to quietly remove a perfect square out of a hardware store window, Nathan started wildly and randomly breaking the windows. On occasions he pointed the pistol right at Dave and would make shooting motions, and when he found a cartridge inside, Dave had had enough. I began trying to keep Nathan only with me and not the others, because I felt I was the only one who could understand and, in some ways, restrain him.

We all had our un-disciplines to deal with. I stole a large quantity of nitric acid from the high school science lab because I wanted to make a well-known explosive and had plenty of the other ingredient. But, not being able to control myself, and besides using it to burn off my fingerprints, I put it in a spray bottle and kept spraying it on things for vandalism throughout the nights, or just into the air so I could see would looked to me like a looming 'cloud of death' go down the road. My lack of discipline probably saved my life, for, if I had used it as intended, I surely would have blown myself up.

CLOSE CALL

I had a lot of other close calls that I can only attribute to some sort of mercy that I didn't deserve, even though my continued freedom was a problem for a lot of people. One night the police had been activated and I was running down the sidewalk with stolen clothes on my back and a bag of loot, and I tripped on the protruding root of a tree, falling face down on the ground. Two squad cars at that exact moment flew directly past me in opposite directions without seeing me, apparently because I couldn't be distinguished from the ground. On another occasion, when the police were thoroughly activated to the point a helicopter came out, Dave and I went off in opposite directions. In that neighborhood the drainage canals were concreted over like the L.A. river, so there was no cover at all and the normal means of escape was unavailable. I could see a pile of sirens in the direction Dave went at the end of the street, thinking surely he had been busted. Meanwhile, I dove deep into some bushes on my end.

Eventually an officer showed up at a sidewalk on the far end of those bushes, and shone a bright flashlight directly at me for what seemed like an eternity. While he slowly moved his flashlight back forth but mostly directly on me, I remained motionless, using a breathing technique where you hardly moved your diaphragm at all, getting just barely enough air through your nose while your external body doesn't move a millimeter. I did not know how long I could go on like this, nor did I have any idea whether he could see me or not. I suspected he couldn't see me at all but knew where I had to be, for I was very deep in those bushes. We were both locked into a standoff. For he had no way of knowing whether I was armed or not or what I might be prepared to do. And I had no idea how he would feel forced to react if I started moving or even tried to surrender. And I did not want to surrender. If this had been a war zone, he could have simply fired into the bushes and be done with the whole situation. But it was not, and so had all the dangers that civilian life potentially held for those officers' future if something went wrong.

Then something happened which tipped me off that they couldn't quite see me but knew in general where I had to be. Two or three of them starting approaching from different directions in a well-planned and steady formation, like a pincer movement, which would eventually leave no ground uncovered, leading to my capture. What happened next was hard to explain to my friends even when it was fresh in my mind, and I could only do it with the aid of drawings. Now after so many years I no longer have the memory to really explain what happened, except to say this. There would be a brief moment of time in their formation where I would be in no one's line of sight. To take advantage of that moment, I would have to get out of the bushes, traverse an exposed clearing between those bushes and the fence, and hop a wooden fence a little taller than I was. As soon as that brief moment came, with 1000 volts of adrenaline, I exited the bushes, leaped and pulled myself over the top of that fence, dropped to the other side with a thud, and was out of there as fast as I could be.

I don't know how it was that they did not see me flying over the top of that fence, but maybe they just did not want to shoot. No one was saying anything; they were all as silent as mice as far as I could tell. I was soon flying through a maze of back yards, sheds, and the like, with no time to give proper heed to whether there was a dog in the yard or not, and eventually made my way all the way home undetected.

The next morning, I saw Dave on the bus and couldn't believe it. "How did you get out?" I asked. "I thought for sure that pile of sirens at the end of the road was you getting busted."

"I thought exactly the same thing about you" he answered. And he told some story about how there was even a helicopter with a floodlight, and yet he still got away.

We continued to do weird and unreasonable things. One night after such activities we were wandering back towards Harry's house through the sports fields at the Catholic school. As we went, Dave looked at me laughing and said "I have an incredible idea. Let's make a monument to the Devil!!!" At that school there were all these games set up, a metal pole coming out of a tire filled with concrete at the bottom and a rope and a ball hanging on it at the top. These could easily be moved. We stacked some tires or something in the middle and wedged the two concrete filled tires diagonally along the bottom so that the two poles came out like horns—and that was our 'monument to the Devil.' The next morning as we passed by on the bus, one of us pointed it out to the other students saying "Look, a monument ... to the Devil!" and we shouted back in reply "Yes, a monument to the Devil, Bar Har Har Har!" as we stomped our feet on the ground, waved our heads back and forth and beat our fists against the back of our seats. If this sounds ridiculous, it surely was. But we were playing with fire, as I soon enough would find out.

EVIL FOR ITS OWN SAKE

One of those days the four of us got together, took out a sheet of paper, and tried to map out what motivated us in our amateur life of crime. To the best of my memory, it went down as follows. Harry said something about money, girls, and being cool. It was the image part that really mattered to him, for Harry was all about the cool. Dave said something about money, parties, girls, perhaps drugs, and Nathan said something about parties, drugs, and revenge.

I said I wasn't really interested in those other things, although I wouldn't mind having money. What I really wanted was revenge. I also said that I was motivated by evil for pure evil's sake, and got preachy, saying that we should all be more devoted to pure evil. By this I may have meant some kind of Joker-like revenge on almost everything and everyone. But I think, more likely, I was looking for some abstract principle to devote my life to and organize it around, something other than following Jesus with all its loving and forgiving and falsely perceived weakness that seemed so intolerable to me.

And yet I continued to go to church every week out of loyalty to my family and my religion. Even then, after that night of apostasy when I vowed never to follow God again, I had not 100% given up on the idea of repentance. Although I don't remember any of the homilies, I loathed what I heard in the songs and in the liturgy about submitting to the will of God, worshiping Him, and being dependent on Him. It all seemed so sniveling to me, in spite of the fact that God was continuing to show mercy to me every day that I went on in this rebellious state. I knew this couldn't go on forever. In my utter blindness, I still hoped that I would repent one day, but only after putting it off as long as possible.

INFINITE CREATIVITY

My issue was I had no understanding of the fundamental goodness and justice of God. My one concern with Him was that He was the stronger and had the power to throw me into hell. In fact, it took me many years to develop an understanding of the goodness of God, even after I was a believer.

When people discuss God's goodness versus His strength, Plato's Euthyphro often comes up. This is a dialogue in which Socrates discusses the question of whether things are just and good because the gods approve of them, or whether the gods approve of such things because they are just and good. I think there are two misunderstandings here. One is that most of the discourse in the Euthyphro relates to polytheism and does not apply to a monotheistic God at all. More importantly, the way the questions of the Euthyphro are often posed in the contemporary world is to ask, "Does God simply define what He wants as good because He is the strongest," or "In approving the good, is He appealing to some standard beyond Himself?" The intent is often to belittle the importance of such things as revealed religion and submission to the will of God.

But the question is one of origin, not of strength. In the true conception of God, He must be the uncreated origin of all things. All other things need something else to account for their existence. But God alone has the quality of simply existing in and of Himself, uncreated, without beginning and without end. He is, in fact, Existence Itself, as His name *Yahweh* indicates.

Because nothing else has this quality of self-existence, all things and their relationships with each other must ultimately come from God and nowhere else. So, it is not simply a matter of God being the strongest man in the room, like Stalin, so that He gets to decide what is good and what is bad because no one can stop Him. Rather, nothing would exist without Him nor would any of the relationships between things making them good or bad have any meaning without reference to Him and the particular ways in which He designed creation. There is therefore simply no possible way that goodness and rightness could be anything other than that defined by God. And there is no way that the ultimate source of all that we desire can be found anywhere else than in Him.

Here lies the inner logic for all those things I was rejecting—to love and worship God and submit to Him, and to seek His will rather than my own at the moment. A thought experiment can illustrate this. Imagine that the Lord gave you god-like powers, to never die, to create things out of thin air and also make them disappear at will—basically to do anything you want. Then He cut you loose in your own corner of the universe. You may have a great run of things for thousands of years, although I doubt it would last that long, for we don't understand how uncreative we truly are.

Eventually, you would run out of new ideas, even with your god-like powers. Then a deep monotony would set in. As the ages wore on, it would be dark, suffocating, crushing, until your whole personality collapsed in on itself like some kind of existential black hole—an endless vacuum that would never cease to implode ever deeper into an uncreative hell of boredom.

Without a complete reconciliation and reconnection to God, what I have described is the least of what will happen to us. We will not be sent off on our own with god-like powers, because we are part of the universe God has created and all its interconnections. However, we are sempiternal—we had a clear beginning but no end, for we were created in the image of God and designed to interact with Him forever. This cannot be undone, so that simple annihilation will never be an option for us. If you die in rebellion against God, you will still continue to exist with your consciousness, like a totaled car in a junkyard that will never run again. As the prophet said:

"And they shall go forth and look, upon the corpses of the men who have transgressed against Me. For their worm does not die, and their fire is not quenched. They shall be an abhorrence to all flesh" (Isaiah 66:24, NKJV).

That will be our fate, if we fail to follow our true purpose from our Creator and Redeemer, the source of all things. But if we are reconciled, the positive side is very literally beyond what we can imagine. Consider what it is that keeps us hooked to video games. It is primarily the prospect of reaching new levels, where things change and we are confronted with new things, and are tested in new ways. Those games that are well designed are the most creative and keep us hooked. On the other hand, tedium sets in when this creative element is lacking, or we reach the last level and there is nothing new to do.

But to walk with God is to tap into the opposite of our lack of lasting creativity: the infinite potentiality of God. In relationship with Him, we will be exploring ever new vistas that are always surprising, ever new depths of understanding that previously could not have been imagined. The wonder, novelty and excitement will never wear off, for we will constantly be infused with new life, no matter how tired we may feel now. We, in fact, have very little in our current life with which to compare the ages to come, precisely because God's infinite creativity is characterized by endless newness and surprise.

We have some inkling of this in the advancement of scientific knowledge. Rather than reaching a point where everything is fully explained and tidied up, on the contrary, ever deeper levels of complexity are always being discovered. This is why the Apostle said, "For since the creation of the world His invisible attributes are clearly seen, being understood by the things that are made, even His eternal power and Godhead" (Romans 1:20). And yet, what we can look forward to in the ages to come cannot be fully compared even to this.

I understood none of this and continued to dissipate. From the time I was cut loose from previous restraints in the 8th grade, all that I did was just consuming and burning up what was already there. I was like a fungus, while those who have been restored to God and have the Holy Spirit are as those who have the power of photosynthesis, and so, with new life, a continual inner moral renovation takes place.

All I had left was a scapular around my neck—a kind of religious talisman with a picture of Mary on one side and words purportedly from her on the other which said something like, "Whoever dies while wearing this will not suffer eternal fire." One night while we were preparing for some crimes, I told Nathan about this and he told me, "If we get shot tonight, I am going to take that thing and put it around both our necks together before we die."

The last shred of the idea of repentance that I was holding onto was about as effectual as that scapular would have been. For, as I said, I hoped to put repentance off as long as possible, until maybe right before I died. But there came a night when it was revealed to me in no uncertain terms how utterly empty that conceit was.

TOO LATE

I was severely sick, unlike anything I had experienced before. This was that third sickness I previously alluded to. I was hugging the toilet, in pain in my chest and stomach but especially my intestines, utterly convinced that I had been poisoned. The first thought that entered my head was "This is probably going to be a long and excruciating way to die. I wonder how long this whole thing is going to drag out." The second thing I thought to myself was, "I guess it's time to execute that last minute asking for forgiveness thing that I have always been telling myself I will do."

That is when I found out that I could not repent. In the very moment when I thought I needed to fear God the most, all such fear left me. I expected to soon be before the judgment throne of God, explaining my life. But a kind of insane arrogance rushed in, an irrational but overwhelming sense that I could talk my way out of it, or weasel out some other way, or that there was nothing to fear for some unknown reason. No matter how I tried, no attempt to fear God or even ask for forgiveness outwardly was even possible to drum up. Finally, I just said to myself, "Let's just bring this on and see what happens."

Most fortunately for me, nothing happened that night, because I wasn't poisoned and I didn't die. The best I can tell, it must have been some very painful form of gas. But I left that night with a very crucial piece of information: God will not be mocked, and I can't just repent whenever I want to. He can take away the organ of repentance from a man who obstinately resists Him, and often does.

My father had a different but related experience one night many years later. Late one night, for the first time in his life, atheism suddenly became very convincing, almost in a flash, for reasons to do with parallel universes or something like that as he dimly recalled. Knowing that he was in trouble, he wanted to call out to God for help but, on the other hand it just seemed too ridiculous to call on someone who didn't exist. He remained in this contradictory state until he overcame his shame and called out to whoever was there to save him. In that moment the mirage broke and he saw things the way he always had. Whenever God offers salvation and repentance on His terms, we had better be ready to take it. If you, reader, have reached a place that you feel Jesus may be calling you to repentance, I urge you—DO IT NOW! There is no telling if you will ever have the opportunity again.

CHAPTER 13

23:00 ON FAT TUESDAY

For we have spent enough of our past lifetime in doing the will of the Gentiles—when we walked in lewdness, lusts, drunkenness, revelries, drinking parties, and abominable idolatries.

1 Peter 4:3

SPRING 1985

Meanwhile, we kept going on the course we were on. My world was in many ways split in two, for I had a separate group of more intellectual friends that I hung out with during school hours. I was still trying in many of my classes, though not as much as I should have. For example, I spent most of my time in my Trigonometry class in the back playing chess or backgammon with a friend of mine who eventually became a Catholic priest. But I was also fascinated by the subject and filled up many pages working the problems at home. I read most of the stuff in English class but failed the Spring semester due to not doing the research paper.

In Latin class I hadn't given up either and struggled through Ceasar's Gallic Wars and Cicero's orations against Cataline. There was another State Latin Convention. I prayed and won first place

127

in Greek Mythology again. This time Dave showed up at LSU where it was held, and we had a lot of fun the whole time, even going out at night to Chimes Street where all the Punk Rockers hung out in those days. But our Latin teacher was incensed that Dave was 'crashing' the convention and made a big stink.

In less than a year my very rapid decline in that Latin class in particular would put me under yet another psychological evaluation. For, without knowing it, I was rapidly approaching another inflection point.

THE DEATH OF THE PARTY

One of many unique things about Mardi Gras, the well-known mass party in New Orleans that means 'Fat Tuesday' in English, is the extraordinarily abrupt manner in which it ends. The carnival goes for days on end, until the clock strikes midnight on the last day finale—and exactly at 0:00 on Ash Wednesday the police pour out, the bars are emptied, everyone is rounded up and sent home; the trucks come out like snowplows to start piling up and hauling out all the trash. In a somewhat metaphorical but less abrupt sense, it also was in the spring of 1985 that the process of winding down our fun-filled year of crime and mayhem concluded.

I think it began with Harry getting kicked out of McKinley for bringing a gun to school. Now various students did this all the time at McKinley, but due to his tendency to boast and all his showing off, Harry got caught and was expelled. He ended up going to a Christian school that took all kinds of expelled students, and I would like to think the gospel that he heard there finally reached him before he died.

Later that year, Nathan and I decided to empty a significant portion of our pantries into our book bags and engage in various food fights at school. We especially liked instant biscuit dough because it was cheap but could make big welts when you hit people with it hard. We went on like this throughout the day, until in one class Nathan rolled up a piece of paper, filled it with flour and blew it all over some kid right in the middle of class. That kid rose up in a rage and Nathan and I got hauled to the office for everything we had been doing that day. We were split off from each other and questioned separately. Nathan's mother was called in, they searched his bags, and he ended up getting expelled. I should have been expelled also but something unusual happened.

Our principal at McKinley at that time, who I will call Mr. Broward, had his personality quirks but was trying to run a tight ship at McKinley. In retrospect, I think he was in some ways succeeding. I will call the assistant principal Mr. Johnston. Johnston was also trying to be a disciplinarian in a sometimes-anarchic environment, had no time for White kids causing trouble, and was eager to see me expelled along with Nathan.

When Dad finally arrived, he was in a foul mood. Not only was there all my antics, but he apparently was not having a very easy day at work either. He had an unbuttoned flannel shirt over a t-shirt, his beard and hair were somewhat unkempt and dirty from whatever he was doing at work that day, and he almost looked like he had just rolled out of a biker bar. And, for reasons that are entirely mysterious to me, Mr. Broward seemed to make some kind of connection with my father, across all lines of race and background.

"Why is it" he asked, "that young men with such promise so often seem to throw it all away?"

"I don't know" Dad said as he shook his head, although he certainly knew experientially, even if it took a lifetime for Dad to begin to know why. And right there Mr. Broward decided not to expel me.

Mr. Johnston came into the office and asked Broward something like, "Let me take over and get this kid out of here."

"No, I got this, I'm going to handle it my own way," answered Broward.

Mr. Johnston was livid but he was overruled. I don't know what my punishment was ... maybe a one-week suspension. But I certainly did not respond with the gratitude that this deserved.

The next big event was going to shut Harry and Dave out of my life for a while. But it took some time to work its way through the court system to the point of keeping us apart. One day Harry, Dave and I were hanging out at Harry's house with this very boastful guy. He was going on and on about all this stuff he was getting when he made trips to Tijuana—switchblades and the like that he was showing us. Then he got into how easy he thought the offices and concessions at the Baton Rouge Zoo were to break into, and how much money he expected to be there. And so we all sat down, made a rough map, and came up with a plan.

On the appointed night, Harry and Dave got together with this guy to carry it out, but for some reason I no longer recall—maybe because my parents caught me trying to sneak out—I didn't make it for this job.

Earlier that night someone had called the police with a tip, saying a bunch of White guys were planning to break into the Zoo and let all the animals out. Who this person was and how he/she got his information is a mystery, but it probably had something to do with all the boasting that guy was doing at Coney Island[1] earlier that night. The result was that the police were ready for

---

1   A local video game arcade combined with a burger joint

my friends when they arrived—really ready. They were lying in wait and had combat boots, long guns, the works. Within seconds of my friends trying to scale the fence, their arms were bound behind their backs and their faces jammed against the links. They were let out of jail but must have been put on probation right away or there was some understanding that we couldn't hang out with each other, including me, as Dave explained when I saw him on the bus and asked about it. This kept us away from each other for some time until compliance with it began to slowly wear off.

Soon enough, Dave would also be gone from McKinley High School. Dave had gotten into one of his many conflicts with his father, and for several months left his home and lived with a mutual friend of ours. This guy's dad was a complete pothead and didn't seem to care who was living in his home or what he was doing there. I would go there from time to time and there were quite a few of our after-midnight escapades that began from that house. Because Dave had semi-permanently moved in there, he got on the school bus each morning from this friend's bus stop instead of his own. This went on for many weeks until one morning the bus driver inexplicably announced to Dave that she was no longer allowed to pick him up. To this day I don't think anyone knows why this happened or who gave this order. But as the school bus drove off, in a scene that is forever fixed in the memories of us all, Dave reeled around, vigorously gave the finger to the bus and everyone on it, and was never seen at McKinley High School again.

ENDGAME

With the last of the old crew gone, I was now spending more time with Chuck Forten, and we came up with a contest to see who could steal the most useless object each day. We would show each other what we stole for the day when we got on the bus home. To put this in context, years ago I had gotten tired of going back and forth to my locker, so I got a large bag to carry all my textbooks and everything in at once, which I lugged everywhere. This contest started small but soon escalated as we were caught in a cycle of one-upmanship. Chuck came with some knick-knack off a teacher's desk. I came with a door knob. He came with a faucet, and I came with a toilet seat, which I somehow managed to jam into my bag. He came with a gas nozzle head that he somehow removed from one of the lab tables for Bunsen burners, I came with a small manhole cover. And, finally, I emptied out my large bag and put in—what else—a very large stolen fire extinguisher.

But this time I got on the bus and sat near enough to the front that the bus driver could very clearly hear the loud clunk when I plopped my bag to the ground. She called in the Principal and demanded an investigation, and so I was caught with the fire extinguisher. Broward still seemed to take it in stride, saying, "We got somebody stealing a fire extinguisher here. Looks like we're going to have to call the FBI." But he only gave me a two-week suspension.

As I waited throughout the afternoon for my parents to come pick me up, I decided I had enough. I was tired of dragging them into this, going through the whole session, pretending like I was sorry, being grounded in perpetuity unless I snuck out, and nothing ever changing. "Why not just go off on my own and be done with the whole charade?" I told myself. And so right then and there, hours before my parents would arrive, I just got up and walked away. I walked all night. I spent some time trying to sleep under a bridge, but then kept going until I got near my neighborhood sometime after midnight. There is a relatively fancy red brick bus stop at the intersection I came to, right next to a gas station at the time, and it provided some shelter, so I spent the rest of the night there. But there was rain that night, so whenever it became too much, I went into the gas station bathroom.

After the sun came up, I headed over to Dave's house. He was out in the living room as I saw him so many times, blue jeans, no shirt, long hair flowing over his shoulders and strumming away on his guitar. His mom gave me some eggs and toast, for which I was extremely grateful, for it had been some time since I had eaten and I had walked for many miles. But not long after this, Dave got into some kind of dispute with his mother, and finally said, "I'm outta here!" So then both Dave and I went off on our own, but not before Dave's mom gave us a truly epic and well-deserved scold about the music we were listening to.

We headed over to the apartment complex where Nathan lived, hung out with him for a while, caused a lot of trouble, and spent the nights in a vacant apartment we found there. We would steal crackers and the like from the nearby convenience store to feed ourselves. At night in that vacant apartment we didn't know who might be coming in there, so we had to take turns keeping watch by the window. Dave would smoke, and those times I would wake up and see him peering out the window with his cigarette was the closest to real camaraderie I have felt, having never seen war. It is hard to relate to how I felt when it was my turn, because it had to be so different than it is now. For now, I almost always feel the Holy Spirit's presence with me, and never feel alone and almost never feel bored. But back then I was cut off from the presence of the Lord and had to do things like count something or concentrate on something or meditate—or just endlessly think through plans or alternate realities.

While we were hanging out at that apartment complex, Dave,

ever the ladies' man, had stolen some guy's girlfriend. This was a big, boastful guy of about eighteen, so Nathan was telling us "You can't take that guy." But the reveal would have to come soon. This was just the kind of thing I wanted absolutely nothing to do with; but Dave was my friend and I would have to follow through. Yet somehow the confrontation never came, because we moved on. In the meantime, a bunch of the guys we were hanging out with in those apartments in those days were doing a lot of overly detailed boasting, saying things like "If anyone breaks into my apartment, I am reaching right into my drawer and getting this gun," or "If anyone breaks in, I am going under my bed and getting that gun."

"Thanks for all that information," Nathan said to himself as he quietly listened to all this bravado—and, as soon as he knew that there was no one in their apartments, he promptly broke in and stole all their guns. There were probably about three, including a .30-06 rifle. Living in a small apartment with nowhere to hide anything, he unscrewed the a/c vent coming into his room on the ceiling, slid the guns into the duct, and screwed the vent back on. Afterwards, there were a couple of occasions when we opened Nathan's window, fired randomly into the apartments, and quickly ducked and closed the window just to see what would happen.

But during that particular period, Dave and I moved on to Johnny Slade. We were often waiting for someone or other to get out of some kind of detention in those days, and Johnny was one of those guys that I was looking forward to meeting. When we did finally meet, he said "Man, I've heard an F** load about you!" and I told him the same. He was the guy whose apartment I stored our loot in, which the cat got into. But I never really got to see him much, either in those days or later while he was still alive, and I regret this. I never got to tell him about my salvation.

Our very brief stint of living as runaways had to come to an end. The police were looking for us and, considering all the trouble Dave was in due to the Zoo incident, we needed a negotiated way out of this. There was a lady the police used as some kind of community youth liaison, and this was the way for everyone to go home without further police involvement. When we went to see her in Johnny Slade's apartment, I thought we would be talking to her about something else, but she quickly convinced us to go back home, describing jail and the like.

And so our wild, criminal year of fun—the very epitome of the pleasure of sin that lasts only for a season—came to an end.

CHAPTER 14

A SATANIC OFFER

So Ahab said to Elijah, "Have you found me, O my enemy?" And he answered, "I have found you, because you have sold yourself to do evil in the sight of the Lord ..."

1 Kings 21:20

SEPTEMBER 1985

When I returned to High School to begin 11th grade in August of 1985, nothing of my old life was left. Yet I still tried to cling to it all in desperate nostalgia quite unnatural for a fifteen-year-old. I need to step back slightly and explain the last few steps towards arriving there. My parents were desperate to get me away from my friends and out of trouble as soon as the summer of 1985 began. They made a decision to send me to my mother's parents, Gramps and Granny, in Florida. At the time they lived in a sandy neighborhood in Fort Walton Beach, far from any beaches, off Beale Parkway.

There I would stay sequestered for almost the whole summer—and I did very, very little. For my old life was shut down, I was far from anything familiar, and I didn't know what I would be doing next. I mostly lay in my room and listened to Heavy Metal all day—with a vigorous dose of onanism thrown in. My grandparents, having grown up in poverty, were amazed that I didn't want to go out and find some may to make money, like selling watermelons on the beaches.

Gramps had a drinking problem, especially since the Guillain–Barré[1], and late at night he would tell me all the bad treatment he believed he had gotten from Granny and her family. And one morning at church Granny was crying over this and had a few things to say of her own. But to me the balance seemed overwhelmingly on Gramps' side. On those nights he also talked of his own upbringing, and the struggles they went through. He spoke of how he was trying to raise chickens as a small child to feed everyone, but the rats kept getting in and eating the eggs. People knew that you handle this with rat poison, he said, but no one told him, and no one cared, and no one understood what he was trying to do. As I looked at his face while he was saying these things, it was like I could see right through to the next generation so that my mother was doing the talking—no one loved me, no one cared, no one understood.

Meanwhile, I was worried about Nathan back in Baton Rouge. I knew that, if he did things on his own without me, he would do them thoughtlessly and without caution, nonchalantly walking into danger as he always did. I begged him and I ordered him, DO NOT do anything for as long as I am gone, do not try to break into anything or even shoplift. But this was all for naught, for Nathan couldn't lay low for long, and he eventually went on a rampage. He stole a vehicle or two and drove wildly through the night. For example, when he saw a bunch of people drinking, hanging out

---

1   A rare nerve disease from a botched flu vaccine, as noted in an earlier chapter

around a pickup truck, he plowed right into that pickup truck for no reason and then kept driving. He fired his guns all over the place, and broke into places all around his neighborhood. When some poor woman looked out her window he held up his axe like he was an axe murderer. He did all this and escaped and ducked down in his apartment while the sirens blazed all around.

And then, in those early morning hours after midnight, he quit ducking and nonchalantly walked out of his apartment to the adjacent convenience store to get a slurpy. As he approached the store, the cops swooped in and apprehended him. They took him back to his apartment and recovered all the stolen goods, including the guns they knew were there, based on all his intemperate detonations. They were familiar with the air-conditioning duct trick and it was the first place they looked. Nathan was detained in a mental hospital to the northeast of Baton Rouge. I only got the story when I got back to Baton Rouge, found out where he was, and called him on one of his once-a-week permitted phone calls.

Back in Florida, I continued to do very little. I half-heartedly broke into a nearby house one night and played the piano. I broke into cars in the nearby neighborhoods, but all I got was some guy's black beret, for this was an Air Force town. And there was a small Pentecostal church on my grandparents' street that I broke into. As I entered, I saw a large mural of Jesus covering the wall behind the pulpit, looking back at me. All I could think of was the story of Nadab and Abihu in the Old Testament[1], and I envisaged a stream of fire at any moment proceeding out of the eyes and mouth of that Jesus mural and burning me to a crisp. I noted that there were musical instruments, but I had no way to get them all the way back home, and that the money in the offering boxes was

---

1   Leviticus 10

not enough to be worth stealing. After a brief amount of hesitation, I left, very relieved to get out from under the watching eyes of that giant Jesus mural.

At the same time, Granny felt the Lord wanted her to make an evangelistic cassette tape for all her grandchildren. She made an original and tasked me with making copies on a double cassette player. With that method, I had to listen to the whole thing every time I made a copy, maybe about six or seven times. On that tape, mostly from a very Catholic Charismatic perspective, she would eventually describe the final fate of the righteous and the wicked. I still have that tape and have listened to it again from time to time over the years, whenever a cassette player is still available. And my summer of isolation finally came to an end.

Some things were proceeding normally, more normally than before. The sequestration that summer had slowed a lot of things down. When I returned home, I was mostly cut off from what I had known before, for I had little contact with my old friends. While I was gone, my friends had organized themselves into a formal gang, but I was never able to fit into that structure.

I did have some contact with my old friends—but a lot less. One evening Dave and I stayed up all night playing a board game called 'Axis and Allies.' I lost, and Dave, true to form, gave me some professorial lectures. "All those missions where no one was allowed to surrender and your armies died to the last man was exactly the mistake Hitler had made," he told me. "There is something to be said for occasionally retreating strategically and living to fight another day." And "I always thought the Empire of Japan was way too overextended in light of the resources they actually had, and your attacks on Australia exceeded their original errors." In an ideal world, where everyone's future lined up exactly with their skill set, Dave would be lecturing in some War

College somewhere. As it was, Dave eventually got his High School diploma, ended up making a decent living on the offshore oil rigs, and has more recently been able to settle down at one of the larger chemical plants. But for me, all this normality was just the calm before a new kind of storm.

I just couldn't let go of all the nostalgia I had for the way things had been the previous year. I continued shoplifting and was arrested again in September. I was at the local Kmart and had stolen some music cassettes. When caught, I ran as fast as I possibly could, into the neighborhood behind the store and towards the drainage canal system. One employee ran behind me and was falling behind, while another jumped into a car and sought to cut me off. He almost did, jumping out and seeking to intercept me before reaching the fence before the canal.

I got around him, but when I was less than ten yards away from the fence and the canal, I miscalculated. I felt my strength waning; yet if I had nevertheless fully pumped up the gas on my running, I likely would have scaled that fence and ultimately reached freedom within seconds. As it was, I infinitesimally 'took my foot off the pedal,' not slowing down enough to be visible to the naked eye, but enough to get tackled. For I foolishly believed I needed to conserve some slight amount of extra strength to go the distance. In a sense, this whole episode was symbolic of my Hamlet-like wavering through life.

They had me subdued until the officer, who was not far behind, handcuffed me, and then I was led back to the store and the squad car. The officer in this case was a tall Black woman. She asked me some questions and I gave her some answers, to which she replied "You seem like a guy who doesn't care about anything."

"That is not entirely true," I replied, "I wish my family didn't have to be dragged into all this."

There was silence and then she broke into some soulful gospel song. But it was more than soulful, it was like a message from another world: even at this point, reconciliation was still possible—it was still possible to repent. But I still wasn't heeding it.

I don't remember much more about that arrest. Since my mother was certain I would be going to prison this time, and would need to defend myself, I went back to doing Tae Kwan Do with Chul Yun on her insistence. A psychological evaluation was ordered by the court, but this process did not begin until November. The events that were about to take place would lead to a second psychological evaluation initiated by the school system, which also would begin that November.

THE DARK SUNRISE

Now, because we are getting near to the point in this story where I will need to discuss Satan, I need to explain some things first. I did not view Satan at the time as I do now—as a creature that is in some sense limited by time and space, not quite in the same way as we are in the realm he mainly inhabits, but analogically similar. Rather, I understood him to be some sort of spirit of evil that mostly pervaded everything, almost as God does—although I did still have the concept that he could be cast out or removed from an area and then force his way back in. But the main point is that, when I was communing with the realm of unclean spirits, I mostly believed at the time that I was dealing directly with Satan.

That is how I will describe such things, in the way I understood it at the time. For to constantly be giving disclaimers as I tell this tale would be tedious. But that does not mean that I now believe that Satan was likely to stop what he was doing, running the kingdom of darkness, and come deal with me. I was dealing with demons to be sure, but who exactly I do not know.

With my old life mostly behind me, I spent most of my time listening to music. I was also spending a lot of time with Chuck Forten, because he was the only one left who was even tangentially related to my old crew. Chuck started telling me about some girl, mostly that she was weird, dressing in black and believing in reincarnation and the like. I could see her on the bus and soon found myself becoming emotionally attracted to her.

This I considered a vital threat. For one thing, such attraction was not compatible with the type of person I had been trying to systematically turn myself into ever since 7th grade. Yes, I was shot through and through with sexual lust for women and had come to accept that this was the way it was going to be. But to actually fall in love with a woman, as was beginning to seem possible at this point, was a mortal threat to the type of untouchable person that I hoped to become.

More importantly, however, I didn't think it was possible that any girl would ever accept me. That would lead to a terrible, humiliating rejection if I ever allowed myself to slip. And it cannot be overemphasized how total, impermeable and invincible this belief of mine was. "They will not accept me, ever," I had told Harry as I tried to get this across to him.

In the end he just had to laugh and say "I guess it's just an ancient tradition, then."

There is one thing that happened which illustrates this. One day I was passed a note, on a sheet of paper covered with writing front and back that was supposed to be from a girl. The idea was that she was some kind of outcast for wearing weird clothes, and that her hope of connecting to anyone was to get to know me. As I kept reading through that note, I couldn't believe it was true. I couldn't deny that it was physically real, and the writing on it had that tell-tale bubbly look indicating that it had been written by a female. And yet my conviction that such a thing could not happen was so invincible that I could only tell myself that it was fake. It could only possibly by some elaborate scheme, actuated by malice against me, to bring about my humiliation if I attempted to follow up. I kept that note in a hidden place, and from time to time I would read it, always wondering if it could be real, and always convincing myself that it could not be, until the end of 11th grade.

Finally, there was the promise I had made to myself that, by the time I was fifteen, I would kill someone. All the previous year there was no fear of failure because I seemed to be on a trajectory that would take me there on time. But the events I described in the last chapter ground the momentum to a halt. Now it was September 1985, meaning I had less than two months before I was sixteen.

Regarding the girl I was attracted to, one of my favorite songs, "The Warning," from Black Sabbath's first eponymous[1] "Black Sabbath" album, was playing in my head: "Now the first day that I met you, I was looking at the sky..." And I began to determine in my heart to kill the girl, in that way eliminating the threat and fulfilling my promise at once. The dread of clocking out on my promise was acute.

I looked to the east and afar off I could see my bus turning the corner, the first light of the sun flashing off its windows. I felt as out of time as Count Dracula would have felt if he similarly saw the rising of the dawn when he was far from the safety of his coffin and would soon turn to dust.

---

1   Basically a thing being named for itself or its owner—like a Black Sabbath album named "Black Sabbath"

Then a voice came crashing into my head that I had not heard since elementary school, if ever. Years earlier I had first left the prayer meetings because I felt under spiritual attack. Something had happened back in the prayer meetings that caused me to recognize that voice—but what, I can no longer recall. Yet I knew exactly who it was.

Satan said, "You must follow me now!"

I was enraged, because I thought I had left this all behind many years ago and would never again experience such things. And I couldn't believe I was dealing with this again. "I am not following you, or God, or anyone else!" I replied. "I want nothing to do with any religion, and will live my life on my own terms!!"

But that rejoinder wasn't going to fly. Satan knew his mark, had in fact been working me for many years, especially in regards to his insane war on femininity.

"Do you think I don't see how you are beginning to feel for that girl?" he said. "And do you not know what that means? You say you don't want to follow God, but do you not see how He is using that girl to bring you down? Do you not realize what humiliations He has in store for you?"

And then he passed before my mind a horrific vision of me ever pursuing after women and ever by rejected by them, forever sniveling in humiliation. This vision was so compelling to me that Satan may as well have shown me a vision of Galadriel tempted by the ring, transmogrified into a terrible phantom and crying out "All shall love me and despair!"[1] If I had seen such a thing, I would have said "All shall love you and despair—except me!"

As it was, the scenes Satan passed before my mind—as one

---

1   https://www.youtube.com/watch?v=HZ7wB4rm5Hw

would see his whole life flashing before him before he dies—thoroughly did the job.

"Follow me," he said, "and I will fill your heart with so much hate that God will never be able to use women to bring you down."

And right there, seconds before the bus arrived and whisked me away, I gave my heart and soul to Satan. Or so I thought.

CHAPTER 15

DOWN THE HALL
OF MIRRORS

And the kings of the earth, the great men, the rich men, the command-
ers, the mighty men, every slave and every free man, hid themselves in
the caves and in the rocks of the mountains, and said to the mountains
and rocks, "Fall on us and hide us from the face of Him who sits on the
throne and from the wrath of the Lamb! For the great day of His wrath
has come, and who is able to stand?"

Revelation 6:15-17

SEPTEMBER 1985 – JANUARY 1986

So began my dégringolade[1]. It started slow but then picked up
pace—very rapidly.

But before I get to the inner, satanic core of my deterioration,
I want to describe the external factors that were weighing in on
me. I also want to delve into other inner aspects of my life that

---

1   A downfall or rapid deterioration, and title of the famous 7th chapter of Paul
Johnson's *Modern Times*

plowed the ground for my satanism. In my own life, several very disparate things were happening, none of them good. You will recall the self-imposed pressure I was under to kill at least someone before I was sixteen? Here is how that deadline got put off.

With the rest of my friends gone I was hanging out mainly with Chuck. One day early that semester Chuck told me that he had fallen in with some guys I also knew of, who were making some very real money selling cocaine. It also involved some very serious violence, as he described it. Then one morning he described a violent experience he himself was involved in the night before, in which they ended up with both the drugs and the money and left someone either dead or for dead. I told him I needed to get involved as soon as possible. We kept talking about how to do that, and how he needed to established himself first. And this gave me hope that with patience I would accomplish my goals after all.

All this, however, soon ended. One Monday morning Chuck showed up with a scar on his face. He had gotten into some kind of conflict with his father on Thanksgiving Day, in which his father gave him a severe pistol whipping. He was out of the house, he said, and would soon be leaving town. Before the end of the week, Chuck was gone. To this day I really have no way of knowing how much of all that Chuck was telling me about his drug dealing was true and how much was just made-up stories. All I know is that, when I told him I needed a gun, Chuck was able to get me one in a matter of days. Right in the middle of history class, he came in from the gym and told me he needed his 'textbook' back right away. My teacher and I had only a second to look on with befuddlement when he said to me, "Come outside for a second with your bag and let's find it." When we briefly stepped outside, without missing a beat, he asked for $50, stuffed the gun in my bag, and I was back in my seat barely before I knew what happened.

I kept up with Chuck for many years after this, calling him from time to time, including after I became a believer. I truly hope I clearly shared to gospel with him, but I can't recall the detail with which we discussed such things. If the things he was talking about before he left Baton Rouge really took place, he seems to have left them all behind at some point and lived a normal life. He was in the National Guard, got married, and was some kind of construction contractor for many years. He even wrote stories for the local newspaper. The last time I saw Chuck was in 1995. He died, I hear, in a very mysterious way, and it is assumed that he took his own life.

BETRAYAL

Other things were going on externally. The principal of McKinley, Mr. Broward, was at this time involved in a big political struggle to keep his job. In a small way—but major for my understanding of myself—this struggle intersected with my own.

Many of the teachers at the school had a serious problem with Broward, and they were campaigning for his removal. He was accused of corruption, which I found hard to believe at the time, because he always seemed like a straight arrow to me. He had a small placard on his wall, for example, titled "Don't do it, son," which then went into all the consequences of smoking weed.

The way this affair involved me had to do with the strange manner in which Dave had been kicked off the bus. No one seemed to know why it happened, but some of the teachers opposed to Broward approached me because of my association with Dave, and told me they believed it was Broward's fault. They wanted me to contact Dave and tell him that they wanted to make his situation part of their case. If Dave worked with them, they said they would help him to get his High School diploma—which he had mostly given up on at this point. I went to Dave and explained this proposal to him. He was very angry, as he often was in those days, and said to me, "Don't you realize that none of these people, Black or White, cares about us at all? I want nothing to do with this!"[1]

At that moment I realized something about myself. For in those days I loudly self-identified as a sociopath, and said I had no concern for any morals whatsoever. Yet it turned out that I was not completely lacking in moral fiber. For, in betraying Broward, it became clear that I had violated an internal code that was, in fact, very important to me. This realization exploded into my consciousness. "Destruction and ruin to all my enemies," I had told myself, "but undying loyalty to those who had shown me kindness." But had not Broward shown me kindness, even against the wishes of his own guy, when he refused to expel me the previous year? I tried to tell myself that I had a greater duty to Dave, to try and help him get his diploma. But I knew this was fake. I saw, in fact, that there was nothing in my heart but rot and fakeness and hypocrisy all the way down to the bottom.

I call this my Romans 2 moment because in that chapter the Apostle explains what Judgment Day will be like:

> For as many as have sinned without law will also perish without law, and as many as have sinned in the law will be judged by the law...for when Gentiles, who do not have the law, by nature do the things in the law, these, although not having the law, are a law to themselves, who show the work of the law written in their hearts, their conscience also bearing witness... their thoughts accusing

---

1   We used more colorful language to describe everyone involved, as we all did in those days.

or else excusing them in the day when God will judge the secrets of men by Jesus Christ... (Romans 2:12-16, NKJV).

This tells us that on the Day of Judgment, we will primarily be judged by the thoughts of our own hearts. It will be revealed that at all kinds of key points in our life, in fact, all throughout our life, we knew that what we were doing was wrong—regardless of what knowledge we did or did not have of the Bible or Jesus. It is important to explain this because sometimes the way we present the Gospel as believers can look absurd—as if God has set a bunch of doors before us as in a game show—one with Jesus, one with Buddha, one with Mohammed, and so on—and with no other information just tells us, "Choose the right door." Then, if we accidentally pick the wrong one, the floor opens and we drop down into hell.

But that is not the way the Day of Judgment will work. Rather, as we saw in Romans 2, it will be the record of our own thoughts, telling us at the time that we were sinning (or excusing us in some cases), by our own standards. That will be the means of judgment. Not that we will be judged solely by our own standard, for we will be accountable to the full weight of God's moral law. But it will be clearly revealed where we veered away from the light that we had, and in the process lost our chance to even understand all of God's righteous requirements.

This realization about myself, without a real understanding of the Gospel to mitigate it, was an occasion for more despair. Such despair spurred my continuing effort to flee from the presence of the Lord. Therefore, in this chapter I must digress to explain how it was that I could have thought that any escape was possible at all. The main narrative continues in the next chapter where we go all the way back again to September to see how my demonization would play out.

FLIGHT FROM REALITY

How could I have conceived the possibility that Satan could end up winning, being more powerful than God in the end? From a straight Christian perspective, this is a metaphysical impossibility. But the mental world that I lived in was very different. First of all, I had imbibed from some people in my church a deracinated[1] Christianity, which saw so much of the teachings of the Bible and about God as mere metaphors of more modern concepts. This was by no means all that I imbibed from my church, for this foolishness was absent from the liturgy. But the notion certainly made its presence felt in other places, particularly in my catechism classes, not from the teachers, but from the materials that were used. In the process, the straight accounts of the Bible were transformed in my mind into something like Jungian archetypes.

Secondly, I had thoroughly imbibed evolutionary thought, with the exception perhaps of its naturalistic, unguided core. Nevertheless, I accepted the basic story, and it is important to distinguish the overall evolutionary Ur-Story[2] from its putative[3] Darwinian core. For the supposed mechanics of how this process took place has and will continue to shape-shift like Proteus[4], so that the line will always be "the Theory is dead; long live the Theory!"

But the unchanging Ur-Story is just a more technically

---

1   Uprooted or removed from one's original, natural environment

2   The Ur-Story, popularized by Joseph Campbell, is a basic storyline that forms the basis of other stories

3   Something that is supposed or believed to be true

4   Proteus was a Greek sea god, who could reveal knowledge, but only to those who could hold onto him as he transformed into various different creatures in an attempt to escape, as Menelaus did in the Odyssey.

sophisticated version of the old Sumerian and Babylonian creation myths, as mediated through the Phoenicians to the Greeks, and through the myths of Hesiod's Theogony[1] to me as a youngster. In these ancient versions of the evolutionary Ur-Story, the gods themselves are naturally emerging out of the primaeval Chaos, and so are themselves created by the universe instead of being the uncreated source of the universe. I partially bought into the modern, scientific version of this story. Perhaps, I thought, God and Satan themselves had somehow evolved through unknown processes. Perhaps, I continued, it was possible for one god to be supreme for a while and then be overthrown by another, as Kronos overthrew Uranus, and Zeus overthrew Kronos.

Finally, I had also bought into a great deal of Eastern thought by this point, much of it Monist[2]. If there was only one consciousness and the rest of the world was an illusion, we could conceivably fight our way through to godhood. For, in the great Hindu epics like the Ramayana and Mahabharata, some of the characters, particularly the villains such as Ravana[3], begin as humans who achieve godlike status through meditation, austerities, and the like—perhaps after going through many lifetimes.

THE SOUL

Reincarnation then, or the transmigration of souls, was an escape option I put some hope in, but not much. This question

---

1   The Theogony contained the origin stories of most Greek gods

2   A worldview which reduces all of reality to a single universal principle or consciousness

3   I had actually never heard of Ravana or the Ramayana when I was in High School, but I definitely had this concept at the time, and I saw the connection when I read the Ramayana about 2 years later.

of reincarnation is deeply bound up in the related question of the nature of the soul itself. I am now convinced that a human mind or soul involves both a physical brain and a non-physical spiritual element, which are so completely intertwined throughout that there is no one point at which they can be separated. This takes account both the fact that our consciousness indicates some non-physical essence, and also that there is no part of our thought processes that can be entirely separated from the physical.

This understanding aligns with the biblical account. I think the translation in the old King James (and ASV) gives the best sense of what man was when God formed him: that he was a 'living soul.' The Soul is where the physical and the spiritual merge. Our physical brain can neither entirely explain that soul, nor can it ever be neatly separated from it at even a single point, as my Venn diagram illustration suggests.

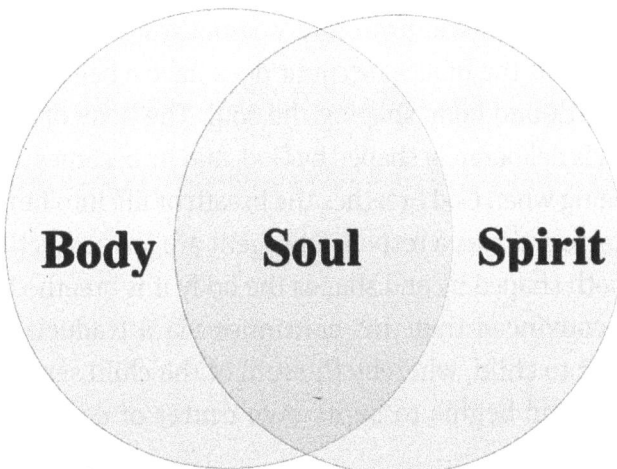

Body   **Soul**   **Spirit**

From this biblical understanding I have come to the following conclusion regarding the transmigration of souls. By its very nature, a soul intertwined with a body and especially its brain throughout its entire warp and woof could never naturally inhabit another body that was not specifically made for it. Now one may say that this is the point of reincarnation, that the soul reshapes itself via the decisions it makes throughout life for good or for bad, and then passes into a new form suited to what the soul has turned itself into based on those choices. But, if we are to take the possibility of reincarnation seriously as a real process and not just some vague theory, I believe we will have to admit that the explanation for an actual mechanism for the new body to be shaped by the soul is lacking. For in this supposed process, the souls are not taking on new bodies for themselves out of thin air. Rather, they are entering the bodies of children being born to other people, and these bodies cannot really be shaped by these souls that are supposedly passing into them.

It is true that demons inhabit bodies that are not theirs (as we see in the New Testament and also my own story), and thereby establish various levels of influence or even control over the host. But this is a violent and profoundly unnatural process.

By contrast, the biblical account does have a believable mechanism for spirit and body shaping the soul. The body of the original man Adam is deliberately shaped by God, and he becomes a conscious rational being when God breathes the breath of life into him. His distinct characteristics as a responsible agent are formed as that breath of life is both shaped by and shapes the body it is breathed into.

I am convinced that this continues via a traducian[1] process from parent to child, whereby the soul of the child separates from the parents and begins to be its own center of consciousness at

---

1   Two main historical Christian understandings of where our souls come from are the 1) Creationist: each soul created from nothing at conception; 2) Traducian: spiritual element is passed from parents to children and they separate/ become individual like the body. (leaving aside the idea of the ancient Christian philosopher Origen)

conception, and thus becomes a responsible agent. Undoubtedly, the Almighty is directly involved in each stage of individuation, as Psalm 139 and Jeremiah 1:5 clearly indicate. But I believe God also does that shaping through a traducian process which necessarily ties all generations into the same original sin. Once we become a responsible agent, however, we will be accountable for what we do with that responsibility in this one earthly life that we are given, when the Great Assize[1] takes place.

Then, as Jesus promised, there will be a resurrection—"those who have done good, to the resurrection of life, and those who have done evil, to the resurrection of condemnation" (John 5:29). In this resurrection, a permanent body will be specifically provided that really is shaped by and designed for each soul—a glorious new body for the redeemed and a ghastly one for the damned.

So having considered for many years how it is that the soul must interact with the brain, and the resurrection of the dead, I have come to the settled conclusion that the transmigration of souls is a metaphysical impossibility. Rather, "... it is appointed for men to die once, but after this the judgment..." (Hebrews 9:27)

Back in 11th grade, having lost my soul, this Judgement Day was the very thing I was so desperately trying to avoid. In those days, I simply conceived of reincarnation as very unlikely, and was therefore unwilling to trust my future to it. My avoidance was just another version of the response we see in Revelation, foreshadowed in the second chapter of Isaiah, where all those alienated from the Lord cry out to the mountains and rocks, "Fall on us and hide us from the face of Him who sits on the throne and from the wrath of the Lamb! For the great day of His wrath has come, and who is able to stand?" (Revelation 6:16-17)

---

1   Another expression for the Day of Judgment

ILLUSION AND REALITY

Here I stood around my sixteenth birthday. I had already given up on atheism as an utterly hopeless pipe dream. I dreamed of rein-carnation but would not put my hope in it. So, desperate for the next available exit, I pursued what I thought was the core, rather than the periphery, of the Hindu point of view: That all the uni-verse was an illusion (maya), and that the only real consciousness was one's own.

To explain this, I will have to say something about the Hindu concepts of Brahman and Atman. Brahman is conceived to be, like God, the fundamental reality and the uncreated source of all that exists. Atman is the individual soul of a person, similar to what I have been trying to describe. There was a famous line in the Upanishads, "That Art Thou," which was given to a student who was seeking to understand what Brahman was. This answer was taken by philosophers like Shankara to mean that Atman and Brahman were the same. While I can't pretend to have a good grasp of Hindu philosophy now, and I certainly did not know much then, what I had heard and understood in my youth was enough to convince me that perhaps it was true that the only real consciousness was my own.

Here was another possible way to escape God and His judg-ment. Or perhaps this putative oneness was a goal to be reached in competition with other beings, I thought somewhat contradic-torily. God seemed to have arrived at that point, but apparently Satan was trying to overthrow Him. Perhaps, I thought, Satan could see some path through self-realization to becoming God's match. Perhaps, like Ravana, I could follow Satan there, maybe even one day be able to challenge them both. I couldn't see that path, but I considered that there were many other things I could not see when I was even younger.

In the beginning, perhaps even before I took the satanic offer, the way I pursued this path was to plunge ever more deeply into my music. The connection was that at this time I began developing my method of using music to enter into altered states of consciousness, unaided by drugs or alcohol. I deeply loved the darkness—the closer to pitch black the better—especially when I was listening to my music. So I was aided in my quest by sensory deprivation. What fueled my quest was, yes, the desire to avoid pain, but more fundamentally, the desire to escape from God. For me both motivations were one and the same.

I think I was mainly using old Black Sabbath songs as a tool to pursue these altered states. "Supernaut" expressed the concept but songs like "Snowblind" and others were more musically useful to me. My idea at the time was that, if the apparent order of things was an illusion, which I needed to break through to achieve my realization of who I really was, I had to break down the normal way of perceiving things. This meant systematically breaking down our basic, God-given sense of pattern recognition. I simultaneously pursued this both through the music and via an intellectual process. This is hard to describe, but it meant carefully thinking through patterns in the visual or audible landscape and gradually convincing myself that the patterns were not expressing actual reality but were arbitrary.

Whenever I reached the goal, my whole experience of reality would dissolve into something like white noise—like the static you saw on your TV screen in the old days when the station would close late at night.

Via these techniques, I developed a way to enter altered mental states without drugs. This became a problem for me, even for the two years after I was saved, for two reasons. First, it could be in times of stress a difficult temptation to resist. Imagine if you didn't have to go out and buy or find drugs, for example, but could just turn on what you were looking for via a mental switch. Secondly, it would sometimes rush in almost involuntarily if not resisted.

SPIRITUAL PATHOGENS

In either case, my techniques were dangerous. They opened a door for unclean spirits to come into my heart and mind. This is because the world we inhabit contains spiritual pathogens just like the physical, microscopic ones we encounter everywhere. And when we break down the normal architecture of our mind as in the way I described just now or through psychedelic drugs like LSD, we break down the God-given protective barriers of our soul and open it to infection. Imagine someone wearing surgical gloves, dipping their hands in raw sewage, and then wiping them across your shirt. It would be nasty, but you could remove your shirt and shower off what soaked through to the skin. But what if the same guy with the sewage drenched gloves started operating on you— your chest, belly and intestines were now open and taking in all the rot and germs. In this case, you would be thoroughly infected. And this is what I did when I broke down the normal barriers of my mind and let the outside spiritual world in.

Besides the practices themselves, the ideas behind them were just as destructive. It is a currently unknowable question, but it almost seems as if Satan himself would have had to have believed something like the options we discussed here to explain his attempt to overthrow the Almighty. If he believed something like atheism—that consciousness emerged from a material universe— then he could think that God Himself had also emerged from the substrate and so could be challenged. But to be any kind of atheist, in the end you must believe what the Buddhists call the doctrine of An-Atman—that the fact that our soul or consciousness exists at all as a unitary being is an illusion. But then who is there to fool? And who is there to be disabused[1] of this false notion? What could it be that believes itself to exist when it does not?

Similarly, if you, or Satan, took it the opposite way around, that your consciousness was first and all the external world was a projection of it, an illusion, you could likewise convince yourself that God could be challenged. You would just have to reach the realization that even He is an illusion. But, if that were the case, if as Atman, you equaled Brahman (your consciousness equaled god), then how could you have ever become confused? How could you have lost, even for a moment, your omniscience?

FULFILLMENT

I constructed this whole hall of mirrors for myself because I did not want to follow God and have my life be found in Him. But there is in the end only one way to account for our existence as we experience it—that we ourselves clearly exist but need an uncreated being outside of ourselves to be the source of our being and hence account for our existence.

God is, as His Hebrew name *Yahweh* indicates, existence itself. More than that, He contains an infinite creativity of new things that will never be exhausted. Our obvious limitations should make it abundantly clear to us that God is the One in whom we need to be completely fulfilled, forever. But I didn't want to follow God because I did not understand His ways and did not want Him to tell me what to do and not do. But what happens, when we make

---

1   to rid of false ideas, undeceive;

our peace with God in the way that He alone has provided? He then becomes a kind of perfect parent that choses what is best for us as no human parent on earth ever could.

Consider my own story. What if Dad had signed me up for boxing as a young child, without asking my opinion? I could have perhaps handily dealt with bullies early on and avoided the whole rotten course of life I embarked on. What if, at the first sign of sloth, my parents had the skills and resources to stop all they were doing to homeschool me and just push me through? But they couldn't see and do all of that. I myself did not fully implement what my own son needed either, much to my regret—regret only for the part I can see. None of us as parents can see and do all these things. However, when we submit our will to the Lord, we enter into perfect training, no matter how long or arduous or confusing it can be. And we also find the fulfillment of all we are looking for in the end.

While recounting that wild year of sin in Chapter 12, I made mention of the opposite of this fulfillment—that vacuum, that uncreative hell of boredom we would sink ever deeper into. I also mentioned a hell far deeper than that, were we to remain cut off from the Lord of life. And in those days, it seemed as if I was already sinking into that hell, even as I walked the earth.

CHAPTER 16

HE DESCENDED INTO HELL

... in which you once walked according to the course of this world, according to the prince of the power of the air, the spirit who now works in the sons of disobedience.

Ephesians 2:2

SEPTEMBER 1985 – JANUARY 1986

And so, through the hall of mirrors, we have come all the way back to my downfall into satanism which began that September in 1985. What I have described so far, such as voices in the head, and even more what is to follow, will cause some people to immediately conclude that I am describing some mental illness, such as schizophrenia, and not demonization. For atheistic or secular people, there can be no question at all. But as I already stated, I don't think an atheistic view of the world can adequately account for reality, particularly the way we experience that reality, in any serious way. On the contrary, as Chesterton suggested, to the extent that secularism focuses like a laser beam on only a few key aspects of existence while ignoring the rest, it seems to itself be a kind of mental illness.

I ask the rest of the world that is more firmly tethered in reality,

161

Christians in particular, to consider how such things are described in the New Testament—especially the Gospels. In one representative case among many, Mark summarizes the ministry of Jesus as follows: "And He was preaching in their synagogues throughout all Galilee, and casting out demons." (Mark 1:39) Clearly demonization was widespread enough for it to be a major part of Jesus' ministry, of which we also see so many direct examples recorded in the Gospels. Consequently, anyone who takes the Bible seriously must decide if today's world is really the way it is described in the Gospels, with widespread instances of demonization, or not.

MOONSTRUCK

Not only this, but the Gospels really do distinguish between demonization and mental illness, although in the terms understood at that time rather than as mental illness is understood today.

> And his fame went throughout all Syria: and they brought unto him all sick people that were taken with divers diseases and torments, and those which were possessed with devils, and those which were lunatick, and those that had the palsy; and he healed them. (Matthew 4:24 KJV)

Note the distinction between those who were possessed with devils, and those which were "lunatic[1]." Note also that there were

---

1   I used the old King James because so many translations render the 'moonstruck' word (selainiazomai/ σεληνιάζομαι) as epilepsy. I think this translation decision is mostly because when the word is used again describing the boy in Matthew 17, the symptoms strike the translators as clearly being a case of epilepsy (though it ends up really being a demon there). BDAG translates it this way also, because there are Greek texts much later than the New Testament that use the word to refer

many more cases of those demon-possessed being healed by Jesus than "lunatics." It is difficult, not only for the secular, but also for Christians to see the world this way as recounted in the Gospels—for me as much as anyone else. For then we all have to confront our seeming powerlessness as we daily encounter people on the streets talking to themselves, screaming into the air, etc., as I could also be seen doing in those days.

It is MUCH easier to walk by, concluding that there is nothing that anyone can do except turn them over to the professionals. There are indeed aspects of modern life that are very different than Israel in the time of Jesus. These include higher levels of family and social breakdown, a dizzying faster pace of life, and also the cushioning of real life while being surrounded by a fake world of entertainment and now, social media. All of this leads to both weaker and more disordered minds. I also have to add that a careful study of many of the words used in the Gospels to describe people being healed of afflictions and torments include mental and emotional suffering and disease within their range of meaning. Most importantly, there are many more people with their minds addled by drugs.

A good example would be Nathan. There was never a time when I sensed him to be under demonic influence, though I may have simply been unaware. But as he aged, he seemed to have increasing psychotic episodes, at least for a season. Nathan already started life with a bad hand because of mental problems. But this was greatly aggravated by later choices, especially his

---

to a disease that does seem to be epilepsy. But I strongly suspect that moonstruck referred not just to epilepsy but also various other forms of madness in the ancient world, all considered to be caused by the moon rather than demons. I still go with lunatic for the translation of the word describing a malady distinct from, although sometimes associated with, demons.

use of drugs such as LSD. Had he given his life to the Lord, he would have needed a certain amount of mental healing along with spiritual healing. The availability of this healing from our Lord belies the suspicion we may have that either the mentally ill or the demonized lack free will or agency.

I strongly suspect that like drugs, involvement in the demonic realm can cause mental damage that in my case needed to be healed. For those demons don't act in a kind of purely spiritual realm, but inside a human mind or soul. As I have previously described, this soul involves both a physical brain and a non-physical spiritual element, which in general are so completely intertwined throughout that there is no one point where they can be separated. That is why I think that my demonization, and also my techniques for entering altered states of consciousness, did do some damage that had to be healed over two years.

UNDER THE LOOKING GLASS

Yet I am absolutely convinced what was happening with me back then was not a case of a mental illness like schizophrenia. For I have not experienced anything like that six months, or the two year healing period that followed, since that time. Rather, I have gone on to live a productive life without any more involvement with the mental health professions after I became a believer.

But here is a unique thing about the story I am telling here. Throughout this approximately six-month period that I am about to describe, I was under not one but two psychological evaluations. One of these was ordered by the family court due to my second arrest, and the other was ordered by the school system due to the rapid deterioration that was taking place in my life, beginning that September. I quote from these reports as I continue to tell my story in order to show what my situation looked like, from the outside and as well as from the inside.

The psychological evaluation ordered by the Family Court was shorter, involving meetings in December and a final evaluation on January 21, 1986. It was over before I became a believer. But because it included some follow-up work to rule out schizophrenia or at least organic lesions in my brain, I will cover it last.

The psychological evaluation ordered by the East Baton Rouge Parish School Board began in October and its final report was disseminated August 1, 1986—but internal evidence from the report suggests that the actual evaluation was complete by the end of May. This evaluation was primarily conducted by the school psychologist, including biweekly therapy sessions about 1 hour in length from October 1985 to May 1986. It therefore covered almost the entire period I am describing in these chapters, until after I had been a believer for about two months.

The two things that initiated the school evaluation were a sudden drop in grades and major changes in behavior. According to the report

> A review of [Ralph]'s grades over the last 3 years reveals a steady decline in performance. In the 83-84 school year, his overall average was B+ while his average fell to C- the following school year. In the 85-86 school year, however, he received F's in the following subjects in the last nine weeks: English, history, calculus, and psychology.

This drop was less steady than it looked. During 10th grade, where I had almost completely lost interest in school and was regularly sneaking out all night and returning the next morning to school with no sleep, I was still able to pull that C-. In contrast, in

11th grade my friends were mostly gone and I was engaging in little outside the house, except that I was going back to Tae Kwon Do until shortly before Christmas. Then that also stopped after I broke my right foot when some guy blocked one of my kicks with his elbow. Yet I was now completely failing most classes. As the report continued, it indicated that my mental state was causing this.

> ...As has been noted, [Ralph]'s grades have fallen this year to the extent that he received failing grades in 4 primary subjects. He continues to experience difficulty with concentration and social interaction (withdrawal)...Though there was no doubt that [Ralph] is a gifted student, there was extreme concern that [Ralph]'s emotional state impinged greatly on his educational performance.

The part of the report written by the school psychologist noted

> Throughout these sessions, [Ralph] presented as a fellow who appeared withdrawn from his peers and family, with the exception of a few boys of his age who, according to [Ralph], were given to "marauding" the neighborhood... In March, [Ralph]'s journal was reviewed...As in therapy sessions, [Ralph] wrote of being taken over by "evil" and obsessional thoughts about a female classmate[1]." "Ms... stated that [Ralph]'s school performance had been deteriorating all year. Suicidal ideation was suspected and supportive-psychological services were requested.

The school psychologist really did suspect schizophrenia. I think this was mainly because of what she was reading in the

---

1   The female classmate referred to here was NOT who I call 'Genifer' later in the book.

journal, where I was probably openly talking about Satan and the like. But this was only as a possibility. As she stated "An interview with [Ralph]'s parents was conducted on May 1, 1986 in order to discuss concerns which emerged in therapy sessions with [Ralph] over a six month period," and I have simply pasted the relevant part of the report below:

```
Presently ███████ has had contact with the criminal justice system and is on a
one-year probation with the Department of Youth Services.  A court ordered
psychiatric evaluation was recently completed which Mr. and Mrs. ███████ pro-
mised to forward to the writer.

Finally the clinical concerns of the writer were discussed with the parents.
Since October, ███████ has been seen by the writer for biweekly therapy sessions
at McKinley High.  Over this period of time, a clinical picture of ███████ as
withdrawn, joyless, and possibly schizophrenic has emerged.  This clinical im-
pression was discussed with Mr. and Mrs. ███████.  Both parents reacted strongly
to this impression, stating that a) they felt that ███████ was "faking" this
malady and that b) he had improved greatly of late due to his involvement with
people from the Jimmy Swaggart Ministries, (or in ███████'s phrase, "the Jesus
people").
```

The court ordered evaluation painted a similar picture:

> According to the family, [Ralph] has been "very depressed, possibly self-destructive." He would not communicate much. On some occasions he had burned cigarette holes on his arms and he used scratch pens as well. He has tremendous difficulty in sleep so he feels excessively fatigued and anergetic. He eats in spurts, skipping an entire day. Subjectively he has been losing weight because he eats very irregularly only. He has felt extremely depressed and entertained suicidal ideation.

Nevertheless,

> [Ralph] is a moderately built and nourished young man in no acute physical distress at the time of his psychiatric interview. [Ralph] is alert, oriented, cooperative and communicative...A diminished

psychomotor activity and inadequate eye contact and a remarkable passivity were notable features of his mental status assessment. Moodwise, he stated "don't feel like anything" which in my opinion indicates more of anhedonia than a motivational state.

When I saw this I asked the school psychologist what anhedonia was. She explained that it meant that I could not feel joy from things that were pleasurable to ordinary people, and that this is why I had previously been going out and doing the 'marauding' and the like. My inward purpose, she suggested, was to push things to the limit so that I could feel these emotions. This made some sense to me, for I have often felt that I was born without enough motivational chemicals such as dopamine or adrenaline. I have nevertheless been able to get through life by the power of the Holy Spirit, as I will describe later.

I have been rather critical of psychology over the years. This is primarily because I understand it to be not so much a science or one of the healing arts, but rather the 'pastoral care' branch of a rival secular religion with a different and competing system of morality. But this does not mean that they have no insights. For they are as good at pattern recognition as anyone else, and can be more so because they do aspire to a scientific method of gathering and systematizing their discoveries. And in the less ideological corners of the discipline, they are gathering some very important insights about the brain.

I speak of pattern recognition because certain traits that I have mentioned in my life, such as anhedonia, difficulty in concentration, invincible beliefs that were, in fact, delusional, and the like, will strike some as a set of symptoms associated with particular mental illnesses. I can see a reason for this which also takes account of the role of the demonic.

A PERFECT TARGET

From the beginning, I was not exactly the same, neurologically, as the general population. This was nothing more than a personality type, a unique combination of strengths and weaknesses. But it did have consequences—a process I call anti-socialization. For my inability to understand or adjust to the outside world led to clashes, as I have recounted. These clashes created a mutual cycle of rejection and resistance, until I abandoned all hope of overall social acceptance early in life. I accepted what I falsely believed to be almost universal rejection as my permanent condition. I adjusted to this condition by adopting an outlaw identity in which I expected to permanently live outside of normal society, with the exception of a few close friends. As such, I became impervious to most social sanctions. And I became very alone.

This opened me to dark spiritual forces, even as a means of escaping this loneliness. I hardly think this process was unique to me. I suspect that throughout history, people born with the type of brain I was born with have had the tendency to be the warlocks or shamans, due to the anti-socialization they would have experienced as they grew up, pushing them towards these dark forces and making them easy targets for Satan's kingdom.

What made me a target for the demonic realm? I suppose a combination of my family history, my psychological makeup, a wounded heart and mind, and spiritual reasons, perhaps my vocation, that I don't expect to know in this life. But it seems to me that this anti-socialization process that I have described results in patterns that can be recognized, resulting in lists of symptoms for perceived psychological ailments. Yet I continue to doubt that the underlying causes for ailments such as schizophrenia, or even epilepsy, are truly understood.

How might the presence of demonic spirits relate to mental health? Consider the relationship between physical wounds and germs. This is not a bad analogy, for beyond what life may throw at us, the sinner does violence to his own soul. Wounds get infected. Likewise, infections cause physical damage, as they cause inflammation and auto-immune responses, release toxins, and destroy cells and bodily functions. This mutual feedback loop means that even when unclean spirits are cast out, there may be a need for a sustained period of mental healing, as in my case. For normal mental and social processes were disrupted, and the demonization may have even caused physical changes in my brain.

Consider the nuances in the account of the healing of the lunatic/demonized boy in the three different gospels where it occurs:

And Jesus rebuked the demon, and it came out of him; and the child was cured from that very hour. (Matthew 17:18, NKLV)

Then the spirit cried out, convulsed him greatly, and came out of him. And he became as one dead, so that many said, "He is dead." But Jesus took him by the hand and lifted him up, and he arose. (Mark 9:26-27, NKJV)

And as he was still coming, the demon threw him down and convulsed him. Then Jesus rebuked the unclean spirit, healed the child, and gave him back to his father. (Luke 9:42, NKJV)

Luke, who was an actual physician of that time, gave a concise account which, taken with the others, indicates the following: the demon was first cast out, and then the boy was physically healed.

What happens to a society when the reality of the demonic is completely denied? Consider again an ancient physician who has access to both passed down knowledge and a lifetime of experience confronting various sicknesses. Yet he is completely ignorant concerning germs. He may be able to thoroughly recognize the patterns and characteristics of various ailments. He may have some partially effective treatments, such as herbs that reduce inflammation or the binding or even cleaning of wounds. But at the same time, he would not accurately understand the actual cause of various infectious diseases, or how and why they continue to spread.

In my case, it is no surprise that the psychologists suspected something like schizophrenia or some form of psychosis—especially in light of their world view. I am explicitly denying this. But I also must admit that based on my behavior, most laymen would not only suspect this but would have come to this conclusion without any hesitation. For in those days I could often be seen having conversations with myself loudly, banging my head against the wall, loudly disrupting class and even slashing myself in the middle of class. And this kind of behavior was far less common in the 1980s than it has become today.

I suspect that the school *psychologist* said that I was 'possibly schizophrenic', not because she wasn't quite convinced, but because she was not a *psychiatrist* and so did not feel qualified to make such a formal diagnosis. This is why she was eager to get the report from the court ordered psychiatrist. He must have known, in spite of the mystery that still surrounds it, that there were certain other indications that should have been present if I was undoubtedly suffering from schizophrenia. He must not have found such clear indications, because in his evaluation schizophrenia was only mentioned as a remote possibility that should be "ruled out."

This court ordered evaluation, noting that "there is no gross sign of a psychotic illness except...borderline features" concluded with the tentative diagnostic impression pasted below:

He also entertained suicidal ideas, serious ones, but is of a chronic nature and does not seem to present an acute risk. Psychosexual identity and psychosocial identity development has been certainly inhibited since a young age. He feels isolate with "some special powers". He also experiences mental confusion and a fear of losing control with paranoid trends in his thinking processes. Future fantasy,thoughts about his ambition and identifications are also poorly developed. Intellectual functioning, speech and vocabulary and language formation seems adequate and intact. Soft neurologic sign screening reveals right handed, right leg and right eye dominance, but cross right-left confusion, finger agnosia, probable left sided elevation in a right handed person on extension test. Short term memory, remote recall, general fund of information, abstract thinking, attention and concentration are intact. There is no sign of gross C.N.S. lesion. There is no gross sign of a psychotic illness except the above mentioned borderline features. He has experimented with drinking and marijuana, but denies other drugs.

TENTATIVE DIAGNOSTIC IMPRESSION:

1) Atypical Depression.
2) Schizoid Disorder of Adolescence.
3) Rule Out Hypothyroidism, Cerebral Dysrythmia.
4) Rule Out Schizophrenia, Residual Type.

I can say a few things about this. I cannot recall ever believing or saying, at any point in my life, that I had 'special powers.' Perhaps at that time I thought I could do something in the demonic realm and said something like that, for I was certainly praying to Satan for power on a daily basis. One thing I tried at this time and was never able to do was to speak in satanic tongues. For on the few occasions when I tried this, it was like trying to push back a bulldozer and I gave up within seconds. I was depressed because I was on the road to Hell and I knew it. The 'Schizoid Disorder' sounds disturbing but despite the similarity in wording is not schizophrenia at all and has nothing to do with psychosis, hallucinations, or the like. I understand it to be more about being detached from other people and introverted. The Cerebral Dysrythmia that they were trying to rule out is, I believe, epilepsy or something like it.

The "ruling out" that they were referring to was done via an EEG (electroencephalogram) and a battery of blood tests. On

February 12, 1986, Ash Wednesday, I had an EEG at the Medical Center of Baton Rouge, now the Ochsner Medical Center on O'Neal lane. They shaved portions of my head and hooked electrodes all over it via some kind of electrolyte paste which both held the electrodes on and, I suspect, helped conduct the signal. The purpose on the paperwork was to "Rule out possible organic lesion," and I remember them recording my brain activity for somewhere between about 30 minutes to maybe a little over an hour. They found nothing. I feel quite certain that they found nothing from any of the blood tests either, although I have no records. By this time, in the middle of February, I was already planning a mass shooting.

VOICES IN THE DARK

And here I must address the 'hearing of voices.' At no point in this account do I speak of hearing actual audible voices that did not exist. Rather, I recount verbal thoughts entering my mind which I knew not to be my own, but rather the voice of Satan. What was really going on? Consider a famous passage from *The Pilgrim's Progress* by John Bunyan, as he allegorically describes a journey through the *Valley of the Shadow of Death*:

> One thing I would not let slip. I took notice that now poor Christian was so confounded, that he did not know his own voice; and thus I perceived it. Just when he was come over against the mouth of the burning pit, one of the wicked ones got behind him, and stepped up softly to him, and whisperingly suggested many grievous blasphemies to him, which he verily thought had proceeded from his own mind. This put Christian more to it than anything that he met with before, even to think that he should now blaspheme him that he loved so much before; yet, if he could have helped it,

he would not have done it; but he had not the discretion either to stop his ears, or to know from whence these blasphemies came. (The Pilgrim's Progress, John Bunyan, par. 101–102)

Like so much in *The Pilgrim's Progress*, Bunyan is here painting allegorically real experiences which he had in his own life as a Christian.[1] Was John Bunyan, author of this great work of literature that shaped the English-speaking world, suffering from some mental illness such as schizophrenia? Or was he describing an ordeal that is part of the universal human condition?

In particular, Bunyan was relating experiences of a Christian seeking to follow the Lord. I must have experienced something similar as a child. But on that September morning, Satan was not trying to bewilder a Christian. Rather, he was communicating with a rebel against God—a rebel who had opened his mind to such infernal communications by deliberately seeking altered states of consciousness, among other gateways to the demonic. With no use for disguise, he announced himself openly as he invaded my thoughts. And unlike a Christian who will resist this, I was willing to listen and get ever more in tune with these infernal communications.

As I did tune in, very strange things began to happen early on. In homeroom English class there was a storage closet where a lot of books and other supplies were kept. Shortly after I made the choice to follow Satan, I began to go into that closet regularly to commune with the demonic realm. This is where it gets very weird. For there was literally a situation, on a daily basis, where I was holding back and forth conversations using my own mouth

---

1   Notes and Commentary on John Bunyan's *The Pilgrim's Progress* by Ken Puls, https://kenpulsmusic.com/pilgrimsprogress54.html

but different voices to speak, depending on who was doing the talking. There was some encouragement expressed, some grooming for a supposedly glorious future. But as time went on, there was also a problem that frequently came up. I really needed to kill at least someone to get on with things, they insisted. They were not pleased with all the planning without any action.

A LINE TO CROSS

Indeed, throughout this entire period there was a constant sense that I had not gone all the way—that I was somehow holding something back and so had not crossed a line. It is hard to understand how this could be the case when I had clearly crossed so many lines, but it was true. There are people in this world who have already completely made their decision, for whom there is no turning back—the walking damned. I had seen what that looked and felt like on that dark night when I realized that at that particular moment, I had completely lost the ability to repent. And yet there was still some invisible line that I had not crossed. I still held onto the possibility of repentance in the deepest recesses of my soul, which I hid even from myself. So I regularly felt an awkwardness when communing with these spirits. It was almost as if, with some kind of sixth sense, I could hear them whispering to each other, 'he has not crossed over', 'he is not really one of us,' 'he is not all in.'

Now I don't want anyone reading this to assume that you have crossed that line and cannot repent—even if you have indeed killed for Satan or done God knows what. No matter how low you may have sunk, if you have even the slightest inkling to call out to Jesus to be saved, do it now! Defect now, and never look back!

As for me, in spite of the doubts, it did seem that I was moving closer to that line. There came a night when I was involved in these meditations and communions. And it was almost as if the words of the Iron Maiden song were becoming real before me

In the mist, dark figures move and twist,
Seem to mesmerize, can't avoid their eyes...

And as I lay in bed in total darkness, I felt like I was spinning, like my soul was going in and out of my body and returning again, like I was ascending into the air, flipping around and descending again. And finally, lying on my back, facing up and feeling in a normal position, I saw what looked like a humanoid shadow descending towards me. It lined up its body in sync with mine, and as it were passed in and merged, a merger which I could in some sense feel. In all those days, that was the closest that I ever came to physically seeing the unseen realm. And things went wild.

During those six to seven months, I was switching back and forth wildly, virtually changing into three and four different people with different belief systems and back again on the same day. Yet I have never experienced anything like that since. But in those days of rapid changes the one metanarrative that would always end up ruling over it all was my decision to follow Satan. And I was always looking for that final act that would bring my undisciplined and scattered personality into coherence, a coherence dedicated to pure evil followed by a lifetime of disciplined preparation for the final war with God to come.

SCREAMING FOR VENGEANCE

All the while one part of me still wanted to hold onto the possibility of repentance, while with another part I prayed to Satan for the fortitude to do what I needed, to cross that line. I wanted revenge, for my ghastly existence, on all that was. I wanted that revenge so desperately that my infernal prayers became ever more frantic. I ran to and frow in circles, collapsing to the ground, getting up, and running in circles again as fast as I could, continually. While I ran back and forth in my back yard, I roared, I cried, I screamed for vengeance.

This went on for hours. And as I cried out to Satan for the power to avenge, horrific images of that revenge rose up one by one and flashed upon the screen of my mind. Mass movements, revolution, war and conquest. Mass enslavement with screens locked across men's eyes and electrodes plugged into their brains, and methods of mass killing much faster than those of the 20th century if you could endure the mess until it rotted clean. And 1980s cameras and computers and satellites watching everywhere, all fed back first to banks of processors and then into my own brain, so that I could chose, beyond my own power of concentration, access to any bit of information I chose.

Especially because I was mostly ignorant of artificial intelligence (AI), the idea of sifting and controlling all that super computing power that I hoped to be able to funnel into my brain seemed to be way too much of a bottleneck. And with that the thought arose of reversing the polarity, and working to completely transfer my essence into something far greater than what I could do as a mere man. Beware, transhumanist! If you attempt to transfer your essence and sentience into some other medium other than the one you have been given, I think we can almost predict with certainty that you will only succeed in completely losing control of your soul, i.e. death, and giving it up into the hands of that great Judge of the quick and the dead. It is a fearful thing to fall into the hands of the Living God!

All my visions began in wrath and ended in fear. For one simulation after another, one dream of widespread revenge after another, one path to power after another ran through my mind as I ran back and forth in circles in that yard. The arcs of whole lifetimes flashed in such rapid vignettes that it would seem that as Thomas Nagel once famously asked what it is like to be a bat, so I was experiencing what it was like to be the AI computer in the 1983 movie 'War Games' as one simulation was carried out in my mind after another in rapid succession. Or perhaps like some hapless computer taken over by a spam-bot to carry out its will.

Yet these were *my* simulations, they were *my* visions, for I was crying out for them. And one by one they ended in defeat. For those whole lifetimes had to end, each and every time, while the people of God who I would oppress would endure. And always the judgment of God would be seen on the horizon in the end. Until finally desperation set in, then exhaustion, and then a kind of final conclusion. There was simply no way to strike back against God except perhaps by confusing or beguiling those He otherwise wanted to save and turning them against Him. I collapsed to the ground on my back and looked up to the sky, where I supposed that my enemy was looking back down on me. And I concluded that there was no way forward for an enemy of God except through the practice of religious deception.

THE HORRIFIC VISION

Around this time I was given, in two separate dreams, my own visions of the judgment to come. In the first dream I was already in Hell while still somehow adjacent to the world of the living, for I could see a room with a Christmas tree off to the side, yet almost in another dimension (it was probably around Christmas when I

178

dreamed). My body was burning, there were actual demons ripping off flesh to the point of my having a partially skeletal look, but they were saying something like "Do not worry Ralph, your flesh won't be gone, for this will last forever."

While that dream was showing me something, I don't actually think it is likely that demons are torturing people in Hell. How would they themselves be judged? In Chapter 12 I presented a thought experiment of what would be an endless vacuum of boredom if we were left to our own devices for eternity. But that only reflects one aspect of our nature—our finite creativity when left on our own. Therefore the illustration barely begins to describe what you will experience if you are ultimately driven from the presence of the Lord. When he was speaking of the Lord to the Athenians, the apostle said "...in Him we live and move and have our being..." (Acts 17:28a, NKJV) In other words, every aspect of our life is wrapped up in God while we live on earth, even if we are not in communion with Him or reconciled.

But if you die in rebellion and are driven away from the presence of the Lord, that deprivation or vacuum will be unimaginably intense. One approach toward suggesting what this will be like is to work through a succession of deprivations. You may, for example, have sexual desires at this moment, but such desires could have been eclipsed, even from the mind of Hugh Hefner in his day, if he had been deprived of food for several weeks. But if, after having no food for five or more weeks you were also deprived of water, in days experiencing a thirst so deep that the walls of your throat would soon be closing in on themselves, you would almost forget the food. And if you could no longer breathe even your hunger and thirst would be eclipsed by an overwhelming desire for oxygen that would be metered in seconds rather than hours or days. And by proceeding from here to the next level of deprivation, you can begin to perceive the outlines of that awful vacuum you would feel if your soul were cast into Hell, away from the presence of "Him [in whom] we live and move and have our being..."—an implosion without end like a moral black hole with no possible hope of annihilation. For we were made as vessels in the image of God to commune with Him throughout all eternity, and a vessel of such weight, when it is thrown away from God to collapse in on itself, can never stop imploding to ever deeper depths.

Besides all this, God by His nature must pour out His wrath upon sin—for as absolutely free as the Almighty is, He will never or could never act outside of His own holiness. We see Him revealing this aspect of Himself to us when he warned the Israelites after the golden calf "for I will not go up in your midst, lest I consume you on the way... I could come up into your midst in one moment and consume you." (Exodus 33:3b,5b, NKJV) Now when God became man in Jesus Christ, and took all our sins upon Himself on the cross, He became in that moment a kind of eternal ground line that was able to discharge an infinite amount of wrath. But if you die in your sins there will be no discharge. Yet if you experienced that awful deprivation and the collapse of your soul in on itself into an eternity of regret, I can almost see how the wrath of God being poured out upon you would be a kind of eternal catharsis. For in a manner similar to those occasions in my own life when I was under such mental or spiritual torment that I was driven to cut or burn myself as a kind of temporal catharsis, perhaps the flames of Hell will be perceived by the damned as the only appropriate response to the intense deprivation within.

Now the second dream that I received in those days was far more forceful, and in a way preternatural. In this dream all my hopes were about to come true, as I was about to seize power in some kind of coup. I turned to my main associate, who in this dream was Dave, and told him 'tonight we must seize power, do not hold back and do not put any limit on how many people we must kill.' And then a very rapid succession of vignettes of exactly this passed before my mind in this dream, with soldiers bursting in and machine gun fire and scenes of mass killing one after another, heavy with women and children. But in the middle of this I turned and everything began to melt away before me and some huge object began to rise out of the ground, and then there was no ground. For I began to see exactly the scene of the Great White Throne judgment as depicted in Revelation—"Then I saw a great white throne and Him who sat on it, from whose face the earth and the heaven fled away. And there was found no place for them." (Revelation 20:11, NKJV)

And there was nothing left but myself and this mighty throne towering ever higher above me, and I could feel the judgment of God driving me down into Hell. But then there arose a horrifying sound, such as I believe has never been heard on earth, nor can I imagine it even now. It was as if thousands, millions of souls were crying out all at once—the souls of the righteous whom I had killed crying for justice and the souls of the damned whom I had deceived crying for vengeance, all in one million-fold scream. And I say that it was preternatural because as I awoke in the pitch darkness my memory has always told me that I could hear the echoes of that scream throughout my room, awake. And I was deathly afraid, indeed afraid of the dark which I had always loved, for what I think was the very first time in my life. And only the words of the Old King James can express my state at that moment, when like Ezra in that pitch darkness I "...sat [laid] down astonied." (Ezra 9:3b)

CHAPTER 17

THE MOTH ALIGHTS

Now then, we are ambassadors for Christ, as though God were pleading through us: we implore you on Christ's behalf, be reconciled to God.

2 Corinthians 5:20

WINTER 1986

At this point we have just about reached the absolute bottom—like the 11th gutter in that long ago journey into the city drainage system. Let's move out of here, reader, as fast as we can, for we had to see this, me to write and you to read, but we cannot linger long lest we completely lose our minds. Let's climb out through a few more chapters until we reach the light at the end of that tunnel. For even then, in the lowest hell, I kept getting signals, like staticky short-wave transmissions sent from a free country to those living under a communist dictatorship, that all was not lost. That in spite of all my enmity against God, and all the opportunities that I had thrown away, repentance was still possible.

I have mentioned the Latin Conventions repeatedly in this tale, and you must have often wondered 'what in the world does this have to do with this story.' Especially when it has reached the point that it has now. Well, the reason I felt compelled to mention these conventions, one by one, was to set the stage for what happened the 5th and final time. For the first time since I had been going, the state Latin convention was held up near Shreveport instead of LSU, and it was in the late Winter rather than Spring. We stayed in a hotel and at night I got drunk and repeatedly used the Gideon Bible in that hotel as an occasion for blasphemy. When the time came when I had always prayed to God for another first-place win, I thought to myself, 'I guess with the way my life is now I have to pray to Satan instead.' But then I was overwhelmed with the utter ridiculousness of it all, asking how it was that I had prayed to God all this past four years and was now going to pray to Satan. And I just couldn't do it. So I lifted up my eyes to heaven one last time and said "Jesus, I know that I am your enemy now, but please remember me one last time, not as I am now but as I used to be. In memory of all that is past, please give a victory one last time." Within minutes, it was announced that I had gotten first place one more time, and specifically that it was the 5th year in a row.

One evening in the midst of all this, while I was listening to some bad music on my Walkman, my father walked in. I quickly turned it off and slipped it away, but he was not coming in to dispute with my music or anything else. He just came to ask if there was anything I wanted to do together—I suppose go to a movie or fishing or something—but I can't remember at all if we ever did go do anything, or even what I said. And yet the moment itself, burned in my memory, was, in fact, one of the most memorable moments in my whole life. It is because my dad just wanted to spend some time with me, and right then an overwhelming sense of sadness mixed with an unbearable longing swept over me. As I looked at him, I knew that there was an unbridgeable gap between us, both because of my mental state and because of the path that I had chosen. I really didn't know that much about my dad and I was convinced that he was going to heaven while I was surely destined for hell.

But in that moment, with all my heart, I did not wish it to be so—I ached and longed and hoped for an alternate reality where we would both make it to heaven, and would be able to spend all the time together we wanted with perfect understanding. I had never longed for eternal salvation so deeply as I did that evening, but certain as I was that it was an impossible dream, that my course was set as surely as if I were already in hell itself, I turned away, crushed with unbearable sadness.

But there was one beacon above all that kept calling to me. There is a line in a well-known hymn which says "Hark, how the heavenly anthem drowns all music than its own." In those days I was given some foretaste of what this would be like. For from time to time, for example on a road trip to see some relatives, the tune from the Christmas hymn "What Child is This?" (sung to the tune of 'Greensleeves') would force its way into my head and drown everything else out. And whenever this song came rushing into my head, it always carried with it an implicit message from the Heavenly realm: "All is not lost! Repentance is possible! Even now it is possible to be reconciled to God once again!"

Then finally there came a message from the heavenly realm that was more than a mere beacon that repentance was possible. For at the end of January Granny had what she called a holy dream. In this dream she saw Jesus with His fingers working on the inside of someone's head, with the back turned to her. Then the head slowly turned around until it was facing her—and it was me, and I was smiling—which is something no one had seen me do for quite some time. As soon as she woke up, she wrote this in her Bible, which was a very large heirloom King James Bible which she had gotten from some televangelist. And then she called my mother, telling her that I was about to be 'healed.'

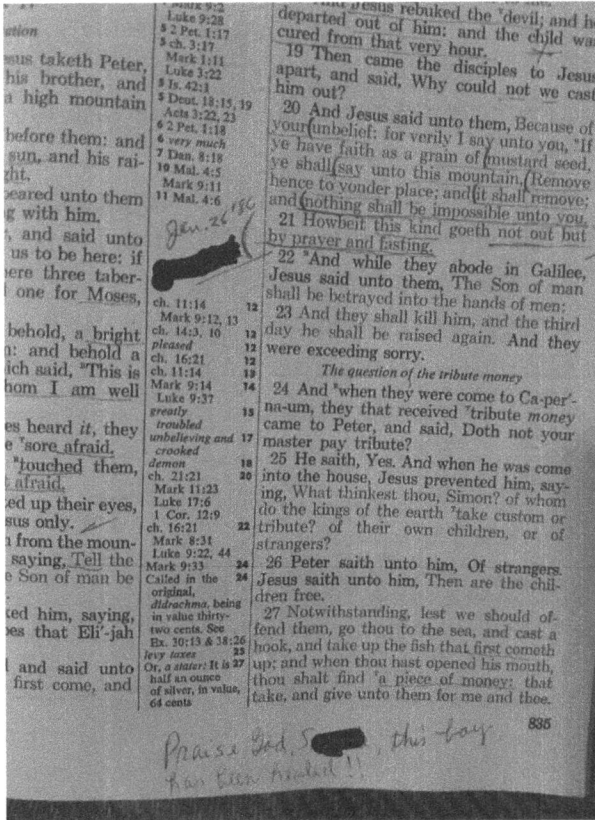

In other words, I was about to become a completely normal person, and not only that, but a believer, living for God and on my way to heaven. And nothing could have been more impossible to believe than this, for I was utterly hardened against God, had sold my soul to Satan, and it was not possible to even conceive of a path back to Him. And yet in barely 2 months it would all come true!

Some of us had often suspected that Granny's religiosity was fake and that she may not have had a real relationship with God. But it couldn't have been more real. Less than perfect, sure, but as real as anything could be none the less. Because between a less than perfect, often flawed and wavering Christian life and actual hypocrisy is a yawning, unbridgeable chasm. For God had revealed something to her in a dream that was otherwise impossible to believe or predict.

Years later, shortly after Granny died, Gramps showed me her things and told me I could take what I wanted. I took her copy of "Pigs in the Parlor," and I also took that old Bible of hers which is with me now. I there found what you can also see, the page where she had written 'January 26, 1986, [Ralph]—Praise God S--- (Mom), this boy has been healed!!'

The moth had alighted.[1] Help was on the way!

---

1   https://www.youtube.com/watch?v=kNnvcs-sQB8

CHAPTER 18

A SHOCKING GREETING

For we are to God the fragrance of Christ among those who are being saved and among those who are perishing. To the one we are the aroma of death leading to death, and to the other the aroma of life leading to life. And who is sufficient for these things?

2 Corinthians 2:15-16

WINTER 1986

Right in the middle of my descent into darkness an event took place in which I was suddenly so shocked and arrested in my thoughts that I was forced to look at the world in a completely new way—a vision completely outside the range of my dwarfed and self-limited imagination. For sometimes an occurrence happens that is considered so completely outside the realm of possibilities that you just have to start over and rethink things. Yet it happened in the most innocuous way imaginable.

In those days a song was constantly playing in my mind as a kind of theme song—Iron Maiden's "Phantom of the Opera." This song came from their first, eponymous[1] "Iron Maiden" album. It seemed to describe my life[2] and I was listening to it endlessly and mulling over it.

There came a day when I was walking back and forth outside the high school cafeteria with thoughts full of hatred and malice. I had my hand on my knife in my back pocket. I was waiting for someone to walk out of that cafeteria, but instead another young lady walked out who I will call Genifer. I had previously known her as a partying kind of girl, and I absolutely considered her to be a kind of natural enemy to myself. I therefore supposed that she would say something to me such as 'you are very low,' or at the least give me what my wife today would call a 'stink face.' As she approached the 'Phantom of the Opera' tune violently forced its way into my head, and I was filled with wrath. I tensed up, 1000 volts of adrenaline shot through my body and... Genifer said 'Hi Ralph' in a very friendly and cheerful manner. And then kept walking.

What the ????????????!!!!

That was not supposed to happen at all. And if you could have looked at that moment into the notional architecture of my mind, as she casually walked away, you would have seen something like castles and towers collapsing and crashing to the ground. Mental structures that I had built to protect myself no matter what the costs, invincible beliefs that no amount of evidence to the contrary could penetrate. I may as well have been a confirmed atheist

---

1   Basically a thing being named for itself or its owner—like an Iron Maiden album named "Iron Maiden"

2   All these decades I thought the words were 'You're the Phantom of the Opera, You're the Devil, *you just have to stare...*" when the actual lyrics, which I only discovered while writing this book, were "You're the Phantom of the Opera, You're the devil, *you're just out to scare.*"

who saw the sky light up with angels the night Christ was born—and was left with the task of refiguring out how the world worked.

I pulled the collar of my jacket over my neck and walked away in shock and confusion, screaming out within myself "what is going on, everything I have believed all my life has got to be a lie!" And it wasn't my voice alone that was screaming in my head.

Whatever awkwardness and silent distrust that I had all this time sensed in the spirit world now broke out into an open cacophony. For apparently what had happened was a three-alarm fire in the kingdom of darkness. "Kill her now, kill her now, end all these cowardly delays!" they screamed.

But I was no longer interested. For one thing, I wasn't interested in tossing caution to the wind, throwing my life away, and abandoning all my bigger plans. Besides that, I wasn't attracted to her yet and didn't expect to have many more dealings with her. So I saw no threat and did not share their concerns. Finally, I simply did not want to harm her because she had shown kindness to me.

A SCORE I COULD NOT SETTLE

Day after day I still went into that closet to speak, but it all just revolved around more demands that I take out Genifer, which would continue throughout the day. I knew that I was not my own man and in control. So as these coercive demands continued, I would sometimes try to deaden myself by drinking whiskey along with antihistamines before I went to school, in an attempt to protect both Genifer and myself. But an event happened around then that I think established that I needed to take no such precautions. Some kid threw a coke on me and for reasons I still don't understand to this day, I froze and did not retaliate immediately. And then I went on for weeks trying to come up with this and that plan to kill him secretly, and then more Hamlet like delays set in. I can now clearly see that my failure to retaliate was really the mercy of God leading ultimately to my salvation. Because like what had happened with Genifer, this failure popped the bubble of so many of my delusions.

Now the veil was removed, and I understood that the gig was up—I would never be some great master of evil. All my life was, in fact, smokescreens and pure gasconade. I had been proven to be an impotent coward, and only an utterly contemptible future awaited me. What this all meant at the time was that I was entering into a vengeance debt, like credit card debt, that was piling up too rapidly for me ever to repay. Like a man drowning in debt who reaches out for ever more get rich quick schemes to climb out, the idea was forming in my mind of way to 'shoot the moon' in order to get out of my dilemma. Life had years ago become so bitter to me, with my extremely limited vision, that of course I wanted it to end—but only with the 'high score'—that is, taking out enough enemies with me to more than cancel out my own life.

And yet before long I would be encountering an entirely opposite way to clear this vengeance debt. Many read the Sermon on the Mount as if it were some kind of unbearable burden placed upon us—that we would soon avenge ourselves and be at peace if only our Lord had not demanded that we be so weak and sniveling. But I want to challenge you to read it from a different perspective—the perspective of those who, for whatever reasons, in all practicality cannot protect or avenge themselves regardless of any commands—that simply do not have the means to do so. To these our Lord says "Blessed are you who hunger now, For you shall be filled. Blessed are you who weep now, For you shall laugh." (Luke 6:21) As He spoke of those who weep NOW, Jesus surely had the words of Solomon ringing in His ears: "Then I returned and considered all the oppression that is done under the sun: And look! The tears of the oppressed, But they have no comforter—On the side of their oppressors there is power, But they have no comforter." (Ecclesiastes 4:1)

Along with this comfort, there is also the command to forgive. Yet even this command comes from a position of strength. With the Lord as our vindication, we have no need to collect from our enemies, just like the unforgiving servant at the end of Matthew 18 had no need to collect from his fellow servant, because his own debt had been cleared in its entirety. I had heard that Jesus had died on the cross to pay for my sins, because of course I had the problem that we all have. I owed a debt that I could not pay. But I also had another problem—I had a score that I could not settle.

And by this time, it seemed to me, one of those with which I had a score to settle was Satan himself. For in the aftermath of these two events, my guiding spirit, which I believed to be Satan, completely changed his tune. There were no more dreamy promises of world power. It was clear to me that Satan had now completely given up on me, whatever plans he may or may not have had for me before. All my hatred and all my malice, which in my swollen imagination was supposed to straddle the globe and slaughter and/or confuse millions, was now to turn and end itself on one young girl. "F--- you, Satan!" I thought to myself— although I wouldn't say such a thing today, due to some serious warnings in the Epistle of Jude.

With that revelation of where I truly stood in the kingdom of darkness, it was like a cloud broke and I saw through the whole con. It was obvious that Satan, if he had power equal to God, would by his nature display it far more openly than he was doing. He just wasn't one to restrain himself without some absolute necessity. In contrast, all that I had heard about God indicated that He was restraining and limiting Himself at all times, to give people room to decide on their own. This much became clearly true to me even though I still believed at the time that God intended to most cruelly triumph over us all in the end. The whole point of giving myself over to evil was not only that I didn't want such restraints as God Himself both practiced and expected, but that I didn't see how I could survive with such restraints in place.

But yet, I now had to admit, the continued existence of the good under such limitations was a clear indication of its overwhelming strength. Then and there it became clear to me that while he was given a great deal of leeway to make havoc, Satan was in some sense being restrained by God. This was not to say that open evil wasn't in plentiful evidence all over the place—simply that by its very nature there should be even more of it, even if it were evenly matched. Nor that the presence of good was universally available—just that by its yielding and self-restraining we should expect to see even less of it. In the end, as has been noted by many, the problem of good became a much more difficult mystery to solve than the problem of evil.

The ultimate implication of all this for me was clear: I had chosen the wrong side, the weaker side, and I was going to lose horribly.

Yet for all this, I was about to get conned again. I confronted Satan. "You never had any intention of giving me any place in your kingdom. And is not everything about you a lie? You are going to lose, and you know it—and you are bringing us all down with you!" "If you want to give up the quest so easily, so be it" was the reply. "If it is as you say, then you and I are the same kind of creatures. You could never follow God's way or bear to live under his rule, and you never will. So we are both, as you claim, doomed to the abyss."

"Let's die with our boots on! Together, you and I," Satan continued. "And if you must end it now, let us do it in such a way as they will never forget, and let those who remain feel the pain that you and I are doomed to for the rest of their lives." With that said, a searing pain came upon my soul, so unearthly that it is difficult to describe to any who have not known it. It is the pain of looking into the abyss, of looming damnation that no consideration can erase. Then the wrath rose within me, the type of wrath I have been subject to at various times in my life, that seems to have no heat to it and turns my blood to ice. And the very beginning of my plans, never carried out, began to take shape.

A KILLER'S PRAYER

I remember those days, walking up and down the hallways of my high school, and desperately plotting my now abortive revenge. On one of those days, I actually lifted up a prayer to heaven, enemy of God though I was, and spoke in my heart as follows: "God, I am about to do a deed of great evil, and I know you don't want me to do it. All this evil and suffering could be avoided if you just allowed one thing which should be easy for you. Simply allow me to kill myself without heaven or hell, but to completely cease to exist. Give me annihilation and no evil will ever come from me again. What, after all, is your purpose in allowing this ghastly existence to go on?"

And in the inner depths of my soul, I roared "why, why can't you grant me this one thing?" And in one of those inexplicable instances where we know that God is speaking to us, though it is heard only within the soul, the Holy Spirit actually spoke back with words to this effect: "I will by no means allow your suicide without damnation. But you may have your request in another way. When a man repents and follows Me, he dies to all that he is, so that he becomes a completely new man. This is what I made possible when I died on the cross. Turn to me so completely that all that you now are dies so thoroughly that it has no more existence at all, and you will have your request." Now if anyone asks why I was given such a word and not others, my answer to you is that if you are reading this right now, God is directly speaking the same thing to you. Be that as it may, in the absence of my immediate acceptance such thoughts passed as soon as they came, and my madness continued.

OTHER DIRECTIONS?

In the midst of all these wild vicissitudes, it would be easy to imagine that there was no path before me that was not depraved, and that there was no part of my life that was normal. But in actual fact a key element of the demonization was that I was changing personality and goals multiple times per day, and sometimes could live a relatively normal life for significant stretches at a time. There were two things in my life which pointed in a somewhat different direction, if only I was my own man and could bring my disordered mind under control.

First of all, there was Physics. I had been allowed into an AP Physics class, and for the first time in quite a spell I found myself not just doing my homework, which I mostly never did anymore, but actually loving it. This was because there was a kind of beauty to the Newtonian Physics that I was learning that could not be denied, and it kept drawing me in. It wasn't entirely enough to overcome my distraction and sloth, and so I began failing in the second semester. But it was coming close, and combined with something else at times it seemed to point toward a different path in life.

That other factor was Chul Yun's Tae Kwon Do classes, which I returned to on my mother's insistence after my second arrest. She felt certain I was going to prison this time and would need this. Chul Yun seemed to point the way toward living an incredibly disciplined life while giving heed to no one. Every day around noon or so he would shut all the doors and windows to his metal building, cut off all ventilation to maximize the Louisiana heat, and work out intensely for about 3 hours to prepare for his series of evening classes each night.

He loved to philosophize via lengthy speeches, given in a thick Korean accent with its own unique phraseology. For he was that avuncular philosophical type very well known among Asians. Years earlier Han Fei and I had spent many an hour in his office listening to these lengthy discourses. Now three years later I got to listen to them on my own. A typical speech might begin thusly: "In our lives we need all kinds of self-defense: physical self-defense, social self-defense, financial self-defense, mental self-defense, and many, many more kinds of self-defense. Physical self-defense, that means Tae Kwon Do!"—and so it would go on for maybe 2 or 3 hours. Beyond that feeble beginning, I really have no way of conveying the simultaneously utterly Korean and conversely utterly sui generis nature of this man.

All I can say is that it was not without reason that Chul Yun was utterly beloved and respected by his students, and had such a legendary awe about him. I got some insight into the man years later, after I was married and was taking his classes again for a season. We had one of our long talks one night, and he showed me some old black and white pictures from Korea. Some were of friends, ROK soldiers from the Vietnam War that he alleged were tougher than him, even though 'they didn't know anything about Tae Kwon Do." Also a woman, and he simply said, "If someone is not interested, why would I ever try to convince her. I will go my own way." In that we truly understood each other. He said that gold has the value that it has because it does not mix or change with anything.

He then spoke about different reasons he loved this country so much. For example, that he could get whatever kind of food he wanted, especially broccoli, which he seemed to think was especially healthy. In a way, the ability to eat all the broccoli he wanted symbolized for him all that he loved about America. Noting that my wife was Asian, he said it is difficult for them to adjust to this country, especially if they had some important position back home. He then became truly animated, saying this is what he loved about America, the Old Republic that still existed in those years, most of all—that you didn't have to kowtow to anyone: "You are very wealthy—So what? - You have a PhD?—Who cares!!" That's when I truly understood why he was so beloved of his local American students: Red-necks, Cajuns, and generic Baton Rouge types such as myself. It was because at his core, underneath vast differences of culture, experience and discipline, he saw the world essentially as we all did. Through mass immigration, mass indoctrination and guilt induction, the hollowing out of the economy and industrial base, along with ever more consolidation and regimentation and credentialism, this old American ideal has been diluted almost to the point of vanishing. But it is worth preserving, as I learned from Chul Yun, in whatever form or background it can be found.

Under his influence, for a time I had hoped to at least be a 'Lawful Evil' type. But after Christmas I was no longer in Tae Kwon Do. In the aftermath of that shocking greeting, limping on my broken foot and failing to get revenge, I was trending toward chaos. Chul Yun was unable to teach me the one form of self-defense, spiritual self-defense, that I most needed. For alas, he was an utterly secular man, or perhaps slightly Buddhist, which is really just the same thing.

What would have been the influence of a Christian Chul Yun in our place and our time—it would have been incalculable—but it was not to be. Nevertheless, I would soon be meeting someone who was equally disciplined and formidable in his own way, even if he was no fighter at all.

CHAPTER 19

BIC

Brethren, if anyone among you wanders from the truth, and someone turns him back, let him know that he who turns a sinner from the error of his way will save a soul from death and cover a multitude of sins.

James 5:19-20

EARLY SPRING 1986

There came a day when I was talking to some girls about Satan, and they wanted to make a joke of it. What they thought would be funniest of all was to see what would happen if I and a foreign student named Bic were brought together. He was from Thailand and Bic was his nickname, as most Thai people have. He was given this nickname by his parents, because he was the oldest, and Bic is just saying 'big' with a Thai accent. It is not possible to understand how it was that I went from being a Satanist to a born-again Christian without understanding Bic's story, which is best given in his own words[1]:

---

1   With only very minor changes made for grammar, spelling, run-on sentences and the like.

Progress and Plan in Buddhism

I was interested in Buddhism when I was young, at the age of 16. My dad was a Buddhist monk in a monastery, as it was a compulsory for every male to be a monk for at least three months, as the way to say thanks to the country and to the parents. When my dad was in the monastery as other monks, they were required to wake up at 3:00 o'clock in the morning to meditate until 5:00 AM. Then at 6:00 AM the monks would go around the temples and villages to receive alms from the Thai people. I remember when the monks and my dad were meditating at 3:00 AM, they were required to stare at the skeletons bones just to remind them how empties and vanities their life are. And I thought that life is just a delusion and to free from suffering I must be detached from desire and the things of this world. From this experience I began my journey to find real peace and meaning in life.

Ever since when I was young, I have a question about life and I began to search for meaning in life through religions. I start to read books on religions like Buddhism and Hinduism. At one time I was a member of the Transcendental Meditation club - to be a member of the group I had to make an agreement of covenant with them. I would spend many hours a day meditating, but the more I meditated I felt emptied inside and the more I meditated, I felt more bondage.

At the age of 16 I decided to be a monk in the monastery, and I want to be a monk for the rest of my life. At the monastery I would spend many hours a day meditating and for most of the day I would meditate in the morning, in the afternoon, in the evening, and at night. Because of doing this my progress in Buddhism was very fast and my headmaster noticed my rapid progress in Buddhism. And I told him that I would be a monk for the rest of my life. But God had a different plan for my life.

After three months into Buddhism my parents asked me to return back to [the USA] to pursue my study in high school. So, I told my headmaster that I would have to leave the monastery, but I promised him that I would return back and resume my monkhood again. And I determined that when I returned to [the USA], I wanted to spread Buddhism in the states.

I went to [the USA] with my head shaven and I ...continued to meditate and read books on Buddhism and Hinduism. I would go to the bookstore to find books on religion, [for] in my mind I was very obsessed with religions, and I wanted to find meaning in life and I want to achieve the height of Buddhism.

I began to talk people into Buddhism and Hinduism, and I would talk to them about life matters and what is the meaning in life. I remember one time I talked to my dad's friends about Buddhism and they were very amazed of my knowledge in Buddhism.

How I Got Saved

Every day when I finished school, I would go to the Episcopal Church[1] on the LSU [Louisiana State University] campus. I would spend at least two hours at a time meditating and I would bring my candles and my incense to pay off respect to Buddha[2]. One Saturday as I went to the Episcopal Church to meditate, I knelt down at the pew in the sanctuary, and I began to look up to see the images of the lamb and of Jesus. I began to pray to God and told God, "If you are really real I want to know you and your

---

1   St. Alban's Chapel, an Episcopal Church that was open 24 hours a day for prayer

2   These meditations took place in an upstairs room at St. Albans' that we later called the "Upper Room."

power. Please reveal yourself to me." And I began to weep and cry. I believe that the Lord heard my prayer, because I got saved later that morning on the same day.

After meditating that day, I began to walk around the LSU campus, and as I was walking, I passed by the LSU [Student] Union. There was a group of students from the Family Worship Center witnessing to people about the gospel of Jesus Christ. There was a lady named Kathy Essex who approached me excitedly, telling me about the good news of Jesus Christ. She told me excitedly that the God who created the heaven and earth loved me and all I had to do is to open my heart and receive him into my heart. And that's what I did. I received Jesus into my heart, and I began to confess my sin and acknowledge that Jesus Christ came to die for me and he has forgiven my sin and granted me eternal life in Jesus Christ. Ever since then my life has not been the same again. I felt his peace and love that flowed into my soul, and I made a commitment to serve him for the rest of my life.

On the next day, which was Sunday, Kathy invited me to go to Family Worship Center. She picked me up at my home and took me to the church on that day. On that Sunday morning the preacher began to preach about Buddhism and Christianity. He preached that Buddha is dead and Jesus Christ is alive, that Jesus Christ has been raised from the dead and He is still alive. After the preacher finished his sermon, he gave an altar call and told that if anyone wanted to receive Jesus into their life, just come forward to the altar. At first, I was hesitant to go forward. But the Holy Spirit began to prompt in my heart, and I went down to the altar and knelt down to pray. As I was kneeling down at the altar, the preacher came and laid his hand on me, and he began to prophecy over me that "you young man God will raise you up to become a preacher." I then began to sense the Holy

Spirit's rushing into my soul like a waterfall and I was electrifying through my body, and I began to shake and weep tremendously and I feel great a peace and felt His great love flooding into my life.

Bic's New Life

After my conversion experience I began to attend church regularly and on every [Tuesday] night I would go to the Bible study[1] near my home. The leader of that Bible study was Gene Mills. I was really hunger for the word of God and I really appreciate Gene Mills for his faithfulness to the Word of God. Every [Tuesday] night he would emphasize the importance of God's Word and he would show me Jesus Christ from the scriptures. Because of that my life grew a lot, and I began to have a better understanding and a better grasp of who Christ is, which strengthened my faith in walk with the Lord.

After my conversion experience, not only I go to church and attend Bible study on Tuesday, but I was also involved in Chi Alpha on Friday night which was a gathering of students on the LSU campus. Many times the preacher would challenge me about the Lord and about evangelism. And on Saturday morning I would go out on LSU campus and began to witness to people about the Lord Jesus Christ. And every day I began to witness in my high school at McKinley high school and many times I would skip lunch, but I will spend my lunch time praying and witnessing to the students at school. Many time I would get up on the table and I began to preach about the Lord Jesus Christ. And that's where I met with my brother [Ralph Tarso]. I prayed to the Lord saying,

---

1   The Bible study was part of Chi Alpha Campus Ministries, a college outreach at LSU.

"Oh Lord that you will save someone this day," and I praise the Lord that God brought him to me and I began to share him about the love of Christ and the gospel of Jesus Christ.

Bic became a believer in October of 1985. Shortly before this, Bic had reached a point where he was meditating up to 16 hours per day. What this meant, if anyone wonders how this was possible while living one's daily life, was that he would remain in a mindful, meditative state at every waking hour, regardless of what activity he was engaged in. So, for example, when he woke up and ate breakfast cereal, he would move his spoon so as to take every single bite in a synchronized, rhythmic way while continuing to meditate, and so on throughout all his daily activities until going to bed. While his discipline was commendable, his forays into the spirit world unfortunately also opened him up to unclean spirits.

But in a twist of fate in which God turned evil into good, these experiences shaped Bic into a spiritual warrior. In the process, Bic became uniquely able to both lead me out of demonic bondage into salvation, and get me through a two-year process of stabilization in which I struggled with, and occasionally gave into, continuing attacks from the demonic realm.

FACING REALITY

It is absolutely necessary that I tell this story as it happened regardless of anyone's preconceived theological notions about such things. AFTER I was born again and all the demons were cast out, there was a two-year period in which the demons would seek to come back in and I would occasionally have a relapse in which they would temporarily gain the upper hand. It is so important to tell this like it was because as ever more demons are unleashed in our putrefying society, we will need to have a realistic idea of what it takes to get the lost and demonized all the way through to the finish line.

We must face reality. We cannot simply ignore real things because they are weird and uncomfortable, and perhaps we may even feel that we don't have sufficiently detailed Biblical guidance to deal with them. CS Lewis famously referred to the demon powers in the world as 'the macrobes', as a way of comparison to the microbes which cause physical diseases. Imagine what would happen if we all suddenly decided that the germ theory of disease was not true. We therefore stopped purifying our drinking water, sterilizing our surgical instruments, washing our hands and dishes with soap, and the like. And in the aftermath, as people all around starting dying of diseases we hadn't seen in such strength in many generations, we just tut-tutted and imagined it was all normal, just a lot of change to be adjusted to.

This is exactly what happened in the spiritual realm when we in the West decided to 'disenchant the world,' and stopped seeing things the way they really are. This 'disenchantment' was in reality a great dumbing down. We built massive armies and economies and systems to protect ourselves from external physical threats, and meanwhile everything rotted out from the inside like a house eaten by termites. Families have broken down, children who can't tell whether they are men or women are being castrated and mutilated, mass shooters are spreading, and everyone is depressed, with many on medications. Jesus also entered into a very broken world in the days of His flesh, and we see He was constantly encountering demons and casting them out. We must ask ourselves, in what way does our theology and ministry approach allow for and confront this fundamental reality, as clearly recorded in the Gospels?

SPIRITUAL WARFARE

But let us continue the story. In the months before we met, Bic also went through some demonic episodes before reaching final deliverance:

> Even though I have been saved for six months, I was still med-itating and at the same time going to church. I would still be reading Buddha and Hinduism book, and I was still meditating and bowing down to Buddha, and I was reading the Bible and worshipping Jesus at the same time. I think because I was not yet growing in the knowledge of Jesus Christ and that nobody has ever told me that I need to go all the way only with Jesus Christ.
>
> Many times, I felt struggling in my spirit. It seemed like it was a spiritual warfare within me and many times I was scared going to bed at night. I cannot shut my eyes and go to bed. Then one night I was really scared and then I called Kathy, the lady who led me to the Lord. I told her about my situations. She began to pray for me and to bind the evil spirit to go away from me. She told me to throw away all the religious books and the image of Buddha, and she told me that I must be exclusively committed to Jesus Christ alone. So on the next day when I woke up I took all my books on Buddhism and Hinduism and I began to burn it. The image of Buddha also burned and I felt great relief in my spirit. But yet I know deep inside my spirit that there is still a spiritual struggle in my soul. I felt like a great bondage is press-ing over me.
>
> Eventually I experienced a great victory and a great sign of relief by the Holy Spirit of the Lord. It happened at the Bible study on Tuesday night, when brother Gene Mills was teaching the word of God as usual. At the end of his teaching, he asked us

if anyone wanted to fully yield and surrender their life totally to the leading of the Holy Spirit and to surrender your life totally to Jesus Christ. At that time, I felt a great struggle (spiritual warfare) in my spirit. I wanted to raise up my hand but there was a voice in me saying don't raise up my hand. Eventually I force myself to raise up my hand and I want to tell Gene that I want to yield and submit my life totally to the Lord Jesus Christ.

Then later I realized that I was struggling inside, and I was shaking and got up uncontrollably. I began to walk toward the door to go outside, and I started to scream from the top of my lungs. Brother Gene Mills and all the brothers and sisters came out to see what was happening to me. And then later I found myself laying down on the floor and brother Gene got on top of me, laid hands on me, and began to cast out the evil spirit out of me. And there was one brother who saw what was happening to me. His name was Joel and God gave him a vison. What he saw there inside of me was a 7 headed green snake. Later, when brother Joel told me about what he saw in me, I realized immediately that it was the seven headed snake that was at the stairs of every Buddhist temple in Thailand, and it symbolized the great serpent Satan itself. The people in the neighborhood came out to see what was happening, and some even called the police. But brother Gene told everyone that it was OK. And I knew right away that the evil spirit was cast out from me. I felt a great, tremendous relief in my soul and I felt like light as feathers and all the heavy burden was relieved from me and I praise the Lord for that.

After my deliverance experience, I began to grow in the knowledge of Jesus Christ, and I felt a great burden to return back to my home country of Thailand. I wanted to go back and tell the Thai people about the love of Jesus Christ, and how that the Lord has help me and saved me, and that Jesus Christ can do it for them too...

And I remember one time after I finish studying in my class-room, at the end of the class I went to the front of the class and there was under the overhead projector a map of Thailand. I knew right away that was God's provision telling me that one day I would return back to Thailand. I praise the Lord that on October 25th, 1985, I accepted Jesus Christ as my Lord and savior, and I was at the age of 18. I returned back to Thailand when I was 22.

ONE MORE ASSIGNMENT

But there was at least one convert Bic needed to make in the USA before he returned to Thailand. In the lead up to that there were other struggles with evil spirits which took place while at school, which put Bic on the radar of just about everyone at McKinley High School:

After I got saved it took me a year to really be delivered from demonic activity in my life. During that first year of my conver-sion, I was still struggling with demonic power, so that's why I was yelling many times at McKinley high school and at Family Worship Center.

There was one incident when I was at McKinley high school during lunchtime. I remember I was yelling in the school and the people took me to the principal's room to find out what was happening to me. They called my dad to come to see what was happening to me, and that day I was sent back home to rest. They couldn't find out what was happening to me, so they thought that I was having some kind of psychological problem in my mind.

There was another incident at Family Worship Center after

the service. A gentleman came to me and he told me that I have some kind of demonic power working inside me. But I was surprised because I already received Jesus Christ into my heart. But he and other guys insist and led me to the back of the sanctuary. With other two or three gentlemen they brought me to a room and they began to pray for me, and at that time my dad was with me. As they prayed for me, I begin to yell. They told me that demonic power was being cast out. But as you know from my testimony, I was not fully delivered until my time at Gene Mill's Bible study place where he cast out the demon out of me. That was when I was fully delivered.

There's one thing I want to praise the Lord about. By God's Providence I was able to gather Christian believers at McKinley high school to have them come together and pray during lunchtime in a room. I asked the principal permission if I can use a room during lunch time to have Christian come and pray, and he allowed me to use it during lunchtime for Christian prayers. We would spend time praying for revival and we would pray for students at McKinney high school to get safe in Jesus Christ

Most of my lunchtime at McKinley high school I would spend time preaching the gospel of Jesus Christ to the students. Many times, I would pray by kneeling down to pray, and people would gather around me to see what was going on with me. As I attracted the crowd, I would share to them about the gospel.

And so Bic became known as a radical Christian at McKinley who had undergone some really bizarre experiences, while I was now well known as a notorious Satanist. Our meeting was about to take place.

CHAPTER 20
A GOD WORTHY TO SERVE

You are worthy, O Lord,
To receive glory and honor and power;
For You created all things,
And by Your will they exist and were created.

Revelation 4:11

MARCH 1986

I mentioned in the last chapter that I was talking to some girls about Satan who ended up, as a joke, bringing me to Bic. I have to say that all these years I had completely forgotten what it was we were talking about, from months after my salvation, when I first started telling my story, all the way until last year, when Bic emailed me his side of the story to help me write this book. I now remember that I was arguing with them about the futility of 'White Magic', and urging them to just go all the way and follow Satan openly. Anyway, Bic describes our encounter as follows:

There was one girl at McKinley high school, she called herself a white magic witch. She told me there was a guy here at McKinley high school that always wore black jacket and was walking around the school. She asked me if I would be interested in sharing the gospel with him, and I say yes. So one day she introduced me to [Ralph Tarso] and then, after that, I tried to share with him the gospel and the love of Jesus Christ. At the end of my sharing, I asked [Ralph Tarso] if he would be interested in receiving Jesus Christ into his heart. Praise the Lord that he accepted Jesus Christ as his Lord on that day.

But I didn't accept Jesus Christ as my Lord on that day—quite the contrary. The way it happened from my point of view was this. One day the girls in question dragged Bic to me. There was some momentary confusion and then Bic asked me something like 'what do you want?' I thought to myself 'why is this foreigner asking me what I want?' But after a brief moment of reflection, it occurred to me that there was something I wanted from him. I told him: 'A bunch of demons have come into my life and they are always tormenting me and telling me what to do. And they keep demanding that I kill a girl that I don't want to kill. If you can use your Jesus powers to cast these demons out so that I can go back to normal life, I would appreciate it.' And Bic rather cheerfully said "I have exactly what you need!" and starting trying to pray the "Sinner's Prayer" with me to give my life to Jesus right then.

"Whoa, hold on!" I thought to myself. I was just trying to get Bic to use his Jesus powers to get rid of the demons, so I could go back to my life the way it was before that September. I had no intention of giving my life completely to Christ. But he did have some Jesus power, enough to keep me mostly frozen when dealing with him. So I tried to sound like I was saying his prayer to get rid of Bic, while I was actually holding on strongly to Satan in my heart.

This was a fiasco. The demons knew that I already wanted out, yet I was unwilling to do the one thing that would deliver me from their power. There was torment, and yet for all this I was still unwilling to give my life to Jesus, because it still seemed an impossibility for me.

I had heard that Jesus Christ had died on the cross to pay the price for my sins, so that if I only believed they would all be washed away. But if He forgives me, I thought to myself, He will just have to forgive me again and again, because all I ever want to do is sin all the time.

CROSSFIRE

It seemed the demons couldn't do much when Bic was around, and neither could I. Because there was a kind of spiritual power that was freezing me, I avoided him whenever I could. On a few occasions during lunch, I would even leave the campus entirely to avoid him. Finally, there came a day when I went into the bathroom and he came in after me, and so there was no avoiding this. He asked me if I wanted to go to Crossfire. This was a youth ministry in town, associated with Jimmy Swaggart's church, that was in the beginning stages of a spiritual revival of teenagers throughout Baton Rouge. I would normally give a fake address to people in situations like this, but I could not think clearly or recall one. I gave him my real address to pick me up, thinking that because Bic was not local, he would surely get confused and never find my house.

I wasn't entirely wrong in my assumption—Bic did drive around fruitlessly for some time before finding my home. When he knocked the first time on a door no one used, Mom did not understand him and sent him away. But he was not to be deterred.

After driving around some more he returned to a different door. My parents were shocked, as I hadn't had any visitors by the light of day for some time—much less a foreigner asking to take me to a religious meeting that I had apparently agreed to. They got me out of my dark room to ask me what was going on. At first I didn't know either, because it was Wednesday now and I had forgotten the whole thing.

Now my parents had a decision to make also, about letting me go. In my father's eyes, going to a Jimmy Swaggart meeting seemed like going to some kind of Marxist group, for Swaggart was loathed by the Roman Catholic population of Baton Rouge. My mother thought it might be an answer to prayer, because the name of the youth group, Crossfire, was similar to a Christian youth group she heard about years earlier that she always hoped I would go to.

If my parents had simply refused to let me go, I would not have put up much of a fight for going to Crossfire. But they both decided that for the most part I was completely out of control and beyond the point of being reached by them. After many prayers my mother had finally given me up to the Lord to do whatever He would do. They decided that anything would be better than where I was right then, so they didn't try to stop me from going.

So I whisked off to Crossfire with Bic and his brother in their little white corolla that night. Although not absolutely certain, this was probably March 12, 1986. On that night I was armed only with a knife in my back pocket. During the whole ride there, the demons inside me were screaming to stab Bic immediately and go running out of the car, doing anything, anything to stop what was about to take place. It is hard to explain to someone who has not experienced demonization how compelling and difficult to control this could be. Yet the demons were already seriously beginning to lose their grip. Once I was in the building, during a brief touch of heaven, they lost their grip entirely.

A CHRISTIAN UNDERGROUND

When I arrived at the Crossfire meeting, I was amazed. For I met people from every background, all very different from each other and yet all very excited about Jesus. They were all in, and I had never seen anything like this before. I had often seen people trying to do everything right. But I frequently sensed from such people that they either wanted to join in with our wickedness but were afraid to do so, or that they wanted some gain from the system. I deeply despised this. But to see people all in for Jesus and excited about it, and wanting nothing to do with the things of this world because they had something far better—this was an entirely different matter.

Several of them had the look, I believed, of people who had recently come out of drug addiction. Besides this, I saw several people I knew of from school, but I had no idea they would ever be involved in anything like this. Finally, I saw Genifer there. This left me particularly amazed, because to me she had an aura of immorality and partying around her. Yet here she was, as excited about Jesus as everyone else. She explained to me that she and her family had become believers over the summer.

I was then struck by the idea that I was in the presence of a Christian underground of young people that I didn't know existed at all, a counterpoint to the wretched world I had always known. I continued to meet various people and took it all in as the meeting was about to get started. Everyone was so kind, especially to a contemptible person such as myself. Some visitors still wanted to look worldly and cool in the midst of all this, and I thought they were ridiculous. We went through some powerful worship songs and then the preaching started.

BELITTLING SIN

The speaker that night, the leader of Crossfire, was Glen Berteau. He had grown up in a neighborhood near mine, went to a high school within walking distance of my house, been a football star there, and lived a wild, brawling, partying life. This all continued in college until he gave his life to the Lord under the influence of a fellow Louisiana Tech football player and preacher named Denny Duron. That night he gave one of the last messages in a series he called "LSD: Lust, Sex and Dating." The primary characteristic of Glen's preaching was that he loudly and defiantly expressed utter contempt for sin, as opposed to fear and loathing of sin. In all that he said, Glen exulted the Lord and belittled sin and the world and the devil. And he was very funny. Nothing impressed me more than the strength and power in which this God was presented, versus the sniveling weakness I had associated with Christianity for so long.

At the end of the message Glen asked everyone to close their eyes and bow their head. He was giving something that is known in Evangelical churches as an altar call, where people are called to stand up, come to the front of the church, and immediately give their lives to Jesus, or otherwise pray for some particular need. But he was explaining everything very carefully in a manner fit for those like myself who had never seen or heard of such a thing.

Although he especially emphasized that he wanted everyone's eyes closed, I just had to keep mine squinted open to see what would happen. Glen then asked people to raise their hand for prayer if they were struggling with various things. At some point he asked people to raise their hand if they were struggling with masturbation, and although I wasn't willing to raise my hand, I did secretly say to God that I wanted to be free from this.

As Glen continued, he finally asked anyone who was involved with homosexuality and wanted deliverance to raise their hand. I saw at least one young lady immediately raise her hand for this. Since this was before the social changes that subsequently took place, I was amazed at three things at once: first, that anyone involved in homosexuality would come to a meeting like this; second, that they would admit it; and third, that they would apparently repent right there on the spot. This told me that even I could potentially repent also.

MUSCULAR CHRISTIANITY

The Crossfire youth ministry certainly epitomized "Muscular Christianity" as it has been figuratively understood. But Crossfire was also a very literal exemplar of Muscular Christianity. The leadership team, from Glen Berteau who had been a star football player at Louisiana Tech, down to the discipleship leaders of small groups, was primarily made up of very muscular young men. If I had spoken to any one of them of my 'mind over matter' philosophy from earlier years, I am sure that they would have replied to me, in tones redolent of Hans and Frans, "Let's not forget muscle over matter!"

One of those muscular young men was Gene Mills. He was at that time also the leader of Chi Alpha (XA), a college Christian ministry at LSU. He had been a big part of Bic's life as a new Christian, so Bic quickly introduced me to him before the meeting started. Gene said some things to me, and I thought to myself "why is this jock talking to me?" But then I thought "why indeed?" For it then dawned on me, as it continued to throughout that evening, that we were in a whole new world here, a whole new community, and that the divisions in the outside world no longer applied. I would soon see Gene again at one of his XA meetings.

A MOCKERY OF SATAN

I actually mocked Satan while in Crossfire that night, thoroughly enjoying the temporary abeyance of his power over me. I suppose King Saul must have done the same when David's music temporarily drove the evil spirit from him, without actually repenting[1]. I mocked Satan's present powerlessness, but mostly that he was doomed to ultimately lose. I paid a heavy price the rest of the week, as the spirits returned in fury to torment me once I was out of this safe zone. This involved a lot of yelling, screaming, and raving on my part, but it was temporary. For God granted me enough peace and lucidity over the next few weeks to really think this through.

There was one more thing that God did that night that served as a token of His power, of all He could do to change my heart were I to trust Him with it all. He broke the power of masturbation off my life for several days in a row. I really wondered why it was that Satan couldn't do this for me. "Aren't you supposed to be in charge of all this lust?" I asked. "The fact that I am hooked on this is an affront to the kind of invulnerable person you are supposed to be helping me to be." I may have been a Satanist, but I would have preferred to be a chaste Satanist.

In contrast, I left Crossfire that night with one conviction firmly settled in my mind—that the Lord Jesus Christ was

---

1   1 Samuel 16:14-23

absolutely a God worthy to serve, that such would be the best possible way for me to live.

If only I could cross that line, if only I could stop sinning! It seemed impossible—and yet... There were those people I saw repent. There was the power that God had shown by ending my masturbation for a week or so. There was a real, vibrant Christian community, so there would be fellowship and support, even for someone as socially unacceptable as myself. This particular aspect was further established the following Saturday morning when a visitation team from Crossfire showed up at my door.

It was a group of about three people, male and female. They were very kind to me, including even the girls, and prayed for me. All that next few weeks, one thought overpowered all others. You must repent, you have got to live for God. There is no other way for you to live, and you must take advantage of this opportunity right now, while you still have it. Morning was about to break.

CHAPTER 21

MORNING HAS BROKEN

Morning has broken, like the first morning,
Blackbird has spoken, like the first bird.
Praise for the singing! Praise for the morning!
Praise for them, springing fresh from the Word!
"Morning Has Broken" a Christian hymn by Eleanor Farjeon

AROUND EASTER 1986

After that night at Crossfire and the visitation, although I did not immediately repent, I began to talk to Bic. I did not go back to Crossfire the following Wednesday, but by the end of that week Bic asked me if I wanted to go to Chi Alpha (XA) with him. This was on March 21, 1986, the Friday before Palm Sunday. Because it is not clear to me exactly when I got saved over about a two to three week period, I have set that date of the Friday before Palm Sunday as the official anniversary of my salvation.

Bic lived in an apartment complex on the other side of the fence from the McKinley High School football field and track. His apartment was also within easy walking distance of Louisiana State University (LSU). It was easy to just go to Bic's house right after school and go to Chi Alpha later that night. That Friday I did this without telling my parents what I was doing.

I went to Bic's apartment first. His parents were there, as his dad was a professor at LSU. He had two brothers, and Bic was the oldest. The first thing we did that afternoon was walk over to St. Alban's Chapel, an Episcopal church on the LSU campus which was open 24 hours a day for prayer. Bic had often meditated there previously as a Buddhist, in an upstairs room he titled the "Upper Room." That is where we now went first, to pray and discuss the things of God. Satan was far from me that whole day until after midnight and into the next day or so.

We then came down from the "Upper Room" to the front part of the main chapel, and sat on the carpeted steps leading up to the altar. There, due to a bit of a language barrier, Bic would just turn his English Bible to one scripture after another and ask me to read it back to him, so that the Bible itself did the talking.

Whenever we finished reading the scripture for a time, we would break off to pray. Though it may seem premature, by this point not only Bic but I also prayed—and prayed and prayed and prayed. For I was beginning to truly understand the Gospel for the first time, and so more than praying, really, I was thinking over the things that I was just beginning to understand. It was a dreamy, ethereal experience. At intervals Bic would go over to the piano that was nearby to the right of that altar and play and worship, while I would lie down on a pew nearby and look up at the ceiling and the stained-glass pictures at the top of the walls of that church. As I looked at those stained-glass windows, hearing Bic pray and play the piano, I thought of all that Christians had suffered and lived and died for over all these many centuries.

FIRST LIGHT

When I say I was beginning to understand the Gospel for the first time, I mean that one or two missing pieces which had previously made it impossible for me to apprehend were finally coming into focus. I had heard so much about the Gospel for many years: How Jesus had died on the cross to pay for our sins, how we only had to put our faith in Him and they would all be forgiven. But there was that one great stumbling block—All I wanted to do was sin all the time, and I couldn't see a way that this could ever change. If Jesus forgave me, He would just have to forgive me again and again, and I knew this couldn't just go on and on with no change.

But on that dreamy, mystical afternoon in the chapel with Bic, there were two doctrines that finally made the way clear for me. The first was the doctrine of man's depravity after the fall. Sometimes the best way to really explain something is to point out its total opposite:

> "Our young people are diseased with the theological problems of original sin, origin of evil, predestination, and the like. These never presented a practical difficulty to any man,—never darkened across any man's road, who did not go out of his way to seek them."[1]

I found reality to be exactly the opposite of these thoughts expressed by Emerson. For when I understood this doctrine of man's depravity, I also realized something about my own particular situation. I was not some special case which could not be explained otherwise than that I was specifically born to be damned. Rather, my life was just one more expression of the universal human condition.

---

[1]   Ralph Waldo Emerson, Emerson: Essays and Lectures, edited by Joel Porte (New York: Library of America, 1983), 305.

I did not come to believe in original sin and its great effect, the depravity of man, because I found these things in the Bible. Rather, I believed the Bible because it taught these things. For by them the entire course of my life up until now could be fully explained.

But there was one more, crucial element: the reality and possibility of the second birth for any who fully surrender to the Lord and call upon Him to give you a new life. For Jesus had said to Nicodemus that "Most assuredly, I say to you, unless one is born again, he cannot see the kingdom of God" (John 3:3) and the Apostle had followed up, saying "whoever calls on the name of the Lord shall be saved." (Romans 10:13, NKJV) Here was the fulfillment of what I had heard in my spirit that day as I walked the halls of my high school, plotting my revenge. Not only was it possible for me to become a completely new person, but it was absolutely necessary for my salvation.

Two scriptures above all made this clear on that ethereal afternoon. I quote these in the old King James Version because that was the translation that Bic was showing me that Friday.

The first scripture was John 14:6: "Jesus saith unto him, I am the way, the truth, and the life: no man cometh unto the Father, but by me."

In other words, there really was a way back to God, even for me. Only one way, to be sure, but nevertheless, there actually was a way. This one way wasn't based on ideals or feelings or values, but was grounded in reality—the way things actually are—and hence was also the truth. This one way also led to real life. Not the temporal life that had become unbearable to me because of its exhaustion. But the never-ending life that will eventually give all the strength and joy and endless creativity that could ever be needed, and even now provides the Holy Spirit to empower us to do what we must each day. All three aspects were bound up in

One person, Jesus Christ, who would freely provide it for whoever asked and completely surrendered to Him.

BORN AGAIN

The second scripture was John 1:12: "But as many as received him, to them gave he power to become the sons of God, even to them that believe on his name:"

This clinched it for me. Here I was, knowing that I was a kind of sociopath that could neither change my ways or even feel genuine contrition, because I had burned my conscience to a crisp. Yet I also knew that Hell was real. And what is a sociopath supposed to do in the face of Hell?

When I read this, I understood that if I believed in the name of Jesus and gave my life to Him, that He would give me a new heart, solving my unsolvable problem. For I understood this power[1] to become sons of God to be the ability to live for God because, through the Holy Spirit, He gives us that new heart, making us new people.

It is important to emphasize this element of being born again, because a writer that I have greatly enjoyed over the last two decades, David Goldman[2] has a theory about a famous piece of literature—which I believe expresses a profound misunderstanding of how all this really works:

Don Juan was the invention of Tirso de Molina, a Spanish monk from a family of converted Jews. Concealed in its puppet-theater

---

1   I know what ἐξουσία (exousia) means, although not at the time. I think my understanding back then was still correct based on scriptures such as Acts 26:17-18 and Colossians 1:13-14, but this is beyond the scope of this book.

2   He previously wrote under the pen-name "Spengler."

plot is a Jewish joke: Don Juan exists to prove by construction that a devout Christian can be a sociopath, and by extension, that the Christian world can be ruled by sociopaths.[1]

And later,

The original Don Juan of the Spanish Golden Age is a believing Catholic, who has no doubt that repentance and forgiveness through the Church can save his soul: For that reason he can devote his youth to evil and repent sometime later. "You're giving me plenty of time to pay up!" ("que largo me lo fíais"), he mocks whomever urges him to repent and save his soul.[2]

But I WAS that sociopath. And I came to thoroughly understand that none of this was going to work out for me until I was changed into a new person from the inside out. I understood on that night of apostasy that no sacramental act without true contrition and a change of heart could save me—A change that I could by no means work up in myself. And I learned during that 3rd sickness on a night a year or two later that such repentance would not be available whenever I wanted it.

ARE WE THERE YET?

I am not sure if I crossed the line to salvation at this point in the story or not. I simply don't know. It would become perfectly clear soon enough.

---

1   Divine Justice, David P. Goldman, Tablet Magazine, October 31, 2011. (https://www.tabletmag.com/sections/arts-letters/articles/divine-justice)

2   Ibid

After we finished praying and going over the scriptures in the chapel, we went back to Bic's apartment and ate some Thai food. Then Bic asked me if I wanted to ride bikes around the lake. He had an extra bike, so I did. As we rode around the LSU lakes, I kept thinking to myself: "This is what normal people do. This is how they enjoy themselves. If I am really going to leave my entire life of sin behind, I need to learn how to do this kind of thing and enjoy it."

By the time we got back to Bic's apartment, the sun was going down and it was time to go to the XA meeting. At that time, it was held in that main central auditorium-style classroom in Coates Hall. I met a few people at the beginning of the meeting, many of whom I had already met at Crossfire. I spent some time talking to some of them and trying to explain my situation. One guy asked me "Have you been saved yet?" I kind of knew what he was talking about, but I thought to myself "that was a rather dramatic way to put it." For I didn't really have the concept of a decisive crisis in which you completely give yourself to God and are changed, and hence saved from yourself. At the time I had a more Catholic mindset, in which you started out as a Christian from birth and may sometimes live completely your own way for long periods of time. Sometimes, I thought, you may be seeking the Lord, and at other times you may be living your life as you want while attending to some basic religious duties. But I had begun to understand what needed to take place that afternoon in St. Albans, and I would be making my own decisive move in about a week and a half.

Gene Mills preached and there was a time of prayer. After that everyone went over to Gene's house on East Chimes Street[1]. There was a meal there like a party, maybe because it was the last

---

1   All the punk rockers and skateboarders were on West Chimes, on the other side of Highland road.

XA before Spring break, which was still always Easter week back then. That house was packed and everyone was having conversations about spiritual things late into the night. I did talk to a few people about what was going on with me concerning Satan and got some prayer. I especially spent a long time talking to a young man who was preparing to go to medical school, who I will call Jacob. Finally, Joel[1] gave me a ride home after midnight.

The next morning my parents asked me where I had been, and I told them I went to some meetings with the Jesus People. My father asked me why, and I told him "Because I don't want to go to Hell." He said something like "Oh no, your not going to Hell." But I think he knew full well where I was going and just responded this way because the directness of my answer took him by surprise, and he didn't know quite what to say.

But I knew I needed to do something soon. I had a lot of time to think about these things because in those days we used to get the entire week of Easter off of school.

The overwhelming thought that had dominated since that first night at Crossfire continued. "You must take care of this, you must completely repent and turn your life unreservedly over to Jesus now. This is THE last chance you will get!" I spent a lot of time on the front porch of our home thinking over what repentance would look like. The biggest obstacle was this—it just seemed to me that I was too lazy to survive any other way than through a life of crime.

SLOTH

Sloth was a major issue for me, for as I mentioned previously when that evaluation had noted the issue of "anhedonia," I have

---

1   The guy who saw the seven-headed snake in Chapter 19 about Bic

often felt like I was born lacking in crucial motivational chemicals such as Dopamine. I prayed a great deal on that porch about this. I sensed the Holy Spirit encouraging me to trust God for everything without reservation, to get me all the way through life. I especially needed to trust Him in changing my heart, regarding both sloth and all other sins.

To step outside the current scope a bit, this issue of sloth and distraction has continued to dog me throughout my life, even to the point of writing this book. Yet I can truly say that the Lord has gotten me through it all, even now in my fifties. He accomplished this in me through various means. In general, I have to continually beat myself every day to keep myself going. At work, for example, I have a spreadsheet that breaks up all my time into 15-minute intervals to keep me on focus. However this may feel on the inside, throughout my working life I have had co-workers tell me that they see me as an extraordinarily productive worker. One coworker even told me he was very envious of my ability to get things done.

More than anything else, though, God has gotten me through life by the power of the Holy Spirit. The Spirit is inside of me now and compels me, so that I have never taken any medicines for mental issues since that night I puked them all out in the 9th grade. In like manner the Holy Spirit has kept believers going throughout the centuries, as witnessed by Patrick also:

After I arrived in Ireland, I tended sheep every day, and I prayed frequently during the day. More and more the love of God increased, and my sense of awe before God. Faith grew, and my spirit was moved, so that in one day I would pray up to one hundred times, and at night perhaps the same. I even remained in the woods and on the mountain, and I would rise to pray before dawn in snow and ice and rain. I never felt the worse for it, and I never felt lazy—as I realise now, the spirit was burning in me at that time.[1]

RESOLUTION

During that Easter week of 1986, I several times fell back into the power of the demons and there would be ranting and raving. But also I would seek to pray to God. Satan just wouldn't give up the con. He changed his tune once again after that first time I went to Crossfire, now saying that it wasn't too late to get back into his kingdom. Glen Berteau was a problem for him, Satan said, and if I killed him, I could eventually get back into my old position— whereas I could never seriously believe that I could serve God. But this was no longer a one-way conversation. The Holy Spirit was also speaking into my heart. On that porch, I believe many strengths and weaknesses were noted, I was warned of many things, and also promised many things by the Spirit of God.

On April 2, the Wednesday after Easter, most of these issues had finally been resolved. By that afternoon, waiting for my ride to go back to Crossfire for the second time, I was determined to get "saved" that night as my new friends termed it. And what a ride it was. Crossfire had sent a guy I will call Sid to pick me up. Sid had been a notorious and vocal atheist at his high school and an out-of-control partier. He was a 1980s punk rocker but more like what would later be called a goth, because he wore all kinds of black eyeshadow and stuff. Don't let the eyeshadow fool you, because he was a big, masculine, Italian guy. He had been very powerfully saved some time previously through the witness of

---

1   Confession of St. Patrick

the campus club that Crossfire had at his high school. Before long he was a kind of protector and leader among the Christians at his high school and in Crossfire in general. Sid and I had a lot to talk about on the ride there.

I don't remember for certain what Glen Berteau preached that night, although I strongly suspect it was his personal testimony of how he himself had become a believer. All I knew was that I was determined to respond to the altar call at the end, for from talking to other people I had come to understand that this was the officially designated way to get saved. Satan continued to fight this and scream in my head and use every possible argument all the way through, even while—especially while—I was walking to the front.

A MOMENT OUTSIDE OF TIME

But I came to understand something very clearly at that moment, between the giving of the altar call and my prayers kneeling down up front. Like one of the dying characters in the 1980s movie "Repo Man", I had often considered society to be at fault for how I had turned out. Now I realized I was in a timeless moment completely outside of the normal course of events. There was Jesus Christ and his death on the cross, paying the price for all our sins. There was His resurrection from the dead, which vindicated all who believed and made it possible for us to be part of a whole new humanity. And nothing I had ever done, and nothing that had ever been done to me, and none of my abilities or disabilities, and nothing about my place in the society around me, high or low, mattered in the light of this. It was like I was removed outside of time and space into my own personal Garden of Eden, and the choice I made right there alone, to believe in and follow Jesus as

Lord or not, was the only thing that mattered and was the one and only thing that would set the course of my destiny.

Pushing through all the screaming in my head, I went to the front and kneeled down, and thus I prayed: "Jesus, I am a complete sinner, and I never want to think about or do anything other than to sin continually. Even now I don't seem to have a conscience left and cannot even feel sorry for my sins as I pray. But I have heard that you died on the cross to pay the price for our sins, that you rose from the dead to give us new life, and that you will give a completely new heart to those who believe in you. So even though I am who I am right now, I believe what you said, and I ask you to give me a new heart and turn me into a new person right now. And I will follow you for the rest of my life."

Right then and there Jesus Christ did give me a new heart. I shed a few tears for the first time since the night of that incident with my father many years ago. I cried out again and again at that altar, telling the Lord Jesus that I wanted to follow Him and serve Him all the days of my life and never turn back, and I asked Him for the strength to do so. In the following weeks as I prayed on my porch, I sensed Him warning me that I would, in fact, stumble and fall many times in the future, but He would pick me up and use me to do His will in the end.

Not many weeks later, Sid asked me when I was going to be baptized in the Holy Spirit. I asked him what that meant, and he told me it was an empowerment of the Holy Spirit that came upon believers that was accompanied with speaking in tongues. I told Sid that this must have already happened because I had already been speaking in tongues for weeks. For I did start speaking in tongues again, as I had when I was a child, not long after I dedicated my life to the Lord.

THE LINE IS CROSSED

I was baptized in water on the evening of Pentecost Sunday, May 18, 1986, in Jimmy Swaggart's church. The guy that was teaching us and preparing us for baptism was an older preacher associated with the ministry named Glenn Miller. Pastor Miller warned me, right before proceeding to baptism, that the unclean spirits I was dealing with previously would seek to come back and promise me all kinds of things, and that I must stand fast. This did, in fact, take place just as he said, little more than a month later in New Mexico.

That very same day on which I was baptized, Pope John Paul II issued his encyclical, *Dominum et Vivificantem* (the Lord and Giver of Life). Whatever disagreements I may have with Rome, concerning which I would soon have to make a final decision, for all that I can hardly find a better expression for what had recently happened to me than the first words of that encyclical:

> The Church professes her faith in the Holy Spirit as "the Lord, the giver of life." She professes this in the Creed which is called Nicene- Constantinopolitan from the name of the two Councils-of Nicaea (A.D. 325) and Constantinople (A.D. 381)-at which it was formulated or promulgated. It also contains the statement that the Holy Spirit "has spoken through the Prophets."
>
> These are words which the Church receives from the very source of her faith, Jesus Christ. In fact, according to the Gospel of John, the Holy Spirit is given to us with the new life, as Jesus foretells and promises on the great day of the Feast of Tabernacles: "If any one thirst let him come to me and drink. He who believeth in me as the scripture has said, 'Out of his heart shall flow rivers of living water.'" And the Evangelist explains:

"This he said about the Spirit, which those who believed in him were to receive." It is the same simile of water which Jesus uses in his conversation with the Samaritan woman, when he speaks of "a spring of water welling up to eternal life," and in his conversation with Nicodemus when he speaks of the need for a new birth "of water and the Holy Spirit" in order to "enter the kingdom of God." [1]

It was around that time, probably a few weeks before, that I was in my room trying to explain to my younger siblings what had happened. I was arrested by the Holy Spirit and told them "there is something I have to do now," and asked them to leave.

I put on my jacket, reached under my mattress, and pulled out the gun which I had gotten from Chuck the previous year. I hid it in my jacket and walked to the nearest canal, where I paused. I thought to myself, 'if you throw your gun in the canal, there is absolutely no going back. Your old life is over.' I would, in fact, remain unarmed for the next twenty-three years. I threw that gun in the canal and walked back home, having never felt so free in all my life.

---

[1]   Dominum et Vivificantem (the Lord and Giver of Life)

CHAPTER 22

THE NEW LIFE

Therefore, if anyone is in Christ, he is a new creation; old things have passed away; behold, all things have become new.

2 Corinthians 5:17

PENTECOST TO CHRISTMAS 1986

I have now answered, in one sense, the question I posed at the beginning of this book: "How is it that I was stopped and they [school shooters] were not?"—I was born again. But how was it that I came to give my life to Jesus? In that other sense the answer is beyond our ken, as it involves the mystery of free will. Our wills, however, are not entirely free—for if our will was 100% free, it would be impossible for a parent to spoil a child. Rather, we are caught up in both an overall miasma of sin and an interconnected web of choices, choices made previously both by ourselves and also by those all around us. And the choices of others impinged upon my own for good or ill, as they do for us all. Or as a relative of mine put it:

Having Bic and the Crossfire infrastructure right where you needed them at the right time certainly comes through. But why did that happen to be set up right when and where you needed it, including those girls introducing you to Bic almost as a joke? And why did you keep getting the strong promptings of the Holy Spirit and why did they breakthrough to your understanding? I personally think prayers really do matter. They are not futile. They make a difference. And I know [your mother] and [grand-mother], and probably many others were praying for you might-ily many times a day for years...My personal opinion is that these years and years of trust and perseverance in prayer has a lot to do with why you and not the others were stopped.

In those early days after I was born again, I simply could not believe my good fortune. Indeed, I wish I still saw and felt this great fact to the degree that I did back then. I was actually at peace with God. The war was over. God actually loved me, He cared for me, whom I considered to be the most despised person in all the earth. I was in a solid community of believers, experiencing real fellowship for the first time in my life. Every time I went to Crossfire on a Wednesday night, there were all kinds of people who were glad to meet me, and also at the other meetings that I will get to shortly.

OLD FRIENDS

One of the first things I did was go to my old friends to announce the change that had taken place. I went to Harry Robinson's house, where Dave also was that night. I did my best to explain to both of them what had happened, and that I wouldn't be par-ticipating in any crimes or sins anymore. Harry made a motion with his leg like he was kicking me in the rear. But I spent a lot of time visiting with them in those early days and preaching, or really teaching. What I would especially always go over is John 15, explaining the difference between just saying you believe in Jesus and actually following him. They all came to Crossfire with me at least once.

As time went on I started to lose contact with them. I didn't see Harry much more over the years but did hear of some drug busts he was involved in. He died weirdly in the hospital of some kind of heart attack in his forties—a consequence of his inordinate desire for big muscles. I had hoped Harry made his peace with God before he died, as he heard a lot both from me and the Christian school he attended after he was expelled from McKinley.

I recently heard that Harry did make it, for as Dave told me recently "Also note that in spite of his vanity, [Harry] had actually rededicated himself to the Lord, and was attending church with his fiancée regularly when he passed away." I think Johnny Slade died around the same time, although I hadn't been in contact with him for many years, since that summer of 1985 that I had been sequestered in Florida.

As for Dave, he came and found me in the late summer of 1991 when I returned from Washington DC. He told me he had given his life to Christ. He had been involved in some drug busts also and underwent a deep reevaluation of his life while spending some time in jail. I went with him a time or two to the rather unusual house church he was attending in those days. He is still alive and I do keep in touch with him sporadically, at least inviting him to Chinese New Year annually, to which he has often come. We had some great talks on the eve of finishing this book.

I also kept in touch with Chuck Forten in the first few years after I became a believer, calling him on the phone from time to time. This gradually fell off. The last time I saw him was at a combined High School Reunion for the classes of 1985-1987[1] that we had in 1995, not long after I was married. He died very mysteriously as I said, but I have only heard second hand.

Nathan was still incarcerated at the time I became a believer, but he was allowed regular phone calls at the mental hospital, and I was able to tell him what had happened on the phone. The first thing I told him was that "I have decided to leave the forces of evil and join the forces of good." He replied "Yeah, let's do it together." But on another phone call where I explained further, Nathan said "I thought you meant we were just going to go around doing good deeds, not all this religious stuff." Nathan had some ideas, typical of him, such as going to the Goodwill, buying a big stack of old coats, and going around and laying them in mud puddles for girls to cross in order to show chivalry. I can't quite remember when, but I think he was free again sometime not long after Christmas, or maybe earlier in order to give him a chance to finish High School. I spent a lot more time with Nathan than my other old friends, as we were always much closer, which I will get to in the final chapter.

CONTINUING BATTLES

One other person I was talking to about my new life was my probation officer. She was a hardcore Charismatic if ever there had been one and claimed some wild spiritual experiences. My case had gone through the Family Court system so slowly that I think I

---

1   This was the practice since we had a bunch of common experiences in the gifted program that were unique to these 3 classes. I was never informed of other ones except for a small gathering in San Francisco in 2005 for those of us living in the Bay Area at that time.

only saw her once before I was saved. The second time I saw her I told her I had been born again and on a later meeting I divulged to her my experiences with satanism. She told me that the first time we met she knew that I was demonized by looking at my eyes.

She continued that she had something like a vision the second time we met. She said she saw an image like a big stable in me that had one big empty pen in the middle and a bunch of smaller pens all around, but they were all empty. She added that now she understood what it meant, that the demons which had inhabited me had been driven out. And I was glad to have someone like this to talk to who somewhat understood my situation until my probation ended.

For though I was saved, there would be many severe battles to come as the demons sought to get back in. I prayed and fought them many times on my front porch, and I would see in my spirit a particularly big one looming over the situation. Sometimes I lost temporarily—either I would slip back through temptation into my self-induced altered states of consciousness, and/or the demons would temporarily overcome me and make some havoc—but only for very short periods of time, normally not more than an hour or two. I was mainly growing and getting stronger and learning constantly in those days, especially with the help of Bic, but many others also.

RESTITUTION

Constant stealing had become such a habit for me that when I became a believer, I found myself constantly taking things and then immediately returning them back. This was so I could go through the motions of my habit without actually committing the act, like a heavy smoker who has quit but keeps pulling a pencil up to his mouth and vicariously taking a whiff. This went on for some time until Bic wrote down a scripture that he said was for me and gave it to me: "Let him who stole steal no longer, but rather let him labor, working with his hands what is good, that he may have something to give him who has need." (Ephesians 4:28)

Now it dawned on me that I didn't have the resources, or even the memory, to make any real restitution for all the damage that I had caused around the city. I just did what I could do to the best of my knowledge at the time. Over several weeks I brought back all the books I had stolen from the library and classrooms, until my shelves at home were almost bare. I tried to give my younger siblings back as much money as I could due to some swindles when I 'auctioned' some items I had stolen. I threw away awards from contests I had cheated on such as the Alabama-Louisiana-Mississippi math exam, as I didn't really know what else to do. Years later I sent money to that kid I bullied the worst in the 8th grade. Hopefully it will somewhat mitigate that accounting that all bullies must give to every kid ever stuffed in a locker on the Day of Judgment, for as the Apostle said "...if we would judge ourselves, we would not be judged." (1 Corinthians 11:31) Beyond this I just tried to do something about the most egregious things whose location I could remember many years later, when I had money.

ROME

I had other issues to deal with and decisions to make very early on. The most pressing was whether to remain in the Church of Rome and, with my new life, fully embrace it. My assumption all along had been that once I made my peace with God, I would quickly reintegrate into the Roman Catholic Church where I belonged. But I had a major issue. It had been outside my church where I got a clearly understandable explanation of the Gospel, a full explanation of the depravity of man, and was shown a clear path to being born again which I obviously needed.

My solution was to dive ever deeper into studying my Bible to come to a decision about this. I had never bought into the idea that we should be wary of the 'private interpretation' of scripture. Rather, what I expected to find, as I had picked up from my family and especially my mother and grandmother, was that the Catholic position would be confirmed as I really studied the Bible. So I began reading as diligently as I could my official Catholic Bible that I had gotten on my Confirmation.

What I found there was not just proof texts but rather, that the inner logic of the Gospel as then presented by Evangelicals was found throughout the entire warp and woof of the Bible, from Genesis to Revelation. This established for me the absolute supremacy of the Word of God above all other possible authority. This did not mean that traditions were bad, or should be avoided, or even that they should not be clung to for dear life in some circumstances, especially when godly traditions were precious to people who had passed through persecution. For in the modern American church, especially after the 1970s, opposition to 'tradition' has itself become a kind of tradition—one that in many ways has run its course and may no longer be helpful. The point is only that the Word of God had to come first and be the judge of all things.

I continued to pray and read and, in the end, upon reading Galatians one more time, I came to the conclusion that I had to leave the Church of Rome. Further discussion beyond this is outside the scope of this book. But this decision was one of the most difficult things I had to tell my family, especially Grandma.

AN ILLUMINATING JOURNEY WEST

Around the time I made my decision concerning Rome, my family made a big road trip out west, toward Yellowstone. It was also a spiritual journey for me. For on that long road trip in a Suburban, I was able to read the whole Bible through in a relatively short period of time, giving me a newer level of insight into how it all fit together.

Secondly, right before I left for this trip, Jimmy Swaggart had invited an author named Dave Hunt on his "Study in the Word' radio show. For about a week they discussed Hunt's new book, "The Seduction of Christianity." When we stopped in Spearfish, South Dakota, to see a famous passion play, I walked into a Christian bookstore. I had a great talk with the lady in there about this book, as I sometimes similarly did together with Bic at the local Christian bookstore that was still on Chimes Street back home. For in those days, before everything was online, the Christian bookstore was often a great place for fellowship and discussion. I purchased this book and also read it through on this trip, and it had a mostly good influence on my thinking. For while Hunt would occasionally go too far on some things, I think reading this early on kept me out of a lot of teachings within the overall Charismatic movement that would have been bad for me.

A third important event which took place on that trip was that somewhere out West I visited a place called the 'Genesis and Geology Museum.' This introduced me to the concept of Recent Creation and thus broke the power of allegorical thinking over my understanding of scripture. This was a crucial breakthrough in my understanding of Biblical doctrine. We often use the word 'literal' in contrast to a more conceptual or allegorical understanding of what the Bible is conveying to us, not because 'literal' is exactly what we mean, but because it is the best word we have. We really mean that the Bible is communicating factually true content in the normal, straightforward way the language would have been understood by the speakers at the time.

Many believe that moving from this understanding of the Bible as a factual, straightforward account, to a more conceptual message of universal truths is an advance in true understanding. What I learned in the summer of 1986 is that the opposite is true.

My previous understanding of large parts of the Bible presenting a notionally true message, while not necessarily being factually correct, could be compared to the vague notions of atomism that had existed ever since Democritus in the 5th century BC. When I advanced to a more straightforward, factual understanding of the Bible, it was comparable to the advance that took place when, for example, scientists actually got down to the business of defining how many molecules were in a mole, or what the actual charge and mass of an electron were. Now actual technological advances could take place. In the same way, my exposure to a believable account of Recent Creation on that trip led to a mighty advance of my understanding of the faith, and my ability to hold onto it intact.

I can give three main reasons for this, among many. First, a cursory reading of Romans 5 and 1 Corinthians 15 quickly reveals that the atoning death and resurrection of Christ can have no serious meaning, that there indeed can be no Gospel, without a literal Adam and Eve.

Secondly, because the way of interpreting scripture that we learn from Jesus and the Apostles only works if the inspiration of scripture extends to such verbal details as:

- The tense of the verb (Matthew 22:32, John 8:58)
- A noun being singular or plural (Galatians 3:16)
- The actual letters of the words (Matthew 5:18)

Thirdly, because an allegorical, big picture conception of the message of the Bible is a wax nose that can be easily assimilated into whatever the prevailing worldview of the day may be. In our day that may be Progressivism, in previous times or places the Divine Right of kings or National Socialism. In contrast, a straightforward, factual understanding of the Bible is simply indigestible—it will not fit into anyone else's system. Such a faith can thus withstand whatever enzymes or acids the prevailing philosophies of the day throw at it and outlast all the lies in the end. And so I returned from my trip that summer greatly strengthened in my faith.

SPIRITUAL INFRASTRUCTURE

Life seemed like heaven on earth in those halcyon days after my salvation. The Crossfire youth ministry and the overall movement had a great deal going for it in those days—much more than the preaching of one man or the one-on-one witness of individuals. In addition to the Wednesday night meetings, there were Friday night "Fellowship Group" meetings held throughout the city where youth worshipped, encouraged each other, and were exhorted to serve the Lord ever more fervently. There were the visitation teams that went out on Saturdays and followed up on people who attended Crossfire, exhorting and praying with them for salvation and encouraging them to come back. There were campus clubs meeting throughout the week in high schools all over town, where more encouragement and collective witness took place.

It was the collective nature of this witness that was so powerful. For I am convinced that without this community aspect of the revival, where so many people were involved exhorting us and holding us together, I would have never gotten saved and would never have lasted if I did.

The leader of my Fellowship Group was a Bible College student from Minnesota and one of the muscular young men. He was tough and mustachioed and resembled Sargeant Slaughter as he exhorted us week after week to give our all to Jesus and serve Him with all our heart. His assistant was equally muscular although perhaps not as tough and, in fact, had a real soft spot for us all. There were others in our Fellowship Group who were on staff at the ministry and provided even more spiritual ballast.

Besides all this, several people involved in the XA campus ministry were also involved in the Crossfire youth ministry, bringing in even more spiritual firepower. XA also had the Tuesday night XA Bible studies at Gene's house, where it was easy to bring the punk rockers from high school and more good teaching and spiritual support could be received.

My point is that all this spiritual infrastructure and collective effort mattered deeply and made everything possible. There were many of us who had come from such difficult backgrounds that they were constantly backsliding and wavering and had to be pulled back in. There were my continuing problems with the demons trying to get back in, although in my case most other Christians did not understand, so I primarily relied upon Bic. Without all this spiritual infrastructure, I think myself and many others could have easily fell through the cracks. Many still did in spite of it all, which just goes to show as the Apostle said that "We must through many tribulations enter the kingdom of God." (Acts 14:22)

But not everyone gets all this support. In fact, few ever do. Who gets to load up their ministry ground force with Bible College students from all over the nation eager to make a spiritual impact? To fight to create and sustain and protect such a spiritual infrastructure is to fight for the souls of men. And in a short while

I would be meeting a man who was committed to build this in places where it did not exist, almost out of thin air.

One more thing I have to say about this spiritual force was that it was deployed with great effectiveness. I spoke in the last chapter of a young guy I called Jacob who was preparing for medical school. I had originally met and talked to him for quite some time at Gene's house after that first night at XA. For a time he took a special interest in me, and within weeks of my salvation, in the midst of discipling me, he was also constantly pointing out to me new people who were coming in. He would be telling me "see where that guy is at", "talk to him about the Lord," "try to get him plugged in," and the like. He was also asking me to constantly follow up on anyone who seemed to be drifting in any way and trying to find out why. Another Bible College student was giving us all rides and constantly focusing on making sure I made it through. For there was a constant state of watchfulness over each other and everyone around us that pervaded the entire ministry culture in those days.

This was extremely important due to the difficult backgrounds of so many who were getting saved in those days. How much more would this be true today! I wish to God we could have kept that momentum and continued to carry out those principles of discipleship, but severe blows, first to myself and then to the ministry as a whole, were about to come. I wish even more that I could see this duplicated in churches and ministries of our current day, for very few of the last two generations after ours seem to have ever experienced such a thing or had such benefits—and it shows.

All that summer it continued to be glorious. Crossfire had a youth camp and it was one of the most spiritually moving experiences I have ever been involved in. I often wondered what heaven would be like when apparently our struggles and wars would be over, and how things could just go on like that, seemingly ending history or any real activity itself.

But one night at that camp there was such a powerful move of the spirit that youth could be seen singing, dancing, and worshiping the Lord, alone or in groups, spread out from the chapel all the way out to the woods and in even in them. It seems like this went on until past midnight. It occurred to me that this is the way things were supposed to be, the true normality, and so I should not be surprised if this is what eternity would mostly be like.

I learned from Bic and Crossfire as a whole to vigorously study my Bible and also to get up very early in the morning to pray. There were, in fact, many mornings when it seemed like I could see a hand coming down to wake me up and pray. Crossfire broke down the basics of the Christian life into 3 main principles above all: Read your Bible, pray, and be a witness of the Gospel to other people.

When I returned to my Senior Year in High School that August, I was eager to be a witness. There were only a few of us at McKinley, so we didn't have a much of a campus club like some of the other high schools. We were kicked out of the library after briefly trying to meet in one of the rooms there, and so began meeting at a kind of alcove in front of a home economics lab that was no longer used. From there we did all we could to reach people, a few times successfully and several times ridiculously.

Finally, the Christmas holiday came and it seemed to cap the whole experience for me. I was listening to Christian radio all I could in those days, and especially Swaggart's daily show with a panel of guests called 'A Study in the Word.' All that Christmas break the topic was the "call of God", and one preacher after another would give their account of how they were called into the ministry. As I listened, I became certain that I was so called also. But I was about to face the most severe trial of my Christian life until this day.

CHAPTER 23

THE PERILOUS ROAD TO NORMALCY

For thus says the Lord to the men of Judah and Jerusalem: "Break up your fallow ground, And do not sow among thorns. Circumcise yourselves to the Lord, And take away the foreskins of your hearts...

Jeremiah 4:3-4a

JANUARY TO EASTER 1987

Several things were going on my last year of High School. First of all, after all the failing that had taken place the previous year during my descent into darkness, I needed a plan to actually graduate. As far as my schoolwork was concerned, I think the enormity of the change that had taken place can best be illustrated by the back-to-back comparison of my Junior year grades to Senior year grades below.

I had of course gotten saved in the second semester of my junior year, but that was after Easter, way too late to recover. But the improvement in going from an F student in 11th grade to a B student in the 12th gave me a lot of sympathy with all my teachers and the school authorities. I was going to need every bit of that

245

sympathy, because to graduate on time took a lot of finagling on their part. By the time this was all stitched together I was able to just squeeze by, graduating from High School with the absolute minimum number of credits and a perfect 2.0.

Having started my new life, there was another dilemma I faced, which I had considered ever since that bike ride around the lakes with Bic. How would I now live as a normal person. How would I engage in normal conversations, when I didn't know what to say and it was so unnatural to me. I then remembered a scene from a movie of the time that hit me like a lightning bolt of inspiration. The movie was "The Terminator", and the scene was when the Terminator was sitting in his apartment with his fake flesh rotting off. His landlord is banging on the door saying, "What do you have in there, a dead cat?!?" The movie then tries to show what is going on in the mind of the Terminator by showing some kind of 1980s computer screen with various choices of how to reply. The cursor moves to one of the choices which the Terminator then verbalizes, which is "F____ Off!"

And there was my solution. I could just use my brain to put words and phrases together and make conversation, even if it was not natural or didn't quite make sense—such as "How do you feel about Big Ben?" I supposed I would just do it until it became natural. Thus inspired by the Terminator, I thought I was well on my way to becoming a sparkling conversationalist.

But in reality I was nowhere near as normal as I now thought I was. I did not know how to interact with people or many aspects of how life actually worked. Yet I was in some ways thrust into a kind of leadership position simply because the story of what had happened to me, the Satanist who had converted to Christ, was so dramatic. This would put me on the forefront of getting up in public settings and sharing my testimony in order to win other people for Christ. The drama of my story even reached the Religion pages of our local newspaper when it did a full feature article on Crossfire[1]. In some ways this actually helped speed up my entry into normal human life by forcing the issue. But in many other ways it was something I was not really ready for.

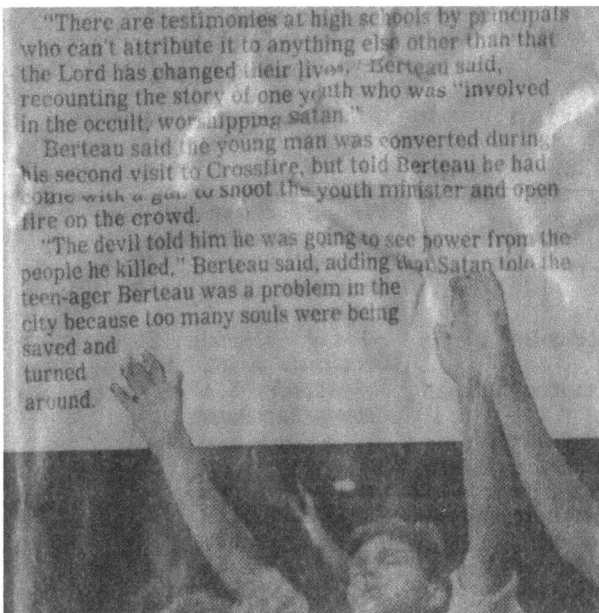

> "There are testimonies at high schools by principals who can't attribute it to anything else other than that the Lord has changed their lives," Berteau said, recounting the story of one youth who was "involved in the occult, worshipping Satan."
>
> Berteau said the young man was converted during his second visit to Crossfire, but told Berteau he had come with a gun to shoot the youth minister and open fire on the crowd.
>
> "The devil told him he was going to see power from the people he killed," Berteau said, adding that Satan told the teen-ager Berteau was a problem in the city because too many souls were being saved and turned around.

---

1 I did not bring a gun on my second visit to Crossfire—by that time I was determined to get saved. But things got conflated as did my best to explain to Glen what was happening between my two visits.

SWEPT AND PUT IN ORDER

There was another way in which I was not normal yet. After I was saved and the unclean spirits were cast out, there was a period of time when they would fight to get back in. I would occasionally lose these fights for a brief season. This could not go on for more than 48 hours or I would not survive, so in some ways this reality kept me seeking God and on the straight and narrow. But when I did succumb this could involve the sin of worshipping the Devil again, though as under compulsion.

I desperately needed the forgiveness of the Lord in those days in order to quickly bounce back—as the Apostle had said "For sin shall not have dominion over you, for you are not under law but under grace." (Romans 6:14). Those times when I could not fight my way back out on my own, I often needed other people, especially Bic, to pray me out. One such attack came on me in the shower one night that was so severe that I almost started biting off my own flesh. But then it inexplicably broke off of me almost instantly without a battle and without a trace. The next morning when I was at church, someone suddenly pointed to me and said "that's him!" This was a lady and her daughter, who explained that her daughter had seen me in a dream and was told to start praying for me at the time the attack suddenly broke off.

There were three main avenues that would occasionally cause these relapses. First, the Heavy Metal songs that had so thoroughly marinated my thoughts over the previous years would come crashing into my mind. Perhaps this was not that different from some advertising jingle you can't get out of your head. But with these songs came my old thought processes, and riding on them, the unclean spirits trying to bring me back into their world. Very closely related to this were the old do-it-yourself methods

I had developed to go into altered states of consciousness, no longer deliberate 'methods' now but just states I could fall into under pressure.

But above all, such stumbles would be instigated by despair. When I saw some area of my life where I wasn't handling things well, or there was some fall into sin, I would project this out into the future to the point that I could not see myself living a life pleasing to God, or even making it to heaven, over the long haul. Then the unclean spirits would come back with all their temptations. And now I was about to face the severest trial I would face as a Christian, even to this day.

INFATUATION

When I describe how this began you may think I am being melodramatic to call this a 'severe trial.' Around that Christmas of 1986, I began to have very strong feelings for Genifer, the young lady who had originally given me the "shocking greeting" in Chapter 18. I talked to her concerning this around New Year's Eve and got an unambiguous no. My feelings continued to grow ever more intense and, with the rejection, drove me to distraction. For I have always been a passionate man in this area, and had not yet learned to handle it normally. In fact, because I had spent my entire life until then suppressing such feelings with all my might, it came back at me with all the more fury.

This became all the worse because we were in English class together where we were reading, discussing, and watching a movie of "The Great Gatsby." And the haunting song of that movie was constantly playing in my head and amplifying all my passionate feelings. I degenerated in many ways and became a bad witness for everyone, especially Nathan. The only mitigating factor at all was that the intensity of the feelings grew to the point of eliminating all physical lust, so that I no longer had to battle this at all, as parts of my mind and body were overwhelmed with the intensity of the infatuation and shut down.

This reached a peak one Friday night at the weekly Fellowship Group. I had come to a point in my desolation and passionate rage that I felt I had been cut off from the life of God and would soon be wandering off into the outer darkness. The half hour of worship that began the meeting was the most heavenly I had ever seen since that summer camp, as I looked at all the faces singing, utterly lost in the wonder and rapture of God's glory. This only increased my desolation and despair, and as soon as the meeting was over, I went out to the porch instead of immediately leaving because I may have been waiting for Nathan and may even have called him from that house[1].

Out there the unclean spirits were running wild with me and the Fellowship Group leader came out with his assistant and some other guys and asked me what in the world was going on. Not long into the confrontation I roared at them with a voice not my own, shouted that Ralph was gone and wasn't coming back, and then lunged at them and attacked. A group of them soon had me tackled to the ground and everyone was praying as hard as they could, in tongues or English. After more praying, I came to and stopped struggling. The fellowship group leader and some other guys counseled and prayed things through with me, while his assistant stood by, simultaneously standing tense and at the ready to jump in if needed, while also weeping and praying in tongues to himself over my soul. And things were made right that night and everything was restored for the time.

---

1   No cells phones back then, if I called him I had to sneak in a phone call from a landline.

FIGHTING TO LIVE

But it turned out that this incident was only a local maximum[1] of what was happening in my life, and the worst was yet to come. This happened in my room at home. I was sitting up and reading my Bible on my bed. I think I either just had blue jeans on with no shirt or my shirt soon got torn to pieces in the midst of what happened. An image of deep desolation at being rejected by Genifer forced its way into my mind. Besides the despairing thoughts, it was like a serum of whatever produces depression and rejection and despair in our mind and body, concentrated many thousands of times, was instantly injected into my bloodstream. And it was intense.

I rolled over face down on my bed, and my spine began to curl backwards as if I was being electrically shocked. I felt like I could barely breath and was gasping for air. When a person feels suicidal, they may ask themselves how many days can they go on, but I was soon counting how long I thought I could last in seconds. There was an overwhelming desire to grab a knife out of my desk, the desk I am sitting at now as I write, and plunge it through the soft spot below my ear. For in the absence of a firearm, that was the quickest and most certain method I could come up with.

Yet in another sense, I was determined not to kill myself. Writhing on the bed, I was counting to myself to try and extend how long I could last, and with one hand I was holding down the other hand with all my strength. I felt like I needed some kind of discharge, like a lightening rod, otherwise the intensity of despair I was feeling seemed like it would burn me to a crisp. So instead of my knife I took a razor blade out of my drawer and started

---

1   This is a calculus term, just means a local peak that is not the biggest peak around.

slashing my chest and my abdomen—not really for the purpose of self-harm but to try and create a distraction and discharge long enough to save my life, as I thought. This did some damage that marks my body to this day, as my body is marked by other sins. Yet nowhere near enough, it was as if this distraction was drawing off just a few amps when I needed it to draw hundreds. In just a minute or two more I would get the discharge I was looking for. But it happened in a most abominable and excretable manner, in a way that would have brought on the death penalty under the Torah. Yet for all that it may have saved my life and my soul.

AN ABOMINATION OF DESOLATION

For at that moment, for some unknown reason, Mom burst through the door and started yelling at me about something. Immediately I leaped for the drawer, pulled out my knife, and was after her. I chased her through the house, smashing a hole in the wall, until at some point Dad came out and started asking me what in the world I was doing. At that moment I threw the knife away from me, fell face down to the floor, and started weeping.

After some time Dad got me up, we both sat down in the den, and slowly began to talk. "What is going on, son?" he asked. "I like a girl" I answered. "I see," Dad said after some pause, "That is not a light or frivolous thing at all. People actually kill themselves over rejected love all the time. As you know, I myself almost killed everyone I loved not that many years ago." "I remember that," I said, and we continued to talk, although I can't remember the rest. But we understood each other. He thought a retreat with some Catholic monks where you remain silent the whole time would help, but I didn't think that was the way to go. I knew I had to overcome, and I had an idea of how which I would begin to execute shortly.

Now I am sure, if I have not completely lost you yet, that you have the same question that I had for many years after this. What in tarnation was going on?!? After many years of reflection, I think I know.

Sometimes when people ask me how it is that God allows Satan to make such havoc in the world, I will begin by saying "because Satan is a really good lawyer." While we see something like real open warfare in Daniel 10, for example, this is by no means unrestricted warfare. We see in the opening chapters of Job that there is a real protocol between God and Satan, which the Almighty maintains complete control of, while nevertheless allowing Satan to make his case. Satan operates by accusing us before God continually and making the case that God, if He is truly just, will allow him to prove how fake we really are. This is what happened behind the scenes when, after Peter's repeated boasting "...the Lord said, "Simon, Simon! Indeed, Satan has asked for you, that he may sift you as wheat. But I have prayed for you, that your faith should not fail; and when you have returned to Me, strengthen your brethren." (Luke 22:31-32)

There is good reason to believe that this process often takes place, not only in the case of a mighty apostle like Peter, but also in the lives of ordinary believers like you and me—more than we know. For when Revelation depicts Satan finally losing his access to heaven it is said "...the accuser of our brethren, who accused them before our God day and night, has been cast down." (Revelation 12:10b)

This is what I suspect must have happened that night. You will recall that when I originally gave myself over to Satan, the offer he made was to bring me to a place of no longer being attracted to women, so as not to experience rejection. While I would claim that he did not do a good job of helping me achieve this, he would say that this was my fault for not taking action to move with his

253

program. However that may be, I imagine Satan's challenge to God must have been something like this: Since Jesus had allowed me to leave my allegiance to Satan and broke his power over me, when I did not deserve this mercy at all, then at the very least Satan should be allowed to give me a full dose of that which he originally promised to protect me from.

This is what I think happened that night. Satan was of course enraged at Genifer for all that had happened, and so he wanted to make her a part of all this. And if he could also pull my mother into it, who had prayed for me all my life—well, that to him would be a royal flush.

A GENUINE STRUGGLE

This was a difficult episode of my life to speak of. Of course, the majority of the life I have described so far was shameful, but this episode was far worse because it happened after I was delivered and born again—and so really should not have happened at all. But as much as I would have liked to ignore this, I share it for two reasons.

First of all, there is a lesson from this that I think the Church as a whole needs to understand. As American society continues to degenerate, more of the people we reach will have very substantial problems that will require a great deal of work to overcome. I believe the days of simply getting people to say a prayer and chalking up 'Decisions for Christ', if this ever had any validity, are now over. We are going to have to work together as a community, or a few strong Christians are going to get very exhausted, while some weaker ones are going to fall through the cracks. There will also need to be a commitment to real spiritual warfare, as potentially exhausting as that sounds to all of us.

Secondly, some of you may be reading this book who have

either had things done to you or made some very harmful decisions that have put you in a really bad place. You may perhaps even think that there is no way back. I thanked God in Chapter 6 that I was born when I was and not more recently. But you were born in the time that you were. Whatever situation you find yourself in, there is still hope of God's total transformation. This indeed begins when you call on the name of the Lord Jesus Christ for salvation and forgiveness, and to give your life to Him without reservation, trusting Him to transform you from the inside out. This is the most important decision you will ever make.

But this begins from the inside, in the inner recesses of your spirit. From there it flows out over time to change everything, mind and body. This process can involve a whole lifetime of struggle, as it has for me in certain areas. Yet through perseverance there will be breakthroughs that you never thought possible, and in the end, eternal life.

Finally, I spoke of coming very close to suicide. I don't want to say anything that could weaken your God-given sense that suicide will lead you to almost certain eternal damnation. I myself have, I believe, truly, eternally lost some people that were once very close to me. And yet for all of this, I still want to say a few things to put the whole phenomenon in context. The Western church got its teaching on suicide primarily from Augustine, I suspect from a chapter in the *City of God*. There he was speaking of the famous suicide of Lucretia after her rape by Tarquin the Proud, the last king of the early Romans. This event was much celebrated by the Romans because Lucretia's demand for vindication, immediately before she killed herself, led them to overthrow the Tarquins and establish the old Roman Republic.

The original context, which led Augustine to comment on this old story, was the mass rape and hauling off into sexual slavery of

Christian women at the time Rome was sacked by the Visigoths. Some pagans were leveling the accusation that God had failed to protect them from this. Augustine's rejoinder was that nothing that was done to the body externally and unwillingly could ultimately deface the soul, and from there he went into his devastating critique of the whole tale of Lucretia, arguing not only that there was no need for suicide but that it was a fundamentally unjust act.

As valuable as this understanding provided by that great doctor of the church is, I think it captures the nature of some but not all suicides. For the whole argument works by describing suicide as a kind of premediated and planned act intended to achieve certain ends, as in a first-degree murder. As such it involves such things as deliberate selfishness, a lack of faith and willingness to trust God, and the like. While I agree that these elements are always present, I think the nature of the sin in many cases is more like falling into something like masturbation or drugs than a premeditated murder. It is still a heinous act, but often occurs when someone knows it is no solution, that is the wrong thing to do, but nevertheless gives in to sudden and overwhelming pressure through a momentary failure of the will rather than through a planned, deliberate act. It is best to warn people severely and yet ultimately wait to see how the Judge of all the earth will handle each individual case without any assumptions.

STRATEGIC WITHDRAWAL

Meanwhile, as I was slowly recovering from all this, the Crossfire ministry under Glen Berteau was reaching its peak. It was hitting over a 1000 young people each Wednesday night, and I remember some services near the end of that school year where God just took over the whole thing. These were moves of the Holy Spirit where immediately after the worship was finished, or in the middle of it, youth would start spontaneously breaking off in groups all over the auditorium praying and preaching to each other, with many getting saved or healed or released from various afflictions. And this would go on until it was time for the meeting to break up with no announcements or preaching or anything except Glen getting up and giving a few words.

Yet I was mostly moving to the outside now, for I was convinced that I needed to create and enforce my own restraining order. On one occasion near the end of the school year I must have taken the city bus as close as I could get and then started walking to Crossfire. Glen was driving in, saw me and picked me up. "Have you gotten your emotions under control?" he asked me. I told him I thought I had, and we talked some more. But I knew that whenever I saw Genifer my feelings were not under control. I understood that to really pull out of the situation I needed to not see her and really needed to do my best to avoid beholding *any* life-threatening beauty that may pull me into the same kind of situation with someone else.

This meant I was going to have to pull out of Crossfire, and gradually even out of the Fellowship Group. This was already the plan I had in mind that terrible bloody night when I was talking over what I should do with Dad. I was going to have to sustain my faith without all the supports I previously had. I didn't know exactly how this would work or what it would look like, but I knew it would be like Ishmael wandering off to his place in the wilderness where he met God.

Before I did this, I wanted to try my chances with Genifer one last time. The Friday before the Easter break in 1987, I woke up late and missed the bus. I was so compelled to try one more time that I walked all the way to school, which took more than three hours. It would have taken even longer if a kindly older man who was fishing had not agreed to ferry me across the pond on the other side of the LSU lakes, taking considerable time off my journey. I arrived around lunchtime. I found Genifer, poured out my heart one more time, and once more got an unambiguous no. I wish I could say that finally ended the matter, but that is not what happened.

While I did mostly pull out, I continued to operate under the delusion that if I just patiently waited from the distance things would eventually work out with her. With the exception of a strange interlude in the Fall of 1991, this foolishness went on for the next 5 years!! The delusion continued because I was regularly conned into believing the Spirit of God was telling me we would eventually be married. Therefore, while I mostly stayed away, I called once a year on her birthday, or maybe twice a year. Finally, via a rather weird intervention from Gene Mills, this finally, mercifully, came to an end in 1992!

A NEW HORIZON

All that was still off in the distance, however. At that time, after the Friday conversation with Genifer, I really thought I was done with this whole matter. I would execute my plan of pulling out, not knowing where I would land. I figured a good first step would be to return to the Tuesday night Bible study at Gene's house that I had not attended in some time, since it involved a whole other group of people not associated much with Genifer. After church on Psalm Sunday, I talked to a Bible College student who used to go to the Tuesday night Bible study. I told her that though I hadn't been at there for a long time, I intended to go back next week. She told me she didn't go there anymore, because on Tuesdays she was involved in a different ministry now. Every Tuesday and Sunday night, she continued, she was going with a ministry team to the Louisiana Training Institute (LTI), which was the juvenile prison.

I instantly realized that this was also exactly what I needed to do, for several reasons. First of all, it was taking me far away from my prior associations to a whole new group of people, where I could completely forget about Genifer. Secondly, there would be no women in that prison at all (worship team excepted). Thirdly, I knew that I owed something to LTI, for I had greatly feared ending up there throughout my earlier life and yet had never gotten caught in something serious enough to land me there. Finally, I knew that the proper way out of the desolation I was feeling was to minister to other people, and the greater the need and the worse the circumstances, the better. In short, I knew that this was exactly what God would have me do. The Bible College student told me when and where to meet, in the lobby of the Bible College dormitory, to go there on Tuesday and Sunday nights.

I went for the first time that Tuesday, and the next time on Easter Sunday, where we had an Easter meal for the prisoners afterwards. Now I was all in. This was one of the most providential things that happened in all my Christian life, for out of the ashes of defeat I would soon be meeting a man that I would be associated with in ministry for many years throughout my Christian life, for a season even all over the world.

CHAPTER 24

A MAN OF STEEL

For behold, I have made you this day A fortified city and an iron pillar,
And bronze walls against the whole land

Jeremiah 1:18a

EASTER TO CHRISTMAS 1987

I began going to the LTI ministry right before Easter[1] of 1987, slightly over a year after I had been saved. There I met George Neau, who was leading that ministry to the juvenile prison. He has been the President or Chancellor of SUM Bible College and Theological Seminary for more than 30 years now. But at that time he was 26 years old and still a Bible college student himself. I think his students now would be surprised to know that the whole SUM began as a practicum, but as one thing leads to another, that is essentially what happened.

George was from Racine, between Milwaukee and Chicago. He had grown up in very difficult circumstances, with his father finally putting a pistol to his head committing suicide dying in his

---

1   April 19, 1987

arms. As his mother cried herself to sleep night after night for all the desolation that had been brought down on their family, he was driven into rage, a life of rock and roll, street fights and terrible sins whose guilt drove him to distraction until the day he found total peace in Christ As he passed through these grueling experiences, adrenaline coursed through his body and changed and shaped him to the point it seemed he could not live without it. For whenever things calmed down and became peaceful it would seem that he was bouncing off the walls and had to go off on some new venture. Yet this first characteristic of his, this constant seeking of new horizons, was the very thing that would shape George into the implement that God wanted him to be and to build the things that God wanted him to build.

Neau played in a rock band and went to a conservatory in Milwaukee for season, for he loved his music and his guitar and poured all his heart and soul into it. But God had other plans. While studying at the Conservatory with his new found faith, he still had the restlessness deep in his heart, that there was something deeper happening within. It was then that he realized that God was calling him into the ministry. As he considered what to do, the one place that seemed affordable and ready to take him was the newly started Jimmy Swaggart Bible College. And so Neau came to Baton Rouge.

But things were still difficult for him. All his dark past lay upon him as he entered Bible college, and he continued to wrestle with the financial pressure which he lived under since his father's death. It sometimes seemed that not a single person there believed that he would last beyond his first year. But by the time I met him, this was all behind and he was wrapping up his time as a student. In the meantime, Neau was supporting himself by working as a mechanic in the garage at Jimmy Swaggart Ministries, as the ministry had many vehicles that needed to keep running. In particular, there was an extensive bus ministry.

Neau had started going to LTI with another man who had asked him to help out there, and after some time this man left and turned the ministry over to Neau. I believe that when this prison ministry began it was a simple visitation ministry. This was an occasion for George to express another characteristic of his—that he would follow up on people relentlessly. He began with one young prisoner who he continuously spent time with every time he went there, and when this young man was released, George took him into his home and then later would also visit him when he moved back to New Orleans. Building on that one young man, George would evangelize and then disciple relentlessly one young man in that prison after another.

These two characteristics of Neau's combined to make a third. I spoke previously of the whole infrastructure that stood behind the Crossfire youth ministry and how effectively it was deployed. George was ever mindful that not everyone had access to this spiritual and ministry infrastructure. This was a fact that ever drove him and still does to this day. And he was committed to do whatever it took to build this in places where it did not exist. There was an unused dormitory on the campus of the juvenile prison that had fallen into dilapidation. Neau told the LTI administration that he would renovate that building himself if they would allow him to use it as a chapel. The prison took him up on the offer. For a season, he worked on that building all by himself, night after night, until he was able to put out an appeal during some of the Sunday night services for a group of men to help him with this project.

Soon the whole building, upstairs and downstairs, was ready to use as a chapel, and the ministry consisted of powerful worship services with altar calls in that chapel rather than just personal visitation. George already had a faithful team of Bible College students by this time. During the Summer of 1987 this had whittled down to almost no one but George and I, and for much of the time, a faithful keyboard player and his wife. Around that time Neau had officially been designated an assistant chaplain, and this gave him the ability to walk the yards throughout the day. By the time the summer was over he had turned the LTI ministry into an official practicum of the Bible college and had a larger stream of student workers.

George was not a perfect man, for he had major anger issues that could cause problems for everyone trying to work with him. He could also be prone at times to an almost titanic pride. But even these things were greatly mitigated and brought under control by a fourth characteristic that he had, for whatever he struggled with on the outside, including constant financial struggles in those early days, George deeply desired to walk with God. Like Glen Berteau, he was always a resolute believer in and advocate of Divine Healing, based on a providential healing he had experienced earlier in life. In all of this can be seen the principle that our entire personality, as shaped by nature and experience, is the package that the Almighty uses to accomplish His will through us.

AN EXISTENTIAL GRADUATION

Meanwhile, when I first began going out to LTI, I had just a about a month left of high school. About a week before I would graduate, I was sitting on a chair in our den reading something when a newspaper came plopping down on top of whatever I was reading. Mom had dropped it and said something to the effect of "You are about to graduate, and if you think you are going to just continue to live here off of us without working, you've got another thing coming. You can see right here in this newspaper that there is a job fair on Saturday in the lobby of this hotel, and you had better be there if you want to continue to live in this house."[1] So I went and applied and started my first day of work at Popeye's Fried Chicken that Monday. My high school graduation ceremony was the following day, on Tuesday[2].

For me that graduation was surreal, what my niece would call existential. For before I was saved, I had reached the point where I didn't really expect to live this long. Yet here I was, on the threshold of a whole life that I had not genuinely envisioned. It is true that after I became a believer, I had all kinds of visions of the future, especially that previous Christmas when I so believed that I was called to the ministry. But on that night, the whole experience of the last five months had all but erased those dreams from my mind. As we poured out of our graduation ceremony, held in the Centroplex[3], I felt like a ghost haunting the streets of Baton Rouge. I had memories of the place but didn't feel like I was really there anymore. It was almost as if I was already gone, just a ghostly phantom watching the world continue to go on in my absence. And I suppose that any potential mass shooter, granted the option to live an entire counterfactual history as I was, would feel similarly.

But what I was really feeling was the sensation of finally putting an old life, my youth, behind and starting on a whole new journey. Nothing would ever be the same. The first decision I had to

---

1   My mother never actually asked for any money from me, she was just trying to get me started.

2   May 19, 1987

3   Now the River Center

make was about joining the military. I had attracted their interest, especially the Marines, because I got every question correct on an aptitude test that they used, called the ASVAB. But as I talked to the recruiter and a young man he sent me home with, an overwhelming sense fell upon me that I was resisting God and that He did not want me to do this. This was very hard for me to understand, because I know that God has two kinds of ministers: Those he has ordained to preach the gospel, and those he has ordained to kill people in order to restrain evil, as clearly explained in Romans 13. I felt this same blockade many other times in life, for example when considering joining the nuclear navy, which has distressed me. I suspect the true explanation is that the Lord simply did not trust me to handle this kind of thing, and we can all see many reasons why.

I worked at Popeye's all that summer, generally about 50 hours a week, not much by many people's standards that I know today, but a lot to me as a rather lazy seventeen-year-old who hadn't worked previously. Since I worked nights, I drifted to my natural rhythm of going to bed around 700 and getting up around 1400, at which point I would rush to work. I still didn't have a driver's license, because my parents never wanted to deal with the extra insurance. But after several weeks of my Dad driving me home from work at night, they signed off on it and strongly encouraged me to get one. For by the time I got off work the buses were no longer running.

That summer I got closer to George Neau because the students were gone and I was one of the few who could go with him to LTI during the day, on those days that I was awake. I tried to stay away from Swaggart's church as much as I could in order to avoid seeing Genifer, so I often visited other churches. But since I needed to be there on Sunday nights to get on the long bus ride to LTI with the ministry team, I was still at Swaggart's church a lot.

One of the people that was part of the regular LTI ministry team in those days was a guy I will call Barnabas. Like me, he was an LSU student rather than a Bible college student. He fell in love with one of the ladies helping out with the ministry at LTI[1]. Barnabas was rejected, and in his desolation, we had a lot in common. I made a deal with Barnabas to rent a nearby apartment with him. This apartment complex was right next to Bic's complex.

OPERATION AMERICA

Around this time Swaggart started a new campaign called "Operation America" in which he would make a big push to establish churches and ministries throughout inner-city America, where crime and violence were continuing to climb toward their early 1990s peak.

While raising money for this campaign, Swaggart established a satellite church that was supposed to be the prototype for this push. This was in a neighborhood known as Mall City which at the time was becoming one of the most dangerous in Baton Rouge. Mall City was a natural place to start because Swaggart still owned a lot of property there. During his rise in the 1970s he had purchased building after building until he owned a great deal of real estate behind the former Bon Marche Mall that the neighborhood was named after. The area was nice at the time but began to decline after the newly built Cortana Mall started taking business away from Bon Marche. In the meantime, Swaggart moved out to his newly built complex on Bluebonnet Road. But he stilled owned a building on Goya Street, and there he set up Goya Family Worship Center as the prototype for "Operation America."

---

1   They were all on the worship team, they couldn't go out to the dorms.

A minister was installed, but what they really wanted was a youth ministry to start reaching that part of Baton Rouge, the way Crossfire was impacting the city as a whole. Just at this time word was getting back to the ministry headquarters of all the constant visits and discipleship that George Neau was carrying on with the former inmates of LTI after they were released, especially the ones who went back to their homes in New Orleans. The story of changed lives that followed led them to install George Neau as the youth pastor of Goya. As soon as he got there, he went to work establishing a bus ministry to bring in youngsters from all over inner-city Baton Rouge to city-wide youth meetings on Friday nights.

I was already going to Louisiana State University (LSU) the first time I visited the Goya Friday night youth ministry, to see if I would get involved. As I sat in the back surveying the scene before the service got started, I could hear some of the youth in the background debating whether I was "Freddy Krueger," a fictional character from a popular horror movie of the time. For in those days I had a fedora that I wore at all times, indoors and outdoors, and to them it made me look like this fictional villain.

One result of having a city-wide inner city youth ministry like this was that you would be bringing in rival gangs out of their normal territory into one central place. So besides the simple fights that would oftentimes break out during the services, there were a few epic group brawls outside in the parking lot. George seemed to thrive in these semi-anarchic conditions, but I found it difficult to negotiate unless I had plenty of time one on one. At the time I decided that this youth ministry, LTI, and LSU all at the same time was too much, so I pulled out of Goya, although I would be returning soon.

Around the middle of my first semester my Popeye's money

was running out, and I needed a new source of income. There was a 24-hour diner less than a 10 minute walk from my apartment, called Louies Café, that famously had been there since the 1940s[1]. I signed on there for a job as a dishwasher and got $3.35/hr and the dog shift, running from 2300 or midnight to 700 AM.

I was mostly avoiding campus life and focusing on the LTI ministry. Because I mostly stayed away from my previous associations, the memory of my infatuation with Genifer finally began to fade away into the River Lethe[2]. On another front the problems I had previously had with demon spirits were also finally fading away, although I did have one relapse at that first XA "Fall Break Away" that I went to with Barnabas and Bic. They prayed through with me, and this was the last time that this type of incident happened, except for one more big test I faced.

---

1   It used to be on State St where it had previously moved from Chimes St, but has moved a second time since.

2   The River of Forgetfulness in Greek mythology

CHAPTER 25

THE END OF THE LINE

... that their hearts may be encouraged, being knit together in love, and attaining to all riches of the full assurance of understanding, to the knowledge of the mystery of God, both of the Father and of Christ, in whom are hidden all the treasures of wisdom and knowledge.

Colossians 2:2-3

JANUARY TO MAY 1988

Around this time the first major scandal with Jimmy Swaggart happened. I was severely tested by this and was tempted to do something crazy. When I returned to my apartment the Saturday night before that famous confession, I found Barnabus, Bic and his youngest brother all gathered and discussing the events of the last few days. Everyone was distraught and trying to comfort each other and come to an understanding of what this would all mean and how to move forward. Bic's brother kept talking about what it was like Friday at school, shaking his head and saying "All Hell is breaking loose! Man, all Hell is breaking loose!"

Even though everyone was in distress and didn't know quite what to do, the depth and reality of the fellowship was beautiful and completely broke me down. I told everyone gathered what I had been planning to do and how the vision of fellowship in God's kingdom that I had just beheld brought me to repentance. Everyone gathered around me to pray. I encourage all Christians, particularly in the USA as we continue to move into difficult times: Hang onto fellowship with other believers at all costs, for without it your light is likely to go out like an ember separated from the pile. As for me, from now on I would be growing more solid in my faith.

For another week I laid low and didn't know what to do. Then George called me and asked "what in the world is going on with you, I haven't seen you in two weeks!" We said some other things, he noted that I was being prideful, and then said "If you are worried about Swaggart, come out to Goya, because he isn't the pastor out here." So I went to Goya the following Sunday and remained there for some time.

I was struggling in some honors classes due mostly to my disagreements with my professor. I soon stopped working at Louie's to try and triage my college classes. I took out a small student loan, but knew I wouldn't last that long financially. So I came to an agreement with Barnabas to move out at the end of May and back in with my parents, and beyond that wasn't sure where things would go.

A CHANGE OF DIRECTION

Then late one night in March I couldn't sleep and I walked down to Louie's to have some eggs and a cup of coffee. It was a weeknight and mostly empty, and there at 200 AM I strangely saw an old acquaintance from high school sitting there and having his own cup of coffee. We started to talk. He was a Physics student, and it was mainly him talking about how cool he thought Physics was, especially quantum mechanics. I was entranced, and he told me point blank that he thought I should switch my degree from History to Physics. By this time I was mostly agreeing with him, wondering why I was in History instead of Physics. For my plan of going to Jimmy Swaggart Bible College after one year of LSU was now over, and besides, I had not expected to do as well in college as I was, in spite of those problems in the Medieval history classes. Yet I wasn't quite ready to make such a decision.

Shortly afterwards, I got confused about the date of my midterm exam in that troublesome honors class, and showed up a day late to an empty classroom where the exam was supposed to take place. Within a few minutes I figured out what happened. As I walked away in dismay, I saw a sign in Coates Hall saying 'Cooperative Education Jobs for Physics, Mathematics and Engineering Majors, up to $1600/month.' I was out of money and out of luck, and as soon as I saw that sign I made an instant decision.

I was in the registrar's office the first thing the next morning, dropped the honors classes while I still had time, and promptly changed my major to Physics. In the process I saved my 4.0 in spite of the ugly Ws. The following day I was in the Cooperative Education[1] room looking for jobs, which, among other things, would soon provide me a financial path for getting through school.

I returned to Crossfire to see how it was doing one night in April, after I heard that Genifer had completely left for another large church to the north of Baton Rouge in the aftermath of the

---

1   The Cooperative Education program was an arrangement where you alternated semesters between working full time somewhere and being a full time student the next.

scandal. That very night, after a completely normal service, Glen got up at the end and said "I am sorry, this will be my last night here. I wish I had more time to prepare everyone but I didn't know this would happen so suddenly." By the last week in April, Glen had his own church meeting at the Rodeway Inn. In the meantime, the senior pastor of Goya stepped down and George Neau took his place. He began preaching inspiring messages about revival and after a period of wavering between Glen's new church and Goya, I settled on Goya due to the revival preaching. I stayed with Neau until he went off to New Orleans to start SUM around the summer of 1991

GRANDPA

While I was at Goya an incident happened later in the year, which although it is not quite in sequence with this tale, I want to describe now. I was concerned for the soul of Grandpa, my paternal grandfather, and expressed in a prayer meeting that I did not know how to speak with him. An older man in the congregation named Jack said he would go with me, and in a few days we were off toward New Orleans.

We spent some time talking with Grandpa, and he described a very early episode in his life. This must have been sometime around 1925 or so when he was about 15 years old, working as a scullion in the galleys of the banana ships of the United Fruit Company. Grandpa told us that as they approached the shores of Nicaragua, he was confronted with horrific scenes of starvation such as he never had known existed. The entire crew, he said, started losing their minds.

As the starving crowds started wading out into the water or approaching the ship in small boats crammed with people, those running the ship, fearing they would be swamped and completely overrun, started dumping the food on board the ship into the sea. Now the whole crew was about to revolt, until the captain or someone calmed them down by saying some kind of service ship would be coming after them to provide food to the starving. I suppose no one genuinely believed this, but it was useful in the face of their inability to do anything about it, and so everyone calmed down.

But Grandpa said that this affected him for the rest of his life. He began drinking a lot and did not want to hear anything about God for many years. For a long time, he was a leader in the Masons in New Orleans and my grandparents were fairly secular. They were fully integrated back into the Catholic Church many years later under the influence of an electrician friend of theirs. But on this day, we were talking about being born again of the spirit, and so we prayed together. Just a few days later I saw him again at their house, he grabbed my hand and said "thank you for that prayer." And those were the last words he spoke to me, for shortly afterward he was back in the hospital and then passed away.

NATHAN

While I was at Goya, which later became Resurrection Life, I continued to try and reach Nathan and kept bringing him there. In those earlier years, I probably spent more time with him than any other person. But I gradually began to have less contact with Nathan after I got that cooperative education job and started going up to DC. My wife and I spent one evening with him not long after I got married. Then again, I didn't have much contact until the middle of the 2010s, when we had a good, long conversation on the phone. Unfortunately, Nathan started going off the rails again not long after that. Dave started warning me that he was threatening death to a bunch of people on Facebook, including me, and Dave and others of my old friends started arming themselves to the teeth.

Although I was still on Facebook in those days, I would only check about once a month or less. On that previous conversation two years earlier, Nathan said for no reason "I see you are going to India a lot." I asked him how he knew, and he cryptically said "I am always paying attention to such things." By this time, I was no longer leaving the country or traveling that much, but I still hesitated for a few weeks, trying to decide what to do. When I did finally reach out, it was too late. He had taken his own life at the end of a high-speed chase with the police.

Did Nathan ever have a chance? I say he did. As I child I feared the illustration of the potter the clay in Romans 9. But Paul had gotten that illustration from the one God gave to Jeremiah, where in chapter 18 it is said:

Then I went down to the potter's house, and there he was, making something at the wheel. And the vessel that he made of clay was marred [ruined] in the hand of the potter; so he made it again into another vessel, as it seemed good to the potter to make.

Then the word of the Lord came to me, saying: "O house of Israel, can I not do with you as this potter?" says the Lord. "Look, as the clay is in the potter's hand, so are you in My hand, O house of Israel! ... (Jeremiah 18:3-6, NKJV)

The Lord in Jeremiah does not use this illustration to say there is no hope, because he is going to make us unto something evil and there is nothing we can do. Rather, he encourages us that if we ask Him and trust Him, He can use His power as the potter to reshape us into something good, even if we are utterly ruined[1] in our personality and soul. He uses this to encourage us to come to Him and be reshaped. We are the ones who say it is hopeless:

> Thus says the Lord: "Behold, I am fashioning [making, as is the potter above] a disaster and devising a plan against you. Return now every one from his evil way, and make your ways and your doings good." And they said, "That is hopeless! So we will walk according to our own plans, and we will every one obey the dictates of his evil heart." (Jeremiah 18:11-12, NKJV)

The case is similar with what could be called the core parable of Jesus—the parable of the sower and the soils. We can read this and imagine it is already set before hand, as if we are like the good soil, or the rocky soil, or the soil with the thorns, simply because that is the way we are. But Jesus was likewise amplifying the Word of the Lord through Jeremiah who had said: "Break up your fallow ground, And do not sow among thorns." (Jeremiah 4:3) I must believe that the Lord's intention for Nathan was salvation, for otherwise why would He have given me that dream so long ago. Surely not to mock.

We all make choices and we all have chances, but those chances are not equal. We are all caught up in the web, not just of our own choices but of others before us and all around us, for good or for ill. That is why the work of the ministers that I have described in this book, to create that patient spiritual infrastructure of church life and fellowship and discipleship, is so crucial.

---

1   The Hebrew gives me the sense of something utterly ruined, not just marred.

As I consider the manner of Nathan's death, I wonder how I may have failed him in the end. This does not absolve him, for he had more opportunities for salvation in a given week than many do in a lifetime. However, in his severest hour of need, I may have faltered. And perhaps you have your own Nathan, and mourn similarly as in the Iliad[1]:

Patroclus indeed they mourned, but therewithal each one her own sorrows

OVER THE MISSISSIPPI

But in the spring of 1988, those storm clouds were still far off in the future. For me, this severe testing phase of my life was about to wrap up, and I would finally find myself on solid footing. The heat of the noonday sun, testing the depth of my soil, was over. A lifetime now lay before me, in which I would either remain true to my mission to the end and bear fruit, or forgetting the mercies I had been shown, drop off into 'ordinary' life and let the thorns grow.

God, seeing that I was now settled in the faith, determined that it was time to send Bic off to the rest of his life's mission. To California first, and afterward off to Thailand. And so late in May of 1988, Bic's whole family packed up a new Toyota pickup with a cover they had purchased for the long trip to California. That whole day Bic and I went around McKinley High School and LSU, taking pictures and remembering all that had taken place. Then it

---

1   Homer. The Iliad with an English Translation by A.T. Murray, Ph.D. in two volumes. Cambridge, MA., Harvard University Press; London, William Heinemann, Ltd. 1924. Book 19, line 303

was time to part. I kept watching them until they turned off July Street, out of sight and over the Mississippi. I knew it was up to me now.

I wouldn't see Bic again for a decade, when I stepped off a train and met him in the main station in Bangkok. But that is a story for another time, for here this tale must end.

AN ADDENDUM: "DAVE BOONE" SPEAKS

The first one to plead his cause seems right, until his neighbor comes
and examines him.

Proverbs 18:17

1981 TO 1986

I worked as hard as I could, as I told this tale, to get the details and
the timeline correct. But that is easier said than done when you
are struggling to recall conversations and events which took place
roughly 40 years ago. So I sent out drafts to friends and family, still alive, who I thought could either corroborate or correct
what I had written. I had to make a few corrections. Sometimes
we simply disagreed and I stuck to my account. Or more likely, I
decided the issue was minor, unresolvable, and did not impact the
story in a substantive way. But usually we could quickly converge,
from our varying points of view, on what must have really happened. The one guy who was in the thick of so much of this who
is still alive is the man I called "Dave Boone." We had some great

conversations, but with his schedule at the chemical plant and mine at my workplace, it simply was not possible to go through each part of the timeline point by point. We came up with another way to cut the Gordian Knot[1]—after 'Dave' read a draft of the book, he agreed to simply write a section from his point of view of all that he was seeing and experiencing at the time. His words are below—let the reader judge how the timelines fit:

Hey folks,

"Dave Boone" here. I have often thought it funny how the rebels of "back in the day" have grown to be the bastions of conservatism today. But then again, maybe no. In this increasingly crazy world in which we live, the very essence of conservative thought and lifestyle seems to have in itself become an Orwellian act of rebellion.

If it ever feels as if I have known Ralph my whole life, it is because I pretty much have. Even before we "formally" met in 2nd period English, I remember seeing the kid with the wild mop of curly orange hair at church. Where others thought him "the weird kid", that never really bothered me because I saw a lot of myself in that. Whether it was how God formed me, a product of my environment and father's influence, I too had an incredibly analytical mind. You weren't just going to throw some kooky statement out and expect me to accept it. You had to show me how and why, prove it to me and if necessary, beat me in the argument.

If it all lined up in my head, then I might accept it. I was quiet, bookish, and completely out of step with most of my peers. It seemed like my mind was always functioning on a level so much

---

1   A legendary, impossibly complicated knot in Phrygia. According to the legend, whoever untied this knot would rule all of Asia. Reputedly, Alexander the Great accomplished this upon his arrival by slashing the knot open with his sword.

higher than the silly things that occupied theirs. I was almost pathologically shy. Within a few years of meeting Ralph, I would take deliberate steps to change all of that.

As years ticked off and we became better friends, Ralph confided in me terrifying encounters with the supernatural from his early childhood. While others may have raised eyebrows and snickered about such things, I was attentive as I too had had a number of such encounters myself on a lesser level. I was very aware of the supernatural world around us, although I rejected the notion of "ghosts" out of hand.

"The kingdom of God is all around you". Years later a pastor I knew suggested he believed the spirit world paralleled our own but moving at the speed of light; occasionally slowing down to allow us glimpses into it, and vice versa. Based on my personal experiences I could, and to a certain extent still do believe this.

Always the outsider, I studied people. I mean I could play the part of the class clown from time to time but there were others who were better than me. I was the guy everyone wanted to sit by and cheat off of at test time. I even had teachers move me away from others during tests because "You know everyone around you is cheating off you, and you are too nice to stop them. I am not punishing you". But they knew I totally got what they were saying, and was actually relieved by the isolation.

But I stayed on the fringes and in the shadows socially. I studied people; their tones of voice and body language. How they looked and acted when they were lying, or happy, sad or trying to hide something. I learned to "read people" and it carried me far in life. Especially when I decided it was time for me to make my entrance upon the stage of life: the high theater of the world we inhabit for a season.

My entry into high school harked back to a number of major

changes in my life. As middle school wound down, my peers were buzzing about the next steps. More than a few were dropping out of the Gifted program to attend their regular district schools. A handful had been accepted to the top-level Baton Rouge High, which only accepted the top 3% of applicants at that time. I realized quickly that the most popular "A list" guys were not going to continue on. I determined that, with a blank slate ahead of me, I was going to fill that void. I didn't really crave attention or recognition per se, but I was determined to "be somebody" without having to tell people I was somebody. And the best way to facilitate that change was to ACT like I was somebody.

I got my first job a few weeks after turning 14 in early April: Five dollars a day watering plants for a starting plant nursery that could not afford an automatic sprinkler system. And the widow across the street had contracted me to cut her yard for ten dollars a week. Two hundred dollars a month seems a trifling amount today, but in 1983, to a young teenager not even in high school yet, it was a fortune. Far over and above that it opened the door to another life-altering situation... it granted me financial independence and a level of freedom most of my peers did not enjoy.

Puberty was finally kicking in for me, later than I would have cared for. But I was morphing from one of the smallest, skinniest kids in my age group to a more athletic build. Hours spent in the summer sun of the Gulf Coast in nothing but sneakers and shorts meant I started high school in great shape with a great tan. I had developed the gift of gab along the way, and a cocky boldness that harbored no place for fear. I would mouth off to anyone, anytime, anywhere and hold my tongue for no one. If it came down to throwing hands, I would in a heartbeat. I refused to back down to anyone. I had been bullied for years as the smallest guy in my class, and had decided I wasn't having any more of it.

Almost everyone I ever had to fight was bigger than me, so I grew past the fear of that rather quickly. I realized size did not equal advantage. Much the opposite; often the bigger guys were slow and clumsy, and my smaller, quicker moves gave me an edge.

My mix of Gallic roots; full Cajun French on my mother's side and Teutonic/Anglo with a touch of native-American on my father's side, blessed me with a handsome look. Delicate, almost feminine features that girls really began noticing. As I grew my hair out and Bon Jovi/ hair metal was all the rage, it got to the point where women were a disposable commodity to me. It was a mentality that would return to haunt me later in life, along with the tag "pretty boy", but that's a different story altogether. In that way Ralph and I differed greatly: polar opposites. I remember he was so awkward around girls and could barely speak to them. But I would brook no criticism, and remember storming away from a number of girls who started with the "Your friend is weird" nonsense.

I did indeed have a number of issues with the Catholic Church, and refused to be confirmed, thinking it the worst hypocrisy to openly declare before the world that I believed things I did not. All the other kids did their compulsory "12 hours of community service" in the goofiest ways. But what did it matter? Nobody was checking up on them. I continued on far past 12 hours volunteering at the soup kitchen.

I liked the brothers: monks who eventually the church disbanded over some dispute on a fine point of theological interpretation. I liked meeting the downtrodden but appreciative diners, many homeless. I even got to see what I deemed a cool knife fight! But it seemed to me to be the same as it ever was... the other kids doing just enough to skate by. Their hearts weren't in it at all, and it didn't make them better anything, including Christians.

My obligatory interview came on a rainy chilly Monday in late winter. At the end of it all when she asked me "So why do you want to be confirmed"? I told her point blank, "I don't". She was stunned, and this launched the final phases of a "ten-minute interview" that had already dragged on over an hour. When she regained her composure and asked me why, I told her flatly, "I don't necessarily believe all of this stuff I feel has been forced on me for years. And I feel like to get up and declare that I DO believe it in front of the world would be nothing if not the height of hypocrisy—and I am not prepared to do that. I believe there is something out there that is right for me, and I will find it eventually. If not, I will return later".

There were a wild 8 years between that, and the day "I found better," sitting alone in my van I had bought to carry my equipment for the lawncare business I had started. No getting carried away in a church. No altar call. Just me sitting alone in my van.

Reading Ralph's book was quite a wild ride down memory lane! What is for you, the reader, the telling of an interesting and hopefully inspirational tale is for me... memories. Memories of a life lived many years ago. But as has been said, if a dozen people view the same event, you will have a dozen versions of what happened. I too have my version of what happened that fateful year.

After the chaos of our freshman year at McKinley High, when the Gifted program was literally being made up as we moved along, our sophomore year was to bring a more determined effort on the part of the Administration to whip things into shape. They were on a mission, it seemed, to bring order and structure to the campus.

This began with the expulsion of Harry Robinson the fourth day of school, a Friday. He had brought a partially loaded .357 pistol to school to sell to another friend of ours. I had stolen it from the back seat of an unlocked car the previous summer[1], in a poorer neighborhood close to ours. The sniveling little guy I was with that night had freaked out, and began crying for me to "Put it back! Put it back!"—but I was having none of it. In my mind, it was an incredible score, better than the junk we usually grabbed. To think now how we literally risked our lives for road maps and the occasional unopened pack of cigarettes seems insane. But we were very young and very stupid, "playing gangsters." Still, this guy idolized Harry and was forever looking for ways to ingratiate himself, so he led him to where I had stashed the pistol. The ways of the Lord are mysterious, but there is always a plan. His expulsion led him to "Christian Life Academy"; the ONLY school in town that would accept him. It was there that the seeds were planted that would eventually lead him to the Lord.

When Harry fell to an ultimately fatal heart attack in Houston a decade ago, he was attending church on a regular basis with his fiancée. Indeed, his Fakebook profile picture was their hands intertwined over a Bible. So I believe one of the guys I considered as close as a brother left us in good standing.

And so it started in the school year 1984-85. They began a systematic program to rid the school of what they deemed the worst troublemakers. Some facilitated their departure by gift-wrapping their stupidity, like blatantly smoking marijuana while sitting on the hood of the principal's Cadillac at lunch, right outside the school offices. Or attacking staff members or one another. Others like me proved a little more "hard targets."

While my troublemaking buddies were being tossed

---

[1] Not the gun we stole from a jeep in Chapter 12, the one that got Johnny Slade, and almost Dave, incarcerated.

unceremoniously out, I was moving into deeper relationships with girls, starting to play guitar after auditioning with a teen band, and other rather tame pursuits. I just wasn't causing the trouble I had the previous year. I wasn't squeaky clean, but it wasn't a daily occurrence like it had been the previous year. And the pranks and trouble were considerably toned down. But because of the sheer amount of trouble I had caused my freshman year, along with an ongoing rebellious spirit, I was still firmly in their sights. And in my own way I delivered the excuse for them to cut me loose with a bow on it. After a particularly bad fight with my father, I "ran away from home" in the winter of 1985.

I bounced around among friends for a week or so before settling in with a couple of brothers and their father who had custody of them. But he was a wild partier and last gasp of the hedonistic 70s, and rarely around.

When I shifted my bus stop to match my new location, my bus driver eventually peeled the reason out of me.

The day she refused to let me on the bus, she said it was "on orders from the Principal." I protested it would be my 10th unexcused absence for the semester and I would automatically flunk. She told me he had told her the only way they would let me back in school was if I went there with my parents. I screamed she knew I wasn't living at home. She shrugged, closed the doors, and drove off. I screamed obscenities and made rude gestures as they pulled away, then stormed back to what was then home. I got as drunk as I could off what was laying around, carved a cross then needled and inked a tattoo onto my chest that remains there to this day. After a few more months and much more drama, including meeting and developing a lifelong friendship with Johnny Slade, I ended up home.

So I started a new school, made new friends, got a new job,

and made the transition of a more stable life. I had rejected marijuana as "turning me into a moron." Even getting drunk was a take it or leave it proposition for me. Others needed it to "loosen up" and be able to be social with some degree of comfort. I didn't. Much the opposite it was easier to talk to girls, and more importantly make them laugh, if you weren't a slurring, stumbling idiot! I had long since ceased to care what anyone thought about me and my long hair and earrings and metal music. So have a drink or no? It was all the same for me.

Ralph was one of the few leftovers from my previous life, and I worried about him all the time. He wasn't particularly street savvy as witnessed by a few days he "ran away from home." Shortly after that episode things took a decidedly darker turn with him. When we did have time to hang out he seemed totally stressed out and agitated all the time. It seemed as if he was trying to crawl out of his own skin.

Now mind you he never got angry with me. It always seemed to me he was trying to ask me for some sort of help but could not verbalize WHAT exactly he needed help with. What little he confided in me about voices, and demons harassing him after years of relative dormancy, deeply concerned me. Although I was very aware of the spirit world, my secular mind could not equate that and I thought I was watching my friend basically have a mental breakdown.

I knew it wasn't academic pressure. We didn't care what we passed or bombed. Ralph was always "math and science guy." I was "history and literature guy" and we complemented one another well for that and flunked our respective uncared-for subjects for years.

Little by little clues came out... "there's this girl". Okay, I get it. Girls can drive you crazy, for sure. But things just kept getting worse. The day he showed up on my doorstep telling me "I know you know people (inference 'criminal element'). I need you to get me a better gun", I was stunned and did something I had never done with Ralph... I lied. I wriggled and wrangled that I had left that life behind, and honestly didn't have a clue where he might be able to get a firearm.

And when I questioned him further as to WHY he felt he needed a firearm, I was shocked and dismayed even further. The "McDonald's Massacre" in San Ysidro, California had happened. Now remember this is the mid-80s and mass shootings were still relatively isolated and even more horrifying events than today. Ralph flat told me he wanted to emulate that type of massacre, then murder a girl and "the Chinese guy who keeps following me around talking about God, and won't leave me alone".

I tried asking why, and did not like the answer at all... "the Devil told me to do it". I tried to deflect with jokes: "What if me and Harry are there just eating Big Macs, and minding our own business?"

"Oh I would never harm y'all... the Devil LIKES you!" Oh. Wow. I didn't even know how to take that. Good on the one hand, but...

But it became more and more clear over the next few weeks that Ralph was serious... this wasn't just another one of his larks. He became increasingly a man at war with himself and forces from within and without. I tried to appeal to his intellect and reason with him. I told him he didn't HAVE to do what the "Devil" or voices were telling him to do. All of these people were innocent of any crimes except in his head, and none of them deserved to be murdered in cold blood. He insisted more and more violently he had no choice and I grew more insistent he did.

As an aside I guess I need to set the stage to the drama that was playing out. I was young, wild, and as rebellious as I ever was. I was calling the shots, and wasn't taking any shiitake mushrooms off anybody. That included God and the Devil! I was a leader, not follower. A decision maker and risk taker, not an order taker.

But at the same time, I was shaping up to tow the line and truly make myself into "a somebody". I had worked steadily from one job to another before settling into working almost full-time at one of the last full-serve gas stations in town with new friends from my new high school. I had secured a transfer through the school board the previous summer to what was geographically the closest high school; but not rejoining my former friends at "my district school" as zoned by the deseg-regation ruling as I entered high school. I had left most of them behind when I joined the Gifted program, and had no ambition to return to the status of "the nerdy guy we like to cheat off of and bully otherwise".

I had money, relative financial independence, and had taken to hanging out with people much older than me and sneaking into bars boldly as if I owned the place, simply by tagging along and acting mature like them. I was told that I was as handsome as a god, with a silver tongue that got me as much attention from women as I could ever want. At first jealousy, but then it became a running joke with my friends... "Dave is always going to get the best-looking girl. But they have friends who aren't too shabby, and all we have to do is kick back and let him literally charm their pants off". I wasn't afraid to approach the most beautiful girls, quickly realizing they were often the most bitterly lonely. The bet-ter looking they were, the more intimidated men were by them... and other girls jealous of them. Along comes this handsome guy with a big smile on his face making them laugh and feel comfort-able; the compliments flowing with sincerity and no pressure for them to do anything but relax and be themselves? They ate it up. "Hair Metal" was huge and here was Bon Jovi's twin hanging out casually with them!

I knew God was real. I knew the Devil was real. I had had my own encounters with the spiritual realm, although none as traumatic as what Ralph had experienced. I was never an actual "Devil Worshipper." Because he was the created, not Creator. He was the servant, not Master. And I had read the Book. Ultimately, he was the loser and I certainly wasn't hitching my wagon to that sort! All the other stuff was just a goof. It was high theater for shock value. It was Alice Cooper and Motley Crue; the heavy metal culture of the 80s.

So long and short? Ralph and I were polar opposites in terms of social skills with the world at large. But exactly the same when it came to loyalty. He was my friend, period. End of story.

Although aware of the spiritual world around us, I still thought "the Exorcist" was hokey and understood the situation with Ralph in secular terms. Even when he told me about the voices, the prodding of Satan, his feelings of being powerless to resist, I sought to "talk him down". I insisted he just stand up to Lucifer or whoever or whatever and tell them to F off. You don't have to do this, Ralph! The more he insisted he did, the harder I insisted he didn't.

I expressed my concern to Harry, knowing they went way back. He thought it was just another goof by Ralph but I insisted no, I have never seen him like this. He looks like he is literally unraveling at the seams. And as "the fixer"; the guy who gets things done, can and will stand up to anyone over anything if he believes he is right... I was at a loss for what to do to help my friend and it bothered me.

Then came the day there was a knock on the door. I usually

camped out in our living room with my guitar and equipment, being too crowded in the room I shared with my two brothers.

I answered it to find Ralph standing there but was immediately struck with how calm and serene he seemed. The wild look in his eyes of the past few months was gone. He wasn't nervous and jumpy. I seem to remember he was carrying a Bible. For someone who had always been socially awkward and oblivious to body language and facial expressions, he was attuned enough to read the puzzled look on my face and simply say, "It's ok, man. I'm okay now and I'm not going to hurt anyone. I got saved".

That's how I remember it all. Ralph did an amazing job of telling what is in some ways not just his story but touches of "our story". Harry suffered a fatal heart attack shortly after his 44th birthday 11 years ago[1]. Johnny Slade died of a stroke in northern Georgia a few months later at the age of 42. Sadly, I heard that Chuck and Nathan took their own lives within a few years of that[2]. Han Fei lives in the Austin, Texas area and actually stopped by a few years ago. He had access to a new HVAC product and a connection to get it factory direct from China. Knowing I was in the business he stopped by while he was in town on other business to discuss it.

I miss those guys, and thank the Good Lord Ralph is never more than a phone call away. It is sad to think we are the last ones left as we enter our latter years. But of course we enjoy the hope of salvation, and looking back... what a ride it has been!

I hope everyone who reads this is inspired and uplifted. I know this book has been a labor of love for Ralph and something he has felt deeply called to do. I think it is an incredible story and

---

1   2013

2   2015

testament to the power of the living God who can and does move the hearts and shape the lives of all who come unto Him. Take care, and

God bless.

9 781961 093782